165

LIKKUTEI SICHOT

An Anthology of Talks

by the
LUBAVTICHER REBBE,
RABBI MENACHEM M. SCHNEERSON שליט"א

VAAD L'HAFOTZAS SICHOS
788 EASTERN PARKWAY • BROOKLYN, NY 11213
5752   1992

LIKKUTEI SICHOS
VOL 4: BAMIDBAR

Published & Copyrighted 1992 by
VAAD L'HAFOTZAS SICHOS
788 EASTERN PARKWAY
BROOKLYN, NY 11213
Tel: (718) 774-7200 Fax: (718) 774-7494

Library of Congress Catalog Card No. 79-93139

ISBN: 0-8266-0503-6

5752 • 1992

Printed in the United States of America

PHOTOCOMPOSITION BY
EMPIRE PRESS
550 EMPIRE BLVD.
BROOKLYN, N.Y. 11225
(718) 756-1473 • FAX (718) 604-7633

PRINTED BY
BOOKMART PRESS, INC.
N. BERGEN, N.J. 07047

LIKKUTEI SICHOT

An Anthology of Talks

Relating to the weekly sections of the Torah and
Special occasions in the Jewish calendar

by the Lubavitcher Rebbe
RABBI MENACHEM M. SCHNEERSON שליט"א

•

Volume IV: *Bamidbar*

•

In English rendition
with Introduction and Notes
by
JACOB IMMANUEL SCHOCHET

TABLE OF CONTENTS

VIII

B"H

PUBLISHER'S FOREWORD

In a continuing effort to bring the discourses and talks of the Lubavitcher Rebbe, Rabbi Menachem M. Schneerson שליט"א — the seventh Rebbe of Chabad — to the worldwide english-speaking public, we hereby present the fourth volume of *"Likkutei Sichot"* — *(Bamidbar)*, a free translation (from the Yiddish original*).

There has been a great and urgent demand of translations of the works of the Rebbe שליט"א. The first three volumes of Likkutei Sichot in English were received with great enthusiasm. It is hoped that this volume, too, will help bring the Rebbe's teachings within the reach of those for whom they have been inaccessible, thereby increasing the "dissemination of the fountains" of Chassidus unlocked by Rabbi Yisroel Baal Shem Tov. Thus it will be instrumental in the actualization and realization of the ultimate goal — the complete and final redemption.

With the publication of this volume we join Jews the world over with our prayerful wishes that the Rebbe שליט"א be blessed with many years in good health, abundance, and success, and may we merit speedily in our days the coming of *Moshiach Tzidkeinu*.

Va'ad L'Hafotzas Sichos

Purim Koton, 5752
Brooklyn, New York

---

* It should be noted that, as in all translations, despite the effort of the translator and editors, a possibility of inadvertent error exists. For this the translator and editors accept full responsibility.

INTRODUCTION

I

The feelings of gratitude and joy in completing the translation of this fourth volume of *Likkutei Sichot*[1] are no less than with its three predecessors.

The sense of *zechut* (merit and privilege) on the one hand, and responsibility on the other,[2] is not diminished by frequency, but enhanced. For "the lover of *kessef* (silver; money) is never satisfied with *kessef*" (Ecclesiastes 5:9): "He who has a hundred wants to turn them into two hundred; and if he has two hundred he wants to turn them into four hundred."[3] Even on the level of the literal meaning of this principle, this is not necessarily a negative attribute: while some are obsessed with their wealth and increase it to their disadvantage, there are others who increase their wealth to their advantage.[4] How much more so, then, on the metaphorical level, of *kessef* signifying Torah and *mitzvot*.[5] True appreciation of Torah and *mitzvot* of itself enhances the desire for ever more.[6]

Thus I pray to merit continuation of this sacred work to facilitate accessibility to the teachings of Torah in general, and the well-springs of *pnimiyut haTorah* in particular, to as wide a circle as possible.

------

1. See *L.S.-Shemot*, Introduction, p. XI.
2. See *L.S.-Bereishit*, Introduction, p. IX*f*.
3. *Kohelet Rabba* 1:13, and *ibid.* 3:10.
4. *Ibid.* 1:18.
5. *Ibid.* 5:9.
6. See *Likkutei Sichot*, vol. XXIII, p. 435. Cf. *The Mystical Tradition*, p. 145*f*.

II

The student of this volume will find here additional discussions of many themes already touched upon in the previous volumes. In view of the principle that it is impossible for a study-session to pass without some novel teaching,[7] however, these are not mere repetitions. They may be the same subjects, but always with something new: a new perspective; further and deeper elaboration; additional meanings and insights. Of this our sages said already that "words of Torah are scant in one place and more substantially elaborate in another place."[8] Like doors, they lead into one another; they *need* one another,[9] for what is closed up by one is disclosed by another.[10]

All this, of course, in context of the special or unique themes of the *parshiyot* of *Sefer Bamidbar*, the fourth book of the Torah, and the special occasions in the Jewish calendar which occur during the period of its readings: the significance of numbering the Jewish people;[11] the festival of *Shavu'ot*, and especially the concept of *matan Torah* (the giving of the Torah at Sinai) and the implications of various aspects related to it;[12] the concept of sin and how it is possible for a Jew to transgress the will of G-d;[13] the deeper meaning of kindling the *menorah* in the Sanctuary;[14] the paradox of great men like the spies sent to investigate the Land of Israel perverting their mission, and the subsequent rebellion of the people;[15] deeper insights into the

---

7. *Chagigah* 3a

8. *Yerushalmi, Rosh Hashanah* 3:5

9. *Midrash Tehilim* 119:61

10. *Tanchuma*, Chukat:23; *Bamidbar Rabba* 19:28.

11. Below, Bamidbar A and F.

12. Below, Bamidbar C, D, F; and the *sichot* on Shavu'ot.

13. Below, Nasso A; see also Shlach A, and Pinchas F.

14. Below, Beha'alotecha A-B.

15. Below, Shlach A, and see there also C.

mitzvot of *tzitzit*,[16] *challah*,[17] and the contributions to be given unto *kohanim* in general;[18] the underlying motives for the rebellion by Korach;[19] the significance and implications of the manna, Clouds of Glory, and the Well, that accompanied the Jewish people during their travels through the desert;[20] the motivations and symbolism of Bilam;[21] the significance and morals of the festival of *Yud-Bet Yud-Gimel Tamuz*, marking the liberation of the *Rebbe Reyatz* (R. Yosef Yitzchak) from his life-threatening imprisonment by the communist regime of Soviet Russia;[22] the zealousness of Pinchas;[23] the relevance of the division of the Holy Land among the tribes of Israel;[24] the spiritual aspect of nullifying spousal vows;[25] and the timeless moral derived from the enumeration of the specific journeys of the Jewish people from Egypt to the Land of Israel.[26]

Unique to this volume are the many *sichot* addressed specifically to women, highlighting their central role in Jewish life, their crucial part in the very preservation of the values and observance of Torah and Jewish survival.[27] In these pages we find also, for the first time, a detailed explanation for the religious significance of birthdays,[28]

---

16. Below, Shlach B.
17. Below, Shlach D.
18. Below, Korach A.
19. Below, Korach A.
20. Below, Chukat A.
21. Below, Balak B-C.
22. Below, *sichot* on Yud-Bet Yud-Gimel Tamuz.
23. Below, Pinchas A-B.
24. Below, Pinchas C.
25. Below, Matot A.
26. Below, Massey A-B.
27. Below, Bamidbar B; Shavu'ot O-S; Beha'alotecha, sect. VI*f*.
28. Below, Yud-Bet Yud-Gimel Tamuz B, and there in *sichah* E, sect. XXIV*ff*.

the awareness and observance of which the Rebbe *shalita* has stressed in more recent years. No less noteworthy is a *sichah* addressed directly to children, with style and language masterfully adapted to its audience, offering inspiring pedagogical guidance.[29]

III

For ever-recurring themes, such as the fundamental principles of *ahavat Yisrael*, personal *avodah*, the dissemination of *pnimiyut haTorah*, and reaffirmation of the belief in—and anticipation of—the Messianic redemption, we find here very important nuances and elaborations.

Ahavat Yisrael is "the great principle of the Torah."[30] The Baal Shem Tov established it as one of the fundamental premises of the teachings of Chassidism.[31] It is an all-comprehensive absolute principle relating to every single Jew.[32] Love and unity of Israel was an essential precondition for *matan Torah*[33] even as it is an assured means to actualize the Messianic redemption.[34]

Ahavat Yisrael does not mean simply an affirmation of the intrinsic sanctity of a fellow-Jew or the recognition of our inter-relationship.[35] It is not only passive but also active, to *demonstrate* our love and concern as we do for our closest and dearest family-members. It involves not only concern for their physical well-being but also their spiritual welfare.[36] It is not limited to becoming involved

---

29. Below, Yud-Bet Yud-Gimel Tamuz C.
30. *Yerushalmi, Nedarim* 9:4; Rashi on Leviticus 19:18.
31. See below, Bamidbar, sect. XIII.
32. See below, Bamidbar, sect. XIV-XIX.
33. See below, Bamidbar, sect. XIII, and *sichot* D and F.
34. See below, Yud-Bet Yud-Gimel Tamuz, sect. XX-XXI; and Pinchas D.
35. See below, Bamidbar, sect. XIV-XVIII.
36. See below, Shavu'ot, sect. XXIII.

when approached, when asked to render assistance, but to *go out*, to seek out anyone and everyone in whatever need; to take the initiative and *reach out* to help them and to bring them back to their roots.[37] Moreover, one must sense a deep feeling of urgency about this: there must be a profound sense that every case of a Jew alienated from Torah and *Yiddishkeit* is a case of *piku'ach nefesh*, endangered life, mandating that everything be done to save him or her.[38] To do so, however, also requires sensitivity to everyone's individuality. Though all of us are essentially one and the same, each one has something unique. The right words and approach must therefore be found to reach, touch and uncover the personal core of the other's mind, heart and soul.[39]

At the same time, special caution is called for not to distort the principles of *ahavat Yisrael* and unity of Israel. It must forever be remembered that the very principle of *ahavat Yisrael*, its significance and primary role, derive from the Torah: *the Torah* mandates *ahavat Yisrael* and establishes its centrality in Jewish life. *The Torah* defines the criteria and extent of *ahavat Yisrael*. The principle of *ahavat Yisrael* thus is wholly and totally dependent on Torah, subject to the rules and instructions of the Torah. It can never be invoked to override, violate or change the Torah or any of those rules and instructions.[40]

The comprehensive principle of unity and *ahavat Yisrael*, the urgent need of outreach-work to befriend fellow-Jews, therefore, are not to be abused for justifying any

---

37. See below, Shavu'ot, sect. XXX; Chukat, sect. VIII; Pinchas, sect. V, and XI-XII. See also Bamidbar, sect. IX and XI-XIII; and Beha'alotecha, sect. I.

38. See below, Pinchas, sect. V-VI. See also Chukat, sect. VIII.

39. See below, Beha'alotecha, sect. I-III. See also Pinchas, sect. I, and VII-X.

40. See below, Beha'alotecha, sect. II-V. See also Balak, sect. III.

modes of behavior which run counter to Torah and Halachah. They can never serve as an excuse to legitimize unacceptable ideas or ideologies under the guise of propaganda-slogans like "harmonious pluralism." No effort must be spared to bring every member of Israel closer to the Torah. The Torah itself, however, cannot be compromised in this pursuit. To compromise the Torah, to amend and modify it in any way, shape or form in an attempt to make it seemingly more attractive or amenable, is to falsify the Torah, to falsify Israel, and to render the principles of *ahavat Yisrael* and unity of Israel meaningless and worthless.[41]

IV

There is another qualification to the *mitzvah* of *ahavat Yisrael*. Concern about others does not override concern about one's own spirituality. One must remain aware of the principle "Do not hide yourself from your own flesh." (Isaiah 58:7) It is self-evident that one cannot offer to another what one does not have. One can hardly explain to another that which one is ignorant about or inspire others to practice that which one neglects. Personal *avodah* is a prerequisite to *avodah* with others; and even in the absence of others one must engage in personal *avodah*, service of G-d through Torah and *mitzvot*, for one's own sake.[42]

To be sure, each one must contribute to the sanctification of the world at large. Indeed, every one has his own share or part in the physical world that he is to sublimate.[43] But before doing so one must first refine and subli-

---

41. See below, Shlach, sect. XVI-XXI; and Korach, sect. V.
42. See below, Bamidbar, sect. X.
43. *Tanya*, ch. 37. See below, Bamidbar, sect. XXIII; Shavu'ot, sect. XXVI and XXXI; Balak, sect. V.

mate one's own material reality, one's own body and *nefesh habahamit* ("animal soul").[44] Before anything else one must develop a sense of *kabalat ol*, total acceptance of Divine sovereignty. There must be a total submission or negation of ego. Not only arrogant self-aggrandizement, but even self-satisfaction from spiritual self-perfection is inconsistent with the ideal of total devotion to G-d.[45]

True devotion to G-d means to give our very best to G-d: the best of our time, the best of our possessions, the best of our energy and efforts, our very being.[46]

G-d-consciousness must be present in all material involvements, as it is said "Acknowledge Him in all your ways" (Proverbs 3:6); but this applies also to all our spiritual involvements. Torah and *mitzvot* must be *lishmah*, for the sake of G-d.[47] Man's *avodah* must be pervaded by a sense of *mesirat nefesh*, self-submission to the point of self-sacrifice,[48] to realize the Divine intent of converting this world into a fitting *dirah betachtonim*, abode for G-dliness in this material world.

Needless to say, this is not an easy task. There are all kinds of distractions and pitfalls along the way. To avoid or overcome these will often necessitate special precautions, protective "guardrails" to prevent sins of omission or commission.[49] Nonetheless, though not an easy task, it is neither an impossible task:

The ultimate goal is within the reach of everyone, regardless of whatever status he may find himself in at the

---

44. See below, Shavu'ot, sect. XXVII.

45. See below, Shavu'ot, sect. XXXIII. See also Korach, sect. II and V; and Balak, sect. III.

46. See below, Korach, sect. I-V.

47. See below, Bamidbar, sect. XXIV; Balak, sect. VI. See also Pinchas, sect. XV; and Matot, sect. II-IV.

48. See below, Pinchas, sect. II-III.

49. See below, Balak, sect. VI; Shlach II and XIV; and Pinchas, sect. XIV-XVI.

present. Just as every Jew partook in the exodus from the physical bondage of Egypt to the freedom and bliss of the "good and spacious land of Israel," so every Jew is able—and thus obligated—to leave any spiritual bondage of *Mitzrayim* (straits and restrictions) for the spiritual freedom of the sanctity of the Holy Land.[50]

Moreover, one must also remember that the human being is endowed with the quality of being a *mehalech*, one that can—and must—keep moving and progressing to ever greater heights. Regardless of past achievements, regardless of whatever accomplishments and perfections already attained, one can—and must—forever keep moving ever further and higher.[51]

V

The calendar-cycle of this volume includes the festival of Shavu'ot, when Israel was given the Torah. Thus it is hardly surprising to find here a special emphasis on the central role of Torah-study in the life of man.

Torah-study, which is "equivalent to everything,"[52] is first and foremost in the practice of *avodah*. It must encompass every aspect of life.[53] Torah is not only a means towards knowing what, when, and how to do or not to do, and the exclusive way to become unified with G-d; it is also an end in itself.[54] It is literally the very life-force of man and the world. Just as vital functions need be preserved every day, so, too, Torah must be studied and pursued every day.[55] Moreover, it is not enough to have curso-

---

50. See below, Massey, sect. VI-VII. See also Bamidbar, sect. XI; and Shavu'ot, sect. XVIII-XX.

51. See below, Massey A-B.

52. *Pe'ah* 1:1. See below, Shavu'ot B, and Balak B.

53. See below, Shavu'ot F.

54. See below, Shavu'ot B, especially sect. VIII.

55. See below, Shavu'ot J. See there also sect. VIII-XI and XLI.

ry *she'urim* (study-sessions) every day to satisfy a minimal legal obligation of *talmud Torah*. Torah requires personal effort and exertion which follow from a deeply felt recognition and appreciation of the fact that the Torah is "our life." As part thereof, each one must have a regular schedule of in-depth study of *Gemara*.[56]

All this applies to both *nigleh* (the study of the exoteric or manifest part of the Torah; Talmud and Halachah) and *nistar*, i.e., *pnimiyut haTorah* (the study of the concealed core or soul-dimension of the Torah). For *nigleh* and *nistar* together constitute the singular Torah given to every single Jew at *matan Torah*. Every Jew shares in both of these, must be made aware of both and influenced by both. Either one of these without the other is incomplete, just as a body without the soul or a soul without the body. Each is a necessary complement to the other, together one singular entity addressing the total reality of man and essential to the self-realization and actualization of man's body and soul.[57]

In this context we find here also an emphasis on *CHiTaT*: everyone can and ought pursue the daily *she'urim* of a) *CHumash*, i.e., learning the *parshat hashevu'a* (Torah-reading of that week) in the order of its division into seven parts, one for each day of the week, along with its primary commentary by Rashi; b) *Tehilim*, i.e., recital of the daily portions of *Tehilim* (Book of Psalms) according to its division for each day of every month (thus completing it every month); and c) *Tanya*, i.e., the daily lesson of this fundamental Chassidic text according to its division for each day of the year. These minimal *she'urim* apply equally to everyone and are of great significance to each one's *avodah*.[58]

---

56. See below, Shavu'ot, sect. IX-XVI and XXXIV.
57. See below, Shavu'ot, sect. XXXV; and Beha'alotecha, sect. V.
58. See below, Shavu'ot, sect. XVII, and XXXVII-XXXIX.

VI

In the present *sichot*, as consistently at every occasion, the Rebbe *shalita* continuously reinforces and revitalizes an unwavering belief in, and anticipation of, the Messianic redemption. We are witnesses to the continuous accumulation of all the signs for the imminent coming of Mashiach.[59]

To be sure, at this very moment we are still in *galut*, a dark and harsh *galut*. This *galut*, however, relates only to our physical reality, our bodies. It does not apply to our souls, to the aspects of Torah and *mitzvot* which are bound up with the soul. The nations of the world may seem to have mastery over Israel, but in reality they do not. G-d alone controls us, and it is by His decree alone (and not because of the nations) that we are still in a state of *galut*.[60] Thus we are able to do something about it:

Awareness of the fact that the *galut* is an abnormal state for Israel must lead to a recognition of its immediate causes. The mourning-period of *beyn hametzarim*, the three weeks between the 17th of Tamuz and the 9th of Av, commemorating the *churban* (destruction of the *Bet Hamikdash* and the subsequent exile of Israel among the nations), is not simply a memorial to this tragedy but more importantly to its causes. Specifically, the *churban* and present *galut* came about because of the sin of *sinat chinam*, gratuitous hatred, divisiveness among the Jewish people. Awareness of the cause reminds us that it can—and must—be nullified: *sinat chinam* is nullified by *ahavat chinam*, gratuitous love of each and every Jew. This love, this peace and unity, is the ultimate means for all blessings, most importantly the blessing of G-d speedily sending us

---

59. See below, Balak, sect. II, and VII-VIII. See also Pinchas, sect. XIII.

60. See below, Balak A.

our righteous Mashiach to redeem us with the complete and ultimate redemption.[61]

The Baal Shem Tov taught that every Jew contains within himself a spark of the soul of Mashiach.[62] Every one of us has the ability to bring this out into the open. Thus every Jew is able to speed up and bring about the actual manifestation of Mashiach.[63] This is our ultimate task and goal.

VII

This volume of *Likkutei Sichot*, like all others, touches upon every aspect of Jewish life from the perspective of all dimensions of the Torah: teaching and enlightening, explaining and clarifying. Above all - it inspires. It exemplifies and demonstrates the unique character of *pnimiyut haTorah*: the very soul of the Torah penetrating to the very soul of man to bond it with its Divine source.[64] The Torah emerges as a *Torat chayim*—a living and relevant Torah that offers practical instruction and guidance, and a Torah that literally infuses, strengthens and enhances life.

Our generation is most fortunate to be blessed with so great and inspiring a leader and master as the Rebbe

---

61. See below, Yud-Bet Yud-Gimel Tamuz, sect. XX-XXI. Note there, end of sect. XXVIII, the remarkable words spoken in 5722 (1962): "The redemption of Yud-Bet Tamuz occurred in our former country [i.e., Russia]. The anticipated manifestations [i.e., of the Messianic redemption], too, will begin in that selfsame land presently suffering the greatest oppression." By now, thirty years later, we have already been privileged to witness the fulfillment of these prophetic words with the miracle of the radical changes in Russia and Eastern Europe over the past few years which affected the formerly oppressed Jews in particular!

62. See below, Yud-Bet Yud-Gimel Tamuz, sect. XXII.

63. *Ibid.*

64. See below, Yud-Bet Yud-Gimel Tamuz, sect. XXVIII.

shalita. He evidences the principle that the leaders, saints and scholars of all generations are extensions of *Mosheh Rabeinu*, Moses, the very first and universal *Rebbe* of Israel.[65] Both on the level of his personal dealings with Jews of all types and ranks, as well as on the level of his formal and informal teachings (as in this volume), we see a manifestation of the qualities of *Moshe Rabeinu* essential to a true leader of the Jewish people. His all-encompassing and unqualified concern for every single individual, man and woman, child and adult, great and small, scholar and layman, those already bound to Torah and *mitzvot* and those not yet, and in his extra-ordinary effort and ability to address and inspire all of these at their individual levels, are the very marks of the authentic shepherd appointed by Divine Providence to guide G-d's holy flock to their destiny.[66]

Very shortly (on the 11th of Nissan) we shall be privileged to celebrate the Rebbe's ninetieth birthday. This is a special occasion to express our deeply felt appreciation and gratitude by thanking Almighty G-d for endowing and blessing us with the Rebbe, and to pray most fervently that our merciful G-d bless the Rebbe with many more healthy years of inspired and inspiring leadership in our midst. Above all we beseech our Father in Heaven that the Rebbe *shalita* will very speedily see the fulfillment of his (and our) most fervent wish and prayer, to experience the *ge'ulah shelemah*, the complete redemption, leading all of us toward Mashiach and into the new *Bet Hamikdash* to be re-established by Mashiach!

J. Immanuel Schochet

Toronto, Ont., 6th of Tevet 5752

---

65. *Tikunei Zohar* 69:112a. See *L.S.-Shemot*, Introduction, p. XVf.
66. *Shemot Rabba* 2:2-3. See *L.S.-Shemot*, Introduction, p. XVIf; and below, Chukat, sect. VI-VII.

PREFATORY NOTES

1. This volume is a free translation and adaptation, thus allowing for the possibility of inadvertent errors by the translator.

2. An attempt was made to make this translation as readable as possible but also to remain fully faithful to the original. As a rule (with, in this volume, one small exception), no parts were omitted, including the few passages which at first appear rather complex or intricate.

Explanatory notes have been added in the margins, along with references to other sources where fuller clarification can be found. The novice to Halachic and Chassidic terminology or concepts may still have some difficulty with a few passages, but this should not intimidate the student of *Likkutei Sichot* because (a) there would be only very few of these, and (b) they can be omitted at first without losing the trend of thought.

3. The original division of the *sichot* into sections and paragraphs was retained practically throughout.

4. To facilitate understanding, I supplemented the original footnotes by

(a) explicating references given, and/or suggesting additional sources relevant to the subject-matter; and

(b) adding sources for quotations in the text which were not annotated in the original edition.

All such additions by the translator are clearly distinguished by square brackets around them. In the first two volumes of this translation (*Bereishit* and *Shemot*), all notes added by the translator were distinguished by alphabetical notations (as opposed to numbers) and smaller type. In this volume, as in the preceding one (*Vayikra*) they are distinguished only by square brackets.

5. There are numerous references to other volumes of *Likkutei Sichot*. To date, 29 volumes have appeared in print. References to parts already translated are to the translations, noted by the following abbreviations:

L. S.—Bereishit, referring to *Likkutei Sichot* in English, volume I: Bereishit;

L. S.—Shemot, referring to *Likkutei Sichot* in English, volume II: Shemot; and

L. S.—Vayikra, referring to *Likkutei Sichot* in English, volume III: Vayikra.

All references to the original volumes of *Likkutei Sichot* in Hebrew and Yiddish are fully spelled out as *Likkutei Sichot,* followed by the number of the respective volume.

While the first three volumes of the translation were taken completely from the original *Likkutei Sichot,* volume I, the *sichot* translated here are from the original volume II. They include the whole section on Bamidbar at the beginning of that volume, as well as all the additional *sichot* relating to the book of Bamidbar and appearing in the supplement at the end of that volume. The latter *sichot* are marked with an asterisk.

6. Many Hebrew and Yiddish words were retained in the translation, rendered in transliteration, because a simple translation would not do justice to them. All such words and terms are dealt with in the glossary.

The glossary also contains the names (and brief biographical data) of the leaders of the Chassidic movement, and other personalities, which are frequently referred to in the text or notes.

J. I. S.

LIKKUTEI
SICHOT

BAMIDBAR   במדבר

A

I. The first precept in the Book of *Bamidbar* is, "Count the number of all the congregation of Israel."[1] The *Gemara*, therefore, refers to this whole book by the term *Pekudim* (the Book of 'Those That Are Numbered;' Numbers).[2]

The act of counting has nothing to do with, and does not indicate the nature of, the objects that are counted. For the sum takes in every component alike, without regard to quantitative or qualitative differences. The greatest or most important does not count for more than one, even as the smallest or least important does not count for less than one. An enumeration, therefore, does not indicate anything about the particular significance of that which is counted.

To be sure, the enumeration referred to above was restricted to those "twenty years old and upwards."[3] This qualification of age, however, does not depend on any effort or personal achievement of the person counted. It is not related to the nature of the person, but comes of itself in the due course of time. A state of prematurity is not the same as the status of insufficient preparation.[4]

---

1. [Numbers 1:1]
2. *Sotah* 36b
3. [Numbers 1:3]
4. [The state of being premature to a stipulated time is not a defect caused by human action, nor is it remedied by human action. Thus it is not the same as insufficient preparation or a default caused by man. See *Pesachim* 90b; *Nazir* 64b; and *Sedei Chemed*, Kelalim, Mem:161 (ed. Kehot, vol. III, p. 1089.]

All this raises a question. An enumeration, as stated, is something external, non-related to essence or significance. Why, then, should something like that be the very first and fundamental precept of this book of the Torah, to the point that the whole book is referred to as the Book of the *Pekudim* (The Book of the Numbered)?

II.   There is a Halachic principle that "Something that one is wont to count does not become nullified or neutralized."[5] The very fact that it is counted shows that its species has intrinsic value, and by virtue thereof each of its entities is counted separately. The counting or enumeration does not indicate anything about the essence or significance of any one part in relation to any other part; nonetheless, it does indicate the significance of the species as a whole in relation to other species.[6]

It would seem, though, that this explanation is not yet satisfactory. An enumeration does indeed show the significance of the species as a whole, but it is no more than an *indication* or *demonstration* of this significance, and not its cause. In other words, the enumeration does not cause or establish significance; it only manifests it.

This would explain the difference between the two standards of "*something* that is subject to count" (i.e., the kind of an object that is *always* sold in specific numbers) and "*whatsoever* is wont to be counted" (i.e., a kind of object that is normally sold in specific numbers, but not always).[7] If the significance of counted objects derives from the fact of being counted, there should be no differ-

---

5. *Orlah* 3:7. *Betzah* 3b (and parallel passages). *Shulchan Aruch*, Yoreh De'ah, sect. 110.

6. [In our context, therefore, the enumeration of the Jews is an indication of the intrinsic significance of the Jewish People. It establishes the people as something that cannot be nullified or neutralized.]

7. See sources cited in note 5.

ence between the two standards of *"something* that.." and *"whatsoever* is.." After all, in this view the only thing that matters is whether or not it has been counted: if it is actually counted it will not be nullified or neutralized.

In fact, however, we do distinguish between these two standards. Quite obviously, then, it follows that the difference depends on whether or not the object has value and significance on its own, and the counting is merely an indication of this value. In the view of R. Yochanan,[8] therefore, an object which sometimes is counted and at other times is not, can be nullified and neutralized because it is clearly not that valuable (and the law follows this view of R. Yochanan[9]).

An enumeration, therefore, is something altogether superficial. Why, then, is the precept of counting the Jewish people so basic that this whole book is referred to as the Book of Numbers?

III.   Nothing is coincidental. All things, and especially matters of Torah and *mitzvot,* are by *hashgachah peratit* (Divine Providence governing all particulars). Thus even signs or symbols have an intrinsic relationship with the things they represent.[10]

This principle applies also to enumerations. The fact that an enumeration is an indication of significance implies that the numbering itself is also of importance.

To be sure, it was stated above that an enumeration as such is not significant; but this refers only to the counting *per se* when it is not related to something of importance. If, however, the counting is related to objects of significance, their intrinsic significance will reflect upon the counting as well. Even so, this "reflected significance"

8. [*Betzah* 3b]

9. [*Shulchan Aruch,* Yoreh De'ah 110:1, gloss of Rema.]

10. *Cf. L.S.-Vayikra,* Shemini-A.

attaching itself to the enumeration is not intrinsic, but superficial.

This explains why the whole book of *Bamidbar* is referred to as the "Book of Numbers." Enumeration on its own is indeed not significant. Nonetheless, the enumeration does indicate the significance of the object numbered, and that is why the whole book is referred to in terms of the enumeration as the "Book of Numbers."

IV. This raises another question. An enumeration, as stated, is something superficial, altogether separate from the essence of the object counted. How, then, can it be the means through which essence and significance will manifest itself?

This question, however, would pose a problem only if quantity and quality were two independent entities. If that were the case, it would indeed be impossible for significance (quality) to manifest itself through numbering (quantity). In our context, however, the subject is Jews and things related to them. Jews are "one nation on earth."[11] The *Alter Rebbe*[12] interpreted this phrase to mean that even "on earth," in all earthly (mundane) matters - that is, material and physical things - they bring about 'one-ness,' joining quality and quantity. With them, therefore, quality can express itself even in quantity.

V. In view of this relationship between quantity and quality, a quantitative increase may also enhance the status of the quality.[13]

---

11. [II Samuel 7:23]

12. *Hayom Yom, s.v.* Elul 27. [See also *Keter Shem Tov*, Hossafot, par. 70.] *Cf. Tanya*, Igeret Hakodesh, sect. IX.

13. This is more readily seen in context of the ruling that even half of a standard measure [i.e., less than legal minimum that would constitute the violation of a prohibition] is alsoforbidden by the Torah [*Yoma* 73b; Rambam, *Hilchot Ma'acholot Assurot* 14:2], because such quantities can complement one another.

For example, there is the concept of a *minyan*. A gathering of ten Jews (the quorum for a *minyan*), regardless of the qualitative status of each of these ten, brings about an indwelling of the Shechinah: "the Shechinah rests on every assembly of ten men."[14] The *minyan* thus allows for the recitation of certain sacred texts.[15] Quantity, therefore, is seen here to cause an increase in quality.

Another example is the recitation of the Grace after Meals. When three individuals eat together they must say grace together (*zimun*). When ten individuals eat together, the Divine Name is inserted in the preamble of *zimun*. In fact, the *Mishnah* voices an opinion that there is to be still another insertion when there are a hundred; and so forth.[16] In other words, a change in quantity brings about a change in quality, because the two are related and quantity is infused with quality.

VI.   The same principle applies also to the observance of *mitzvot*: "While occupied with the observance of one *mitzvah*, one is exempt from fulfilling another *mitzvah*."[17] In other words, while occupied with whatever *mitzvah*, one is exempted from observing another *mitzvah* regardless how great it may be, even in terms of distinctions between "the simple and the most severe *mitzvot*."[18]

---

14. *Sanhedrin* 39a. [See below, note 28]

15. [The recitation of certain sacred texts requires the presence of a *minyan*. *Berachot* 21b and *Megilah* 23b; *Shulchan Aruch*, Orach Chayim, sect. 55.]

16. *Berachot* 49b [*Shulchan Aruch*, Orach Chayim, sect. 192.]

17. *Sukah* 25a. *Sotah* 44b.

18. [All *mitzvot* derive from G-d. Thus one cannot "weigh the precepts of the Torah" to distinguish between "light (minor)" and "heavy (major)" *mitzvot*. Nonetheless, our sages still use expressions like "the most simple and the most severe *mitzvot*." *Yerushalmi, Pe'ah* 1:1; *Tanchuma*, Ekev:2; *Devarim Rabba* 6:2; and *cf. Avot* 2:1.] *Yalkut Shimoni*, Yitro:298, and Mishlei:937.

Moreover, while preoccupied with the observance of a *mitzvah* one is exempt even from the study of Torah! This exemption holds notwithstanding the fact that the relationship of *mitzvot* to Torah is like that of the body to the soul,[19] and like that of the limbs to the "blood which is the life-force"[20] within the limbs.[21] This relationship is analogous to that between quantity and quality. Nonetheless, preoccupation with even a 'minor' *mitzvah* will at the time exempt from the study of Torah. The reason again is because quantity is infused with quality.

VII.   This principle is found also with *matan Torah* (the Giving of the Torah). *Matan Torah* required the presence of 600,000 Jews. If just one had been missing, even if that one had been the least significant of the tribe of Dan,[22] the Almighty would not have given the Torah, Heaven forbid, to the Jewish people,[23] not even to the greatest among them. The lack of even one would have diminished the quantity of 600,000. Likewise, the blessing of *chacham harazim* requires the presence of no less than 600,000.[24]

VIII.   The numberings in the Book of Bamidbar tie in with the subject of the tribal standards.[25] The *Midrash*

---

19. See *Tanya*, ch. 23.

20. [Deuteronomy 12:23]

21. *Likkutei Torah*, Bamidbar, p. 13a. [Note *Tikunei Zohar* 30:74a that the *mitzvot* are compared to limbs.]

22. [Dan was of the "lowest of the tribes," being of the sons of the handmaids; *Shemot Rabba* 40:4; Rashi on Exodus 35:34.]

23. *Mechilta*, Yitro, Bachodesh:ch. 3. [See also *Mechilta deRashby* on Exodus 19:11; and *Devarim Rabba* 7:8.]

24. [When seeing a large crowd of at least 600,000 Jews one is to recite the blessing of "Blessed are You . . who discerns the Secrets," i.e., who knows what is in the heart of each one of these in that crowd.] *Berachot* 58a, and Rashi there.

25. [Each of the tribes had its distinct standard or banner (Numbers ch. 2). As each tribe is assigned its standard, the Torah reiterates the number of its members.]

relates: at the time of *matan Torah* the Jewish people had a vision of the *merkavah* (Divine chariot) and of legions of angels "all arrayed under separate standards.. Thus they longed for standards, and said, 'Oh that we also could be arrayed under standards like them.'" The Holy One, blessed be He, then said to Moses, "Go, arrange them under standards as they desired."[26]

Even as *matan Torah* required the amount of 600,000, so also the arrangement under standards - which originated with *matan Torah*. Our sages thus said that the number of people arrayed under the standard for the camp of Judah corresponds to the number of angels in the camp of Michael; and so forth.[27] In other words, that particular quantity effected a specific quality.

IX. The above teaches us the following:

We live in a time when quantity is viewed as more important than quality. Thus we must see to bring ever more Jews under the standards of Israel, regardless of their condition and status. As the quantity increases, this will eventually enhance also the quality.

Initially it is not important to consider how profoundly they will be affected quality-wise. The immediate concern is to bring Jews into the camp of Israel. The *Alter Rebbe* explains that the principle of "The *Shechinah* dwells over every gathering of ten"[28] applies even when they are not occupied with Torah: the very fact that there is a gathering of ten is sufficient to bring about an indwelling of the *Shechinah*.[29] Likewise in our context: the greater quantity in the camp of Israel will have a qualitative effect. This, in turn, will lead to the realization of the ultimate goal that

---

26. *Bamidbar Rabba* 2:3
27. *Zohar* III:154a, see there.
28. [See above, note 14.]
29. *Tanya*, Igeret Hakodesh, sect. XXIII. [See *Korban Ha'edah* on *Yerushalmi*, *Eruvin* 1:10, s.v. vekamah; *Tossafot*, *Nedarim* 8a, s.v. tzarich.]

"The Holy One, blessed be He, desired to have a *dirah betachtonim* (an abode in the lower world)."[30]

X.   Even so, one must remain aware of the principle of "Do not hide yourself from your own flesh."[31] To prepare for *matan Torah* means not only working with others, but also with oneself. The *Midrash*[32] tells us that at the time of *matan Torah* none were deaf, blind, or otherwise maimed and handicapped, G-d forbid. Everyone was healed. For the giving of the Torah one must come with all limbs fully intact, without any blemishes or handicap.

As for *others*, one is not to be scared by their deficient quality. *Every single* Jew must be befriended and brought close. Thus it was at *matan Torah*: "Israel camped,"[33] in singular tense, all of them as one.[34] As for *oneself*, however, careful stock must be taken of one's own condition. Any kind of blemish must be corrected, whether it be in one's vision, hearing, or whatever.

B

XI.   The two *sidrot* of *Bamidbar* and *Nasso* deal with the *mishkan* (sanctuary) in the desert, and the division of duties related to moving the sanctuary from place to place.

This emphasizes that even in a desert Jews have the ability to establish a place of sanctity—a *mishkan*—for the *Shechinah* to dwell among them in general, and within

---

30. [*Tanchuma*, Nasso:16. See *Tanya*, ch. 36-37.]

31. [Isaiah 58:7]

32. *Mechilta*, Yitro, Bachodesh:ch. 9; *Bamidbar Rabba* 7:1 (cited by Rashi on Exodus 20:15). *Yalkut Shimoni*, Yitro:300.

33. [Exodus 19:2]

34. [*Mechilta*, Yitro, Bachodesh:ch. 1; Rashi on Exodus 19:2. See also below, note 40.]

every Jew in particular.[35]

Just as there is a physical desert, a wilderness governed by extreme climates and all kinds of threats, so, too, there is a *spiritual* desert which is governed by the most harmful ideas. The latter may exist even in a land that is physically a blooming garden.

Our holy Torah thus teaches us that when we find ourselves in a spiritual desert, we can—and thus *must*—establish a sanctuary. Moreover, we can, and thus *must*, carry it forward, walking in the footsteps (as it were) of the *Shechinah*,[36] until we reach the Divinely blessed Holy Land, i.e., the true and complete redemption through the righteous Mashiach.

XII.   This is a lesson for *all* Jews, but above all for Jewish women. For the women were the very first to respond when it came to building the *mishkan*.[37]

In the spiritual wasteland of certain circles, governed by desolation and emptiness in matters of *Yiddishkeit*, let alone with respect to a Chassidic way of life, women have the great and perpetual merit to be among the first to establish a *mishkan* for the Divine Presence.

Special attention must be given to the very young children in particular. For quite evidently, raising a child properly from the earliest age guarantees much more success, greater and better results.

---

35. [See Exodus 25:8, "They shall make Me a sanctuary, and I shall dwell among them": it does not say "I shall dwell *in it*" but "*in them*", i.e., within every single one of Israel. *Reishit Chochmah*, Sha'ar Ha'ahavah, ch. 6; *Shenei Luchot Haberit*, Sha'ar Ha'otiot, *s.v.* lamed, and *ibid.*, Masechet Ta'anit (*s.v.* me'inyan ha'avodah), and Terumah, *s.v.* Torah Or.]

36. [When Israel left Egypt, the Shechinah led them throughout their journeys to the Holy Land. See Exodus 13:21*f.*, and *Mechilta*, Beshalach, Shirta:ch.3; Exodus 33:14, Onkelos there, and *Midrash Tehilim* 90:9.]

37. [*Midrash Hagadol*, Ibn Ezra, and Ramban on Exodus 35:22.]

C

XIII.   Today is *Shabbat mevarchim*, the Shabbat of blessing the month that includes the day on which our Torah was given. This Shabbat, therefore, also marks the beginning for the preparation towards the giving and receiving of the Torah.

Peace and unity are the preparation and instrument for the giving of the Torah. Our sages thus state in *Mechilta*,[38] quoted in the commentary of Rashi:[39] "'Israel camped there [before the mountain]'—as one man with one mind." Another Midrash states: The Holy One, blessed is He, wished to give the Torah unto Israel immediately when they left Egypt, but they were divided among themselves.. When they came to Sinai, all reconciled to become a singular band.. Said the Holy One, blessed is He: "The whole Torah is 'peace,' thus I shall give it to that nation which loves peace.'"[40]

The peace and unity which serve as a preparation for the giving of the Torah must be in the context of Torah and *mitzvot*, as it is said: "Israel camped there (in singular tense, indicating unity; and they did so for the purpose of being—) before the mountain"[41] (signifying[42]) the Torah and its precepts).

By means of peace one is able to achieve desired objectives, as it is written, "Ephraim is united in idol-wor-

---

38. [*Mechilta*, Yitro, Bachodesh:ch.1.]

39. [Rashi on Exodus 19:2.]

40. [*Tanchuma*, ed. Buber, Yitro:9. Cf. *Vayikra Rabba* 9:9.]

41. See Rashbam on this verse: "Before the mountain" that was mentioned earlier (Exodus 3:12)—"When you will take the people out of Egypt, you will serve G-d upon this mountain."

42. See *Shemot Rabba* 2:4 and 51:8, and *Bamidbar Rabba* 1:8, that all names of that mountain relate to Torah and *mitzvot*.

ship, let him alone,"[43] in context of our sages' interpretation of this verse.[44] Likewise, by virtue of being "of one
language and unified words"[45]—"they are not precluded
from anything they have devised to do."[46] Nonetheless,
the peace in those contexts has no permanence. It is cer-
tainly not the way to induce, as it were, Heavenly effluences, let alone when desiring the Torah of which the
Almighty said, "I Myself have written, have given,"[47] as it
were—i.e., the very core, as opposed to an encompassing
aspect.[48] One can elicit these only when the souls are rooted in the Divine Essence, as explained in context of the
concept "Who did He consult? The souls of the righteous."[49] Unity, therefore, must be in the context of Torah
and *mitzvot*; the sense of *ahavat Yisrael* must manifest itself
especially in efforts to bring others close to the Torah.

The above is said for a practical purpose:

Shavu'ot is the time of *matan Torah* for the year as a
whole (in addition to the more specific aspect of *matan*

---

43. [Hosea 4:17]

44. *Bereishit Rabba* 38:6 ["Great is peace, for even if Israel practice
idolatry but maintain peace among themselves, the Holy One, blessed
is He, says, 'I have no dominion over them because there is peace
among them.'"]

45. [Genesis 11:1]

46. [Genesis 11:6.] *Zohar* I:76b. [*Cf.* also *Zohar* I:75b: "As all are as
one, in unity, they succeed in their deeds."]

47. *Shabbat* 105a [reading "*Anochi* (I)," the first word of the Ten
Commandments revealed at Sinai, as an acronym for this expression],
in context of *Tanya* ch. 47 ["He has given us His Torah, and in it His
Will and His Wisdom which are united with His Essence and Being,
blessed be He, in absolute unity. It is as if He gave us His very self, as
it were."]

48. On all the above, see *Tanya*, ch. 32; *Torah Or*, Noach, p. 11a-b.
Torat Chayim, and *Likkutei Torah-Shalosh Parshiyot*, end of Noach.

49. [*Bereishit Rabba* 8:7; *Ruth Rabba* 2:3. See *Likkutei Sichot*, vol.
XX, p. 279; and *cf. ibid.*, p. 370.]

Torah relating to every single day, as expressed in the text of the blessing "Who *gives* the Torah," in present tense[50]). The days between now and the morning of the festival of *Shavu'ot*, therefore, must be utilized to the fullest extent, and especially on the Sabbaths when assemblies of the community are gathered together,[51] as follows:

All those who have some influence over Jewish men and women must inform them, and give them to understand, that especially during this period of time it is their duty and merit to make intensified efforts with regard to *ahavat Yisrael*. (This, of course, is in addition to the duty and merit to do so every day. It is well-known that the *Alter Rebbe* wrote in his *Siddur*, which he composed for everyone and which applies to all equally: "It is proper to say before prayer: 'I hereby accept upon myself the commandment[52] 'Love your fellow like yourself.'"[53])

One must explain this in terms of *ahavat Yisrael* being a preparation for the giving and receiving of the Torah.

---

50. *Likkutei Torah*, Sukot, p. 81c; also *ibid.*, Nitzavim, p. 46b. [*Cf.* *Turei Zahav* on *Shulchan Aruch*, Orach Chayim, 47:note 5.]

51. [*Yalkut Shimoni*, beg. of Vayakhel:408. *Midrash Hagadol* on Exodus 35:1. Rashi, *Shabbat* 115a, *s.v.* bein she'ein.]

52. [Leviticus 19:18]

53. [Beginning of Morning Prayers]. Note *Peri Eitz Chayim*, Sha'ar Olam Ha'asiyah, end of ch. 1 ["Before starting with any prayer of the Morning-Prayers it is incumbent to accept upon oneself the precept of 'Love your fellow like yourself.' One is to have in mind to love every single Jew like his own soul, for thus his prayer will ascend compounding all of Israel, and therefore is able to ascend to be effective and to succeed."] See also *Sidur Ha'arizal*, Tefilat Ha'asiyah ["Before praying one should have in mind to accept upon himself the positive precept of 'Love your fellow like yourself.' His prayer will thus be compounded with the prayers of all of Israel, as the merit of the multitude is attributed to him. Thus one should say, 'I hereby accept upon myself the positive precept of 'Love your fellow like yourself,' and hereby I love every single Jew as my soul and my might.'"]

One must make known and explain the saying of the *Alter Rebbe*[54] that "The precept 'Love your fellow like yourself' is a means and tool to the precept of 'Love *Hashem*, your G-d.'[55]" The implication is that love of G-d, love of Torah, and love of Israel are entirely one![56]

One must disseminate the teaching of the *Maggid* on the words of the *Mishnah*,[57] "Know what is above [from] you": "Know that everything from above is all from you," i.e., it depends entirely on each individual.[58] Our sages thus taught that man should regard the world as equally balanced [between merit and guilt], and a *single* deed will tip the scale either to the side of merit or..[59] In our context, too, one single deed can cause and effect the giving of the Torah.

This applies especially to actions relating to peace and *ahavat Yisrael*, which the *Baal Shem Tov* established as one of the fundamental principles of the teachings of Chassidism.[60] Such actions compound one in the other so that one is no longer a singular entity.

This is the proper preparation for receiving the Torah. For the whole Torah was given for the purpose of establishing peace in the world[61]—in the world at large (macrocosm), as well as in the 'miniature world' (microcosm),

---

54. [*Torat Hachassidut*, ch. 30; *Hayom Yom*, s.v. Tishrei 6. *Cf. Keter Shem Tov*, Hossafot, par. 18 and 141.]

55. [Deuteronomy 6:5]

56. [See below, note 79.]

57. *Avot* 2:1

58. *Likkutei Amarim*, sect. 198; *Or Torah*, sect. 480. [See also *Tzava'at Harivash*, sect. 142; and *Hayom Yom*, s.v. Iyar 13.]

59. *Kidushin* 40b; Rambam, *Hilchot Teshuvah* 3:4.

60. See *Sefer Hasichot 5701*, p. 153ff.; *Sefer Hasichot 5705*, p. 66. [*Cf.* also *Sefer Hasichot 5703*, p. 161.]

61. Rambam, *Hilchot De'ot* 4:14. See also *Sifre*, Nasso, sect. 42. [*Cf.* above, note 40; *Gitin* 59b; *Zohar* I:197b and III:176b.]

i.e., man[62]—to establish peace between the Creator and His creation.[63]

Every one should relate and publicize the above, especially those who will speak in public during these days.

Thus we can be assured that all of us, among all of Israel, will merit that which my father-in-law, the *Rebbe*, expressed in his blessing of *"receiving the Torah with joy and inwardness."*

D

XIV.   *Ahavat Yisrael* is a prerequisite to *kabalat Hatorah* (receiving the Torah). This can be understood in context of *matan Torah* requiring the number of 600,000 Jews, without regard to any differences between them.[64]

Any difference between one Jew and another relates to individual potentials. In terms of the soul *per se*, however, all are equal. In terms of essence, the souls are "all of a kind, and all having one Father."[65] At *matan Torah*, therefore, when the Almighty bound up His essence—*Anochi* (I, Myself)[66]—with the essence of the Jews, all 600,000 Jews were equal.

Thus we can understand why *ahavat Yisrael* is a preparation, a prerequisite, to *matan Torah*. For *ahavat Yisrael* evokes the essence of the soul, as will be explained further on.

XV.   My father-in-law, the *Rebbe*, quoted a teaching

---

62. ["Man is a microcosm"—*Tanchuma*, Pekudei:3; *Zohar* III:257b; *Tikunei Zohar* 69:100b. See *Avot deR. Nathan*, ch. 31.]

63. See *Sanhedrin* 99b. *Likkutei Torah*, Matot, p. 88.

64. [See above, note 23.]

65. *Tanya*, ch. 32.

66. [See above, note 47.]

of the *Baal Shem Tov*[67] about *ahavat Yisrael* relating also to simple folks:

The *Gemara*[68] says, "What is written in the *tefillin* of the Master of the universe? 'Who is like Your people Israel, the one nation on earth.'[69]" The Jewish people are the Almighty's *tefillin*. In *tefillin* there are the *tefillin* of the hand and the *tefillin* of the head. Each of these is a *mitzvah* and requires a *berachah* (blessing)[70] [with differing opinions whether one must recite one or two blessings[71]]. The donning of the hand-*tefillin* precedes that of the head-*tefillin*.[72] The same applies to the *tefillin* of the Master of the Universe: the hand-*tefillin*—which signify the 'masters of good deeds' (simple people who observe the commandments), precede the head-*tefillin*—which signify the intellectuals (scholars knowledgeable in Torah).

This teaching evoked in many a sense of *ahavat Yisrael* towards simple folks, by virtue of its premise that 'masters of good deeds' stand higher than scholars. Many sources explain this in terms of simple people having a manifestation of the simplicity of essence.[73]

XVI.   The saintly R. Zusya related to the *Alter Rebbe*[74] that he heard the following from his brother, the saintly R. Elimelech: The disciples of the *Maggid* attended to their master in prearranged shifts. Once, when it was R.

---

67. [*Keter Shem Tov*, Hossafot, sect. 70, and see there note 71.]
68. *Berachot* 6a
69. [I Chronicles 17:21]
70. [See *Menachot* 44a; Rambam, *Hilchot Tefilin* 4:4; *Shulchan Aruch [Harav]*, Orach Chayim 25:13 and 26.]
71. [See *Shulchan Aruch [Harav]*, Orach Chayim 25:13-14 and 23.]
72. [*Ibid.* par. 12.]
73. [See *Keter Shem Tov*, Hossafot, par. 154, and note 164 there; *Likkutei Sichot*, vol. XXIV, p. 567, note 50. See also below, sect. XXIV and note 102.]
74. *Sefer Hasichot 5700*, p. 116f. *Or Torah*, Hossafot, par. 42.

Elimelech's turn, the *Maggid* called him in and said: "'Melech, do you hear what they say in the Academy On High? '*Ahavat Yisrael* means to love a *rasha gamur* (an altogether wicked person) just as a *tzadik gamur* (an altogether righteous person)!'"[75]

This maxim of the *Maggid* goes beyond that of the Baal Shem Tov. The *Baal Shem Tov* referred only to simple folks. The *Maggid* included also the altogether wicked, and furthermore, that the love towards a *rasha gamur* is to be the same as towards a *tzadik gamur*.

XVII.   The *Alter Rebbe* states that *ahavat Yisrael* relates to "both the great and the small," a love as among "real brothers"—thus a truly intrinsic love.[76] This is the meaning of "Love your fellow as yourself"—literally "as yourself." Love of self—"like yourself"—is an intrinsic love, independent of any external factors or calculations. That is why "love covers all transgressions"[77]: even when one recognizes and admits that there are transgressions—(he is in a state that even self-love cannot deceive him into thinking that certain actions are not transgressions)—self-love will still somehow cover these and excuse them. For that love penetrates to a point so deep in the soul that transgressions will not touch it. This is the extent of the obligation of loving a fellow-man.[78]

[To be sure,this kind of love can be evoked only through rational contemplation (as explained further on); even so, by means of contemplation one can reach an intrinsic love which transcends reason.]

---

75. *Cf.* R. Mosheh Cordovero, *Tomer Devorah*, beg. and end of ch. 2. [*Cf.* "The Dynamics of Ahavat Yisrael," in *Chassidic Dimensions*, ch. IV and XI, and note 126 there.]

76. *Tanya*, ch. 32.

77. [Proverbs 10:12]

78. [See *Derech Mitzvotecha*, s.v. Ahavat Yisrael, cited and translated in "The Dynamics of Ahavat Yisrael," ch. XIII.]

How can one the love toward another be as intrinsic as love toward oneself? After all, the other is not oneself!

There are two ways of explaining this:

a) Love of Israel, love of Torah, and love of G-d, are altogether one.[79] A Jew's love of G-d is intrinsic, for "You are children unto G-d, your G-d,"[80] and a child and its father are one essence.[81] Thus it follows that the love of Israel, too, which derives from the love of G-d—"loving that which the beloved loves"—is also an intrinsic love.[82]

b) On a deeper level: All Jews are a singular entity.[83] There is *one* essence manifesting itself in each of the different parts.[84] Thus it is not really love toward *another*; it is love toward *oneself.*[85]

XVIII.   It would seem that the statement of the *Alter Rebbe* goes beyond that of the *Maggid.*

The maxim that one is to love a *rasha gamur* just as a *tzadik gamur* is based on reason and a calculated judgment. This is seen by fact that a distinction remains by saying that he is to be loved *'just as* a *tzadik gamur.'*

A love "like yourself," however, is not subject to any calculations, because there is an intrinsic love of self, of

---

79. [See *Likkutei Sichot*, vol. II, p. 499*ff.*, cited and translated in "The Philosophy of Lubavitch Activism," in *Chassidic Dimensions*, ch. I, and see the notes there.]

80. [Deuteronomy 14:1. See *Kidushin* 36a.]

81. [*Cf. Tanya*, ch. 2.]

82. See *Kovetz Michtavim-Amirat Tehilim* [appended to *Tehilim Ohel Yosef Yitzchak*], p. 192.

83. [*Mechilta deRashby* on Exodus 19:6. See "The Dynamics of Ahavat Yisrael," ch. IX, and the sources cited there.]

84. [Note the teaching of the Baal Shem Tov that *etzem* (essence) - [another version: *achdut* (unity)]—is indivisible; when seizing any part of it, one seizes all of it. *Keter Shem Tov*, sect. 250, and *ibid.*, Hossafot, sect. 116.]

85. *Likkutei Sichot*, vol. II, p. 435.

one's very being. It is likewise with the love of *real brothers*.

XIX.   This explains the connection between *ahavat Yisrael* and *matan Torah*: *ahavat Yisrael*—"'Israel camped there' as one man,"[86] without distinctions—evokes the very essence of the soul (and all of Israel constitute one essence as stated above). This allows taking, as it were, the "I, Myself"—the Divine Essence, which through the Torah is given to the essence of Israel.

E*

XX.   This *sidrah* relates that after Moses counted the Jewish people G-d said to him: "Bring near the tribe of Levi.."[87] The tribe of Levi was chosen from among all the Jewish people to be "brought near" to conduct the service in the *mishkan*, and later on in the Sanctuary. This became their task. They were to conduct the service in the *mishkan* and *mikdash*, as deputies of all of Israel. Thus they elicited for Israel all the Divine blessings that were effected through that service, for all of Israel.

XXI.   The Midrash[88] relates this prooftext to the verse, "The *tzadik* (righteous) flourishes like a palm-tree, he grows tall like a cedar in Lebanon."[89]

This year, the first day of *Shavu'ot*—the day on which we were given the Torah[90] which offers instruction[91] to all

---

86. [See above, notes 38-39.]

87. [Numbers 3:5]

88. [*Tanchuma*, Bamidbar:15; *Bamidbar Rabba* 3:1.]

89. Psalms 92:13

90. See *Shulchan Aruch [Harav]*, Orach Chayim 494:1.

91. [See *Zohar* III:53b; Redak on Psalms 19:8; R. Judah Loewe, *Gur Aryeh* on Genesis 1:1 — and his *Netivot Olam*, Netiv Hatorah:ch. 1 and Netiv Ha'emunah:ch. 2 — that the term *Torah* means instruction. Cf. *L.S.-Bereishit*, Introduction, p. XV.]

Jews to the end of time—marks the 200th anniversary of the *hilula*[92] of the *Baal Shem Tov*.[93] He interpreted[94] this verse as follows:

There are two kinds of *tzadikim*: one is compared to a palm-tree, and the other is compared to a cedar.

A cedar has many qualities: it is strong, tall and beautiful.[95] However, it does not bear any fruit. A palm-tree does not possess all those qualities. Nonetheless, it has the advantage—[and this is a fundamental advantage]—that it flourishes: it brings forth beautiful and sweet fruits[96] which contribute to the strength and health of those that eat it.[97]

It is the same with *tzadikim*—a term applied to all Jews, as it is said, "Your people are all *tzadikim*."[98] There are two ways of serving G-d:

One kind of *tzadik*, says the *Baal Shem Tov*, is compared to a cedar. He does not produce fruits. He studies

---

92. [*Hilula* (lit., joy; wedding). The passing of a *tzadik* from this world is designated as a *hilula*, signifying the joy of the *tzadik* whose soul returns unspoiled to be rejoined with its Maker. (*Cf. Zohar* I:98a and 245b; also *Zohar* III:296b.) There is an element of joy also for the *tzadik*'s disciples and followers who (a) share in his joy, and (b) the merit of the *tzadik* reflects upon them as well (see *Tanya*, Igeret Hakodesh, sect. XXVII). Thus they celebrate the anniversary of his passing (*yahrtzeit*) with reflection upon their master's teachings and instructions, and resolve to follow in his righteous ways to enhance their observance of Torah and *mitzvot*. See also *L.S.-Vayikra*, Lag BaOmer, note 61; and *The Great Maggid*, p. 220, and notes 28-29 there.]

93. [The Baal Shem Tov was born on the 18th of Elul 5458 (1698), and passed away on the 6th of Sivan (first day of Shavu'ot) 5520 (1760; see *The Great Maggid*, p. 87, note 6.]

94. *Tzava'at Harivash*, sect. 125.

95. Ezekiel 31:3*ff.*

96. [*Pirkei deR. Eliezer*, end of ch. 19.] *Yalkut Shimoni*, Tehilim:845.

97. *Ketuvot* 10b

98. Isaiah 60:21

Torah, he observes *mitzvot*, but it is all for himself. He does not influence others. To be sure, he is a *tzadik* and will receive a Divine reward, "he grows tall like a cedar"— strong, tall, and beautiful; but this is not the goal intended by G-d.

G-d wants man to "flourish like a palm-tree," to produce good and sweet fruits. In other words, G-d demands that one is to give from one's own time, abilities and energy which could have been used for personal pursuits. One is to utilize these to influence others, so that they become that which the Almighty regards as good and sweet fruits. He who influences others is referred to as a palm-tree, to which Scripture ascribes the quality of *"flourishes like a palm-tree."*

XXII.   The *Baal Shem Tov* passed this interpretation on to his disciples and to their disciples, including the *Alter Rebbe*, and onwards unto my father-in-law, the *Rebbe*. It teaches that one can serve G-d in the first of those two ways, and still be regarded as a *tzadik* with all the qualities of height, strength and beauty. Nonetheless, this is not the goal and principal way demanded by G-d. The Almighty demands that one do not withhold any time or effort, but to utilize these with the innermost energy of the soul, to influence others, to influence one's whole environment.

The *Baal Shem Tov* himself followed this way, and he passed it on to the leaders of general Chassidism as well as to the leaders of Chabad, and to all Chassidim: every one of these is to follow this path. It is the illuminated way, the way that converts darkness to light.

XXIII.   This is also the special way and task of the tribe of Levi,[99] for themselves personally as well as in their function as representatives and guides of all Jews.

---

99. See Deuteronomy 33:10. Rambam, *Hilchot Shemitah Veyovel* 13:12 [and see there also 13:13, cited below (note 107)].

To be sure, there are 'different tribes,' Jews who have not yet reached the realization and conviction of this principle. We, however, must conduct ourselves according to the way shown to us by the *Baal Shem Tov*. We must work on ourselves and on others, to make of ourselves and of others such that "flourish like a palm-tree" with good and sweet fruits. This must be done with soul and vitality, evoking one's innermost energies, to influence our total environment. Each one must contribute his share to make this world more pure, more sublime, more radiant and more holy.[100]

F*

XXIV. *Parshat Bamidbar* relates the counting of the Jewish people. In this enumeration all were counted equally, from the greatest to the most simple. The greatest of all did not count for more than one, even as the most simple did not count for less than one.

This enumeration also serves as a preparation for *matan Torah*. Our sages thus said[101] that if there had been 600,000 less one, then, G-d forbid, the Torah would not have been given, not even to Moses.

This idea is related to the concept of the integral simplicity of the soul, common to all Jews alike. Thus it was said by the *Baal Shem Tov*, the *Alter Rebbe*, and all the *rebbes* to my father-in-law, the *Rebbe*, that the integral simplicity of the ultimate Essence is bound up with the integral sim-

---

100. *Tanya*, ch. 37. [Each *neshamah* descended to this world "to be vested in a body and natural soul for the sole purpose of mending them .. to elevate his natural soul together with *its portion* that belongs to it of the totality of the world.."]

101. See above, note 23.

plicity of a Jew.[102] In this there are no distinctions between them.[103]

Thus all were counted equally. Nonetheless, the enumeration of the Jewish people as a whole included only those of twenty years and older.[104] The members of the tribe of Levi, on the other hand, were counted from the age of one month old and up: infants of one month old were counted equally with the greatest.[105] In the view of one opinion, Aaron [the High Priest], too, was included in this enumeration. (Moses, though of the tribe of Levi, was not included; but with regards to his brother Aaron there are two opinions.) Thus it follows that an infant of one month old was made equal in number to Aaron.

The tribe of Levi, as stated in Scripture, is to serve G-d.[106] Rambam thus states that "any individual whose spirit moves him to serve G-d" is like the tribe of Levi.[107] Service of G-d implies not only a service of Torah-study and prayer, but to "Acknowledge Him in all your ways."[108] There are thus no distinctions among those who devote themselves to the service of G-d. Even a child of one month old has the same numerical value as the very greatest.

Students raised in the pure spirit of our sacred tradition, imbued with a sense of serving by way of "Acknowledge Him in all your ways," are like members

---

102. See *Likkutei Diburim*, vol. III, p. 491b. [See there also vol. IV, p. 578b; and above, note 73.]

103. [*Cf.* above, note 84.]

104. [Numbers 1:3. *Cf.* Exodus 30:14.]

105. [Numbers 3:15]

106. [See above, note 99.]

107. [Rambam, *Hilchot Shemitah Veyovel* 13:13.]

108. [Proverbs 3:6. "All your ways" refers to all of man's involvements, including all mundane preoccupations such as eating, sleeping, conducting business, and so forth; see Rambam, *Hilchot De'ot* 3:2-3.]

of the tribe of Levi among which there are no distinctions from the age of one month old.

Of the Levites it is said that "they are wholly given unto Me *from among* the children of Israel."[109] The tribe of Levi thus represents, and works for, all of Israel. The references to 'separating' the Levites[110] do not mean that they are detached and removed from the Jews. Their distinct *avodah* affected *all* Jews, and had an impact on *all* of them. Any division falls by the side by virtue of a manifestation of the integral simplicity of the soul shared by all Jews alike.

XXV. In context of *matan Torah* there is the principle of "Our children will be our guarantors."[111] The children brought about the manifestation of *matan Torah* for all Jews.

This is one of the reasons why the *Rebbes* put so much emphasis and effort on *chinuch hakasher* (proper education) in the pure sense of our sacred tradition: to instruct children specifically with the phonetic method—"kometz-aleph o,"[112] making them aware of the sanctity of the consonants and the sanctity of the vowels.[113] For the education of children affects all of Israel.

---

109. [Numbers 8:16]

110. [See Numbers 8:14; *ibid.* 16:9; and Deuteronomy 10:8.]

111. [*Shir Rabba* 1:4; *Midrash Tehilim* 8:4; *Tanchuma*, Vayigash:2. Prior to giving the Torah to Israel, G-d demanded from them some surety that they would keep and observe it. The people of Israel proposed a number of sureties which were unacceptable to G-d, until they said: "Our children shall be our sureties."]

112. [Phonetic reading (which emphasizes each letter and vowel), as opposed to sight-reading (which ignores the individuality of the letters and vowels).]

113. See R. Mosheh Cordovero, *Pardes Rimonim* 28:1: "It is accepted knowledge among all the sages of Israel, by unbroken tradition going back to Ezra the Scribe who had an unbroken tradition going back to Moses who received from G-d at Sinai the different

The days of *matan Torah* are approaching. The preparation for *matan Torah* begins with the Shabbat upon which we bless the month of Sivan. It applies even more so from *rosh chodesh* Sivan [as it is written, "On that day they came to the desert of Sinai,"[114] which the *Gemara*[115] interprets (by an analogy of the phrase *"that* day") to refer to the day of *rosh chodesh*], and still more so in the 'three days of set boundaries.'[116]

As these days, and more particularly the festival of Shavu'ot itself, are soon upon us, the above serves as a lesson for every one of us. We must awaken the pupil within ourselves, as well as "'You shall teach them diligently to your children'[117]—i.e., your students"[118] in the literal sense, to arouse and manifest the integral simplicity of the soul within them. This will also effect a manifestation of the integral simplicity of the soul in all of Israel, which, as stated above, is not subject to any distinctions. This is a preparation towards *matan Torah* of which it says, "Israel camped"[119]—in singular tense:[120] all stood there together for one purpose, and with one mind, to receive the one Torah from the One G-d.

By virtue of this we shall merit—in the words of the blessing of my father-in-law, the *Rebbe*—"to receive the Torah with joy and inwardness."

kinds of vowel-points.." [See *Zohar Chadash*, Shir Hashirim, 65d and 73b.]

114. Exodus 19:1

115. *Shabbat* 86b

116. [The three days preceding Shavu'ot are called the "three days of set boundaries" (based on Exodus 19:12). At the time of *matan Torah* these days were devoted to preparing for *matan Torah* (see Exodus 19:10*ff.*; and *cf. Shabbat* 87a), and so every year again.]

117. [Deuteronomy 6:7]

118. *Sifre*, Va'etchanan, par. 34; Rashi on Deuteronomy 6:7.

119. Exodus 19:2

120. See above, note 34.

SHAVU'OT   שבועות

A

I. The Torah was given in the month of Sivan, the third month.[1] The Torah is thus connected with the number 'three.' This follows from the principle that everything — and especially anything pertaining to Torah and *mitzvot* — is by way of *hashgachah peratit* (Divine Providence relating to all particulars). Indeed, there is an *explicit* reference to the connection between *matan Torah* and the third month in the expression of our sages, "The three-fold Torah to a three-fold people in the third month."[2]

This raises a question: what is so special about the *third* month? After all, the purpose of Torah is to to use the 'one Torah'[3] to manifest in the world the reality of the 'one G-d.' The uniqueness of Torah, therefore, lies in unity, in oneness, and not in the number 'three.'

Furthermore, the third month is related mainly to Torah, as stated in the quote of "The three-fold *Torah* .. in the third month."

Mitzvot had been ordained already before *matan*

---

1. [Exodus 19:1]

2. *Shabbat* 88a. ["Threefold Torah" as the Scriptures divide into the three parts of *Torah* (the Five Books of Moses), *Nevi'im* (the Books of the Prophets), and *Ketuvim* (Hagiographa; the Holy Writings). "Threefold People" as the Jewish People divides into the three general classes of *Kohanim* (Priests), *Leviyim* (Levites), and *Yisra'elim* (Israelites). Notealso *Tanchuma*, Yitro:10 for further instances of 'threefoldedness' in our context.]

3. [See Numbers 15:16. *Tanchuma*, Lech:1; *Bamidbar Rabba* 13:15.]

Torah: the precepts commanded unto the descendants of Noah;[4] the precept of circumcision;[5] and the precepts ordained in Marah.[6] To be sure, these precepts were not equal to those ordained at Sinai, not even in the cases of the self-same ones that were commanded again at Sinai.[7] Nonetheless, the general idea of *mitzvot* was already there. The principal novelty of Shavu'ot in the third month, therefore, was the giving of the *Torah*.

The advantage of Torah over *mitzvot* is explained in *Tanya*[8]: By means of *mitzvot* one becomes a *merkavah* (chariot) to Divinity. A chariot stands in total self-negation to the charioteer, yet it remains distinct, it does not become a singular entity with the charioteer. Torah, on the other hand, literally unifies with the Almighty.

This fact in itself, however, strenghtens the difficulty raised by our question: how is it that the Torah, by means of which one becomes unified with the Almighty, was given specifically in the *third* month?

II.   This principle can be explained as follows.

The ultimate goal is to establish unity, to preclude any dualism. However, unity is recognized as real and proven only in the face of some other entity which will not distract and divert from the affirmation of that unity. When altogether unaware of anything else, there is no evi-

---

4. [The seven precepts revealed to Adam and Noah, and incumbent upon all mankind. *Sanhedrin* 56a*ff*, based on Genesis 2:16-17 and 9:4*ff*.]

5. [Genesis 7:9-14]

6. [Exodus 15:25. See *Mechilta* and Rashi on this verse; and *Sanhedrin* 56b.]

7. See Rambam, Commentary on Mishnah, *Chulin* 7:6. [*Cf. Encyclopedia Talmudit*, vol. I, *s.v.* ein lemeidim mikodem matan Torah; and *L.S.-Bereishit*, Vayetze-C.]

8. *Tanya*, ch. 23; and see the glosses of Tzemach Tzedek on this chapter [*Kitzurim Vehe'arot*, pp. 19*f*. and 104*ff*.].

dence that there is a true affirmation of unity; for, in such a case, there would be no way to know how one would react when becoming aware of some other reality.

There is a parable relating to the descent of the soul to this world: to test the loyalty and bond of a king's son to his father, the prince is removed from the royal palace to be among lowly people in a far-off place. If he will conduct himself even there according to the norms of a prince, it is evident that he is truly bound up with his father, the king.

It is likewise in our context. When one is exposed to dualism, when confronted with situations opposing the reality of unity, and still remaining steadfast in the conviction of unity, this would show that one is truthfully absorbed in it.

A situation like this can manifest itself in two ways: a) One can negate the opposing reality, ignoring it altogether; or b) one can turn that reality itself into an instrument for unity.

The second way goes much deeper and is more truthful. To ignore an opposing reality does not remove it: the reality contradicting and opposing unity remains, except that it is ignored. If, however, the concept of unity penetrates to the point that all perceived realities become themselves instruments for unity, that is true and ultimate unity.

III.   The above aspects are signified by the three months of Nissan, Iyar and Sivan.[9]

Nissan is the *first* month. In Nissan occurred the exodus from Egypt, when "the King of all kings, the Holy One, blessed is He, revealed Himself unto them."[10] That was a revelation from above without any regard to the

---

9. *Cf. L. S.-Vayikra*, Emor, sect. IV*ff*.
10. [*Haggadah for Pesach*, p. 30; *cf.* there p. 24*f*.]

world below. Thus it is said, "The people had fled,"[11] that is, a flight from everything below to become attached to Divinity.[12]

Iyar is the *second* month. In this month there is a daily counting of the *omer*,[13] which signifies a refinement of the emotive attributes of the animal soul.[14] There *is* involvement with the mundane, thus suggesting dualism, but the mundane is sublimated. Even so, the mundane retains a sense of reality of its own and is not absorbed in Divinity. This is alluded in the very name of this month. For Iyar is an acronym for 'Avraham, Yitzchak, Ya'akov, Rachel,'[15] the four supports of the *merkavah* (chariot).[16] A chariot stands in self-negation towards the charioteer, but it is not unified with him.

---

11. [Exodus 14:5]

12. [See *Tanya*, end of ch. 31.]

13. [*Sefirat Ha'omer*, the counting of the days between the first day of Pesach and Shavu'ot, begins on the 16th of Nissan (Leviticus 23:15; see *Sifra, Lekach Tov,* and Rashi on this verse; *Menachot* 65a), spanning the three months of Nissan, Iyar and Sivan. Of Nissan and Sivan, however, only parts of the months are involved in this counting, while in Iyar this *mitzvah* is observed every day of the month. See *L.S.-Vayikra,* Emor, sect. I (p. 156).]

14. [The seven weeks of *Sefirat Ha'omer* signify the seven *midot* (emotive attributes) of the *Sefirot,* and correspondingly of the soul-faculties. Each of these seven subdivides into seven sub-categories, just as each week subdivides into seven individual days. See *L. S.-Vayikra,* Emor, note 23. The counting of each day signifies the refinement and sublimation of its respective attribute. See *Zohar* III:97a-b; and also ibid. 189a; *L.S.-Vayikra,* Emor, pp. 168*f.,* 171 and 174*f.,* and the notes there.]

15. [*Kohelet Ya'akov, s.v.* Iyar; *Bet Shemuel* on *Shulchan Aruch,* Even Ha'ezer, sect. 126, note 20. *Cf. Me'orei Or, s.v.* aleph, par. 84.]

16. [The three patriarchs and Rachel signify the compound of attributes which constitute the *merkavah,* the Divine Chariot. See *Zohar* I:150a (and *Sha'arei Zohar* on *Bereishit Rabba* 47:6) with regards to the patriarchs; and *Zohar* II:29b and III:244a with regards to Rachel.]

Sivan, the *third* month, is the month of *matan Torah*. The two aspects of 'above' and 'below' are taken together and converted into a third aspect, which transcends both of them: true unity and absorption in Divinity.[17]

IV. This explains why the Torah was given in the third month. For Torah signifies unity. Observance of *mitzvot* involves self-negation with respect to the *mitzvah*, but it does not mean a unification with it. With Torah, however, man's intellect is unified with the "wisdom and will of the Almighty."[18] This is the concept of the 'third': man's intellect and G-d's wisdom are taken, as it were, and turned into a new, a third reality, becoming altogether one.

This concept is alluded in the expression of "Moses received the Torah from Sinai."[19] *Mitzvot* had been given at Marah as well, but Torah is exclusively from Sinai. Sinai is the "lowest of all mountains,"[20] a unification of two opposites.[21] This unity, therefore, was manifested specifically in the Torah.

B

V. The *Zohar*[22] states that the festival of Shavu'ot is more sublime than all the other festivals. It is celebrated

---

17. [See *L.S.-Emor*, sect. XV. For more on the concept of *matan Torah* joining 'above' and 'below', see below, Massey, note 31.]

18. See *Tanya*, ch. 5: "This is a wondrous union like which there is none other, and which has no parallel anywhere in the material world.."

19. [*Avot* 1:1]

20. [*Midrash Tehilim* 68:9]

21. See *L.S.-Vayikra*, p. 192*ff*.

22. *Zohar* III:96a, see there at length. See also *Torah Or*, Yitro,p. 109d*ff*.

between Pesach and Sukkot, because it is the very center of all; for Torah is the central point of everything.

Shavu'ot is but one day, unlike Pesach and Sukkot which are seven and eight days respectively. This does not detract from its significance, for the one day of Shavu'ot establishes the fact of "Who is like Your people, like Israel, *one* nation on earth."[23]

This is the very concept (discussed in the preceding *sichah*) that ultimate unity is to be found in the Torah which was given specifically in the third month.

VI.   Centrality, to be in the middle, has two advantages: a) The central position is more distinguished than the two extremities on its sides. The *Gemara* thus states that "the master goes in the middle, the senior disciple on the right and the junior disciple on the left."[24] b) The center is the root for all other directions, for it ascends to *keter*, the root and source for all the *sefirot*.[25]

The centrality of the festival of Shavu'ot has both these qualities: a) Shavu'ot is itself more sublime than the other festivals; and b) on Shavu'ot we were given the Torah which contains *all* the festivals.

The main aspect of Shavu'ot, as stated, is Torah. The advantage of Torah-study over observance of *mitzvot* is manifest in both of those qualities: a) Torah-study is greater than all *mitzvot*, as our sages said, "The study of Torah is equivalent to all of them."[26] b) Torah-study is the root leading to all *mitzvot*, as our sages said, "Torah-study is greater because it leads to performance."[27]

VII.   To explain all this:

---

23. [II Samuel 7:23]

24. *Yoma* 37a

25. [See *Mystical Concepts in Chassidism*, pp. 69f. and 100, and note 157 there.]

26. *Pe'ah* 1:1

27. *Kidushin* 40b

The 613 precepts correspond to the 613 components in the human body: 248 commandments corresponding to the 248 organs, and 365 prohibitions corresponding to the 365 veins.[28] Torah corresponds to the brains, the intellect.[29] The advantage of the intellect over the components of the body is two-fold: a) The vital force of the brain transcends that of all other parts. b) The brain compounds the vitality of all other parts and is a root to all of them.[30] Analogous to this is the cited advantage of Torah over all other *mitzvot*.

VIII. Centrality has the additional advantage of ascending to the very core and essence of *keter*, which transcends even the level of the root and source of the *sefirot* in *keter*.

The same applies to Torah. The two qualities of "leading to performance" and "superseding all *mitzvot*" are qualities in the *mitzvah* of Torah-study. Torah, however, has the additional advantage of its own, of being the very "wisdom of the Almighty": "I am with Him as a craftsman.."[31]

This, indeed, is the true meaning of studying Torah *lishmah*, "for its own sake," i.e., "for the sake of the Torah itself." The implication is that one does not learn for the sake of acquiring knowledge on how to conduct oneself, nor for the sake of observing the *mitzvah* of Torah-study, but purely for the sake of Torah itself.

---

28. *Zohar* I:170b

29. [Torah is *chochmah*, wisdom (*Tanchuma*, Vayelech:2), identified with—and deriving from—the Divine *chochmah* (*Zohar* II:62b and 85a). See also *Zohar* III:85a. Torah-study (specifically of the Oral Torah) requires intellectual understanding; *Magen Avraham* on *Shulchan Aruch*, Orach Chayim, sect. 50, note 2; *Hilchot Talmud Torah [Harav]* 2:13.]

30. *Tanya*, ch. 51.

31. [Proverbs 8:30. *Tanchuma*, Bereishit:1; *Bereishit Rabba* 1:1.] See *Likkutei Torah*, Bamidbar, p. 12a*ff*.

This can be compared to a child that has not seen its father for a long time and calls out for him. When seeing him, the child will hug its father, embrace and kiss him. The child will do so not because of any benefit it itself will enjoy from him, but strictly for the father's own sake.

It is likewise with a Jew: whenever he has a free moment affording the opportunity to grasp his Father, the King, by means of Torah — as our sages expressed it, "You are taking Me"[32] — he does not think of anything else. He will not think about guidance for action, nor about fulfilling the precept of Torah-study. He grasps the Torah itself, for "the Torah and the Holy One, blessed is He, are entirely one."[33]

IX.   This explains the Talmudic statement that "The poor will be held accountable by virtue of Hillel, and the rich will be held accountable by virtue of R. Eleazar ben Charsom."[34] When the poor or the rich will argue that they were unable to study because of their respective preoccupations, a counter-argument will be brought against them from Hillel and from R. Eleazar ben Chisma.

Offhand this statement appears difficult. If these peoples' argument is fallacious because they could have found the time to study, we do not need the examples of Hillel and R. Eleazar. After all, there is the explicit obligation of "you shall meditate therein day and night."[35] Thus if they failed to utilize any opportunity to study, they are

---

32. [*Vayikra Rabba* 30:13] *Shemot Rabba* 33:1. *Tanya*, ch. 47 [citing *Zohar* II:140b].

33. *Tanya*, ch. 23, citing the *Zohar* as source. [See *Zohar* I:24a; and *ibid*. II:90b.]

34. *Yoma* 35b. [Bet Hillel and R. Eleazar devoted themselves fully to Torah in spite of the dire poverty of the former and the immense wealth of the latter.]

35. Joshua 1:8. [Rambam, *Hilchot Talmud Torah* 1:8; *Shulchan Aruch [Harav]*, Orach Chayim 155:1.]

in the category of "He has scorned the word of G-d."[36] If, again, they did not have any free time to study, how could they be criticized?

However, there are indeed situations of being legally exempt from the *mitzvah* of Torah-study. Nonetheless, the fact remains that "The Torah and the Holy One, blessed be He, are entirely one." With regards to the intrinsic fervor and delight required for Torah, therefore, one must seek involvement with Torah even when legally exempt.

X.   This explains why the Torah is referred to as *emet*, truth, as our sages said, "There is no truth but Torah."[37]

Truth means consistency and permanence, without interruption. Anything subject to interruption is relative, thus not true, as known from the concept of "rivers that fail."[38] Truth means "established forever."[39]

This is alluded in the letters *aleph-mem-tav* which make up the word *emet* (truth), as stated in *Yerushalmi*:[40] *aleph* is the beginning of the alphabet, *mem* is the middle, and *tav* is the end. For truth means that it remains the same: at the beginning, in the middle, and at the end.

Torah is thus referred to as *emet*. For the Torah is not subject to any restrictions. *Mitzvot* are restricted. They are subject to time and space. Even the *mitzvah* of Torah-study has its temporal limitations (as, for example, those preoc-

---

36. Numbers 15:31. *Sanhedrin* 99a.
37. [*Yerushalmi, Rosh Hashanah* 3:8] *Berachot* 5b.
38. [Certain rituals require the use of *mayim chayim*, naturally running waters. The waters of a "river that fails," i.e., a river that dried up (thus 'fails' in its natural flow) even once in seven years, are called *mayim hamechazvim*, waters that fail (based on Isaiah 58:11) and do not qualify as *mayim chayim*; see-] *Parah* 8:9. [*Cf. Likkutei Torah*, Matot, p. 83cf.; and *Likkutei Sichot*, vol. VI, p. 92, note 38.]
39. Proverbs 12:19. See *Tanya*, ch. 13.
40. *Sanhedrin* 1:1

cupied with actions sanctioned by Torah-law are exempt from Torah-study during that time, as defined and explained in *Shulchan Aruch, Hilchot Talmud Torah*). The *mitzvah* of Torah-study is also subject to spatial limitations (one is not allowed to study Torah in places of impurity[41]). The Torah itself, however, is not restricted. It has neither temporal nor spatial limitations (as stated in the *Gemara*, "it is different when done involuntarily"[42]).

XI.   Practically speaking, this means that one must study Torah continuously.

One is not to learn just to fulfill a legal obligation defined by the *Shulchan Aruch*. (When looking strictly at legal duties, one may ultimately be led to dispense his obligation by learning the minimal "one chapter in the morning and one chapter in the evening".[43]) Before anything else, one must ascertain whether his considerations about his 'legal obligation' are correct according to the *Shulchan Aruch*. It is quite possible that he does have more time available, which means that even the law itself obliges him to more extensive study. Moreover, even if he is correct in his considerations, the delight and fervor intrinsic to Torah require continuous learning.

One is not to regard the importance of Torah-study in terms of it providing man with guidance for his conduct. That kind of approach implies that when problems arise about actual practice, he will sit down to research the sources in the *Chumash* and the *Gemara*, with all the commentaries of the *rishonim* and *acharonim* up to the final decisions stated in the *Shulchan Aruch* of the *Alter Rebbe*; but when there are no problems affecting his conduct, then he will not learn.

---

41. [*Berachot* 24b; *Shulchan Aruch [Harav]*, Orach Chayim 85:2.]
42. *Kidushin* 33a
43. [*Menachot* 99b; *Hilchot Talmud Torah [Harav]* 3:4.]

One must realize that the principal aspect of Torah is "Torah for the sake of Torah." Thus one must learn continuously, every moment, making the Torah "great and glorious."[44]

XII.   In this context we can understand the difference between Torah and *mitzvot* with regards to minors.

Minors are exempt from all *mitzvot*.[45] There is a *mitzvah* to train and educate them; but a) this is merely a rabbinic precept,[46] and b) this is incumbent upon the father, and not upon the minor.[47]

Of Torah, however, it is said that "There is a positive precept, incumbent upon a father, to teach Torah unto his minor son,"[48] and there is also an obligation on the child's part "to learn for himself when realizing [a deficiency]."[49]

This distinction follows from the fact that *mitzvot* are generally restricted. The Torah, however, is not restricted, and thus it relates to all Jews [adults as well as minors].

XIII.   *Matan Torah* thus required that the children would serve as guarantors.[50] When *mitzvot* were ordained at Marah there was no demand for any surety. This happened only at *matan Torah*. For the basic principle of *matan Torah* is not a "giving of *mitzvot*," but the "giving of the Torah" which relates to minors as well. As minors, too, are obligated to study Torah, its special quality appears specifically in their context.[51] The Midrash [about the chil-

---

44. [See below, sect. XV.]

45. [*Chagigah* 2b]

46. *Shulchan Aruch [Harav]*, Orach Chayim, sect. 343. [See glosses of the *Rebbe* on *Pelach Harimon*, p. 294.]

47. [See *Encyclopedia Talmudit*, *s.v.* Chinuch, sect. 1.]

48. *Hilchot Talmud Torah [Harav]* 1:1.

49. Rambam, *Hilchot Talmud Torah* 1:3. See *Piskei Dinim -Tzemach Tzedek*, p. 339, on this ruling.

50. *Shir Rabba* 1:4. [See above, Bamidbar, note 111.]

51. See *L.S.-Bereishit*, Vayechi, sect. XVII.

dren being our surety] thus concludes by adducing the verse, "Out of the mouths of babes and sucklings You have *established oz* (strength, i.e., the Torah)."[52]

XIV.   The Torah is thus referred to as *emet* (truth). Truth extends from *aleph* (the first letter) to *tav* (the last letter), from the highest levels to the very lowest ones. Torah represents the most sublime extremity: it is beyond "knowledge how to act," transcending all aspects related to action. On the other hand, Torah is also in the lower extremity, relating to minors who are exempt from all *mitzvot*.

XV.   This explains also why we find the phrase "He makes the Torah great and glorious"[53] in two opposing contexts.

On the one hand we find this expression in the context of teaching young children. By virtue of the principle of making the Torah "great and glorious" it is ruled that the professional activity of teaching children is not subject to the laws of encroachment.[54] Here we speak of the very beginning in learning Torah, the lower extremity.

On the other hand we find the same expression in the context of the signs of kosher fish. The *Gemara*[55] notes that all fishes with scales also have fins. Why then does the Torah state the requirement of fins also? It does so in order to make the Torah "great and glorious!" In other words, here we speak of Torah on its own, beyond the concept of offering knowledge for proper action.

On all levels of Torah-study, therefore, from the highest to the lowest, there is the concept of making the Torah

---

52. [Psalms 8:3. The Midrash cited above, note 50, refers to this verse as a prooftext.]
53. [Isaiah 42:21]
54. Rambam, *Hilchot Talmud Torah* 2:7.
55. *Chulin* 66b

"great and glorious" and the concept of "You are taking Me."

Scripture thus states also, "G-d is close to all who call upon Him, to all who call upon Him in truth,"[56] and "there is no truth but Torah."[57] This means that "G-d is close," i.e., one takes, as it were, the Divine Essence, regardless of the approach used—"to *all* who call upon Him"—provided that it is "in *truth*," i.e., Torah. For *etzem* (essence) is the same everywhere, and when grasping any 'part' of *etzem*, one holds it all.[58]

XVI. May the Almighty grant an involvement with Torah-study on all levels, and in each of them in the sense of "making the Torah great and glorious." This will make the "'Day of His Wedding'—i.e., the giving of the Torah"[59] result in offspring that is alike to His blessed Essence, and achieve the "building of the world"[60]: the world below, and thereby also the world above, will become an abode unto Him, may He be blessed.

C

XVII. Shavu'ot is an auspicious time to reinforce one's observance of the daily *she'urim* (lessons) instituted by the *Rebbe*, my father-in-law, in *Chumash*, *Tehillim* (Book of Psalms), and *Tanya*. In *Chumash*, one is to learn every

---

56. [Psalms 145:18]

57. [*Yerushalmi, Rosh Hashanah* 3:8; *Tanya*, end of ch. 37.]

58. *Keter Shem Tov*, Hossafot, sect. 116. [See above, Bamidbar, note 84.]

59. ["'On the day of his wedding' (Song 3:11)—this refers to (the day of) *matan Torah*;" *Ta'anit* 26b.]

60. ["What are *bana'im*? Said R. Yochanan, These are *talmidei chachamim* (disciples of the wise; Torah-scholars) who are engaged all their days in the upbuilding of the world;" *Shabbat* 114a (and *cf. Berachot* 64a). See *Sefer Hama'amarim- Kuntreisim*, vol. I, p. 16b.]

day one portion of the weekly *sidrah* with the commentary
of Rashi: on Sunday, from the beginning to *sheni;* on
Monday, from *sheni* to *shelishi;* and so forth. In *Tehillim,* one
is to recite every day, after the morning-prayer, the appropriate psalms as they have been apportioned for all the
days of the month. [In *Levush*[61] there is a reference to reciting *Tehillim* before prayer, but that is something else altogether. The *Rebbe* instituted a recital of the daily section of
Tehillim at the conclusion of the prayers.[62]] In *Tanya,* one is
to learn a daily lesson in *Tanya* as this work was divided
into portions for each day of the year.[63]

The *Chumash* was given on the festival of Shavu'ot
through Moses.

Tehillim was authored by King David, whose birthday
and day of *hilula* are on Shavu'ot.[64]

Tanya relates to the *Baal Shem Tov* (for the teachings of
the *Baal Shem Tov* were made manifest through the teachings of *Chabad*-Chassidism, and especially through *Tanya.*
This is noted in the well-known allusion in one of the
approbations for the *Tanya:* "Now *Israel* shall rejoice as *his
saintly words are revealed*"[65]); and Shavu'ot is the *hilula* of
the *Baal Shem Tov.*[66]

Shavu'ot, therefore, is an auspicious time to reinforce
these *she'urim,* which apply to everyone equally. This is in

---

61. [*Levush Hatechelet* 1:9]

62. *Cf. Sefer Hamaamarim 5708,* p. 264, note 1.

63. Published in the *Moreh She'ur* appended to all recent editions
of *Tanya.*

64. [King David was born on Shavu'ot—see *Sha'arei Teshuvah* on
Shulchan Aruch, Orach Chayim, sect. 494, note 6; and below sect.
XXXVI. His *hilula* (day of passing; see above, Bamidbar, note 92, for the
term *hilula*) is also on Shavu'ot, as stated in *Ruth Rabba* 3:2, and in—]
Yerushalmi, Chagigah 2:3, cited in *Tossafot, Chagigah* 17a, *s.v.* af atzeret.

65. [Approbation of R. Yehudah Leib Hacohen, *Tanya,* p. 2b;
alluding to R. *Israel* Baal Shem Tov.] See *Likkutei Diburim,* vol. I, p. 61a.

66. [See above, Bamidbar, note 93.]

addition to reinforcing any *she'urim* in Torah, each one according to his level and capacity. For as Shavu'ot marks the giving of our Torah, the *whole* Torah—including "all that a diligent student is yet to discover,"[67] it is self-evidently the appropriate time to do so.

The observance of these three *she'urim* will effect "*chitat Elokim—(chitat* is an acronym for *Chumash, Tehillim, Tanya*[68])—the dread of G-d was upon the cities."[69] This, in turn, will allow that "they journeyed,"[70] i.e., setting out for the Land of Israel with tranquillity, with the complete and true redemption. Thus it was said to Jacob, "Travel on and let us go,"[71] which will happen speedily in our very own days, "and saviors shall go up on Mount Zion to judge the mount of Esau."[72] The study of Torah and the observance of *mitzvot*, and following the prescribed practices mentioned above, will bring about the coming of our righteous Mashiach, here on earth, speedily in our very own days.

---

67. [*Yerushalmi, Pe'ah* 2:4; *Vayikra Rabba* 22:1. See *Likkutei Sichot*, vol. XIX, p. 252f, and notes 20-21.]

68. See *Sefer Hasichot 5696*, p. 145 ["'*Chitat* (the dread of) G-d was upon the cities round about them' (Genesis 35:5); *chitat* is an acronym for *Chumash-Tehilim-Tanya*, and 'the cities round about them' signify hindrances and obstacles. The letters of *chitat Elokim*—i.e., *Chumash-Tehilim-Tanya*—repel those (hindrances and obstacles)." See also *Igrot Kodesh—Maharyatz*, vol. IV, p. 368.]

69. [Genesis 35:5]

70. [The first word of the verse cited ("They journeyed, and the dread of G-d was upon the cities.. "), and the next verse reads "And Jacob came to Luz, which is in the land of Canaan (i.e., the Land of Israel).. "]

71. [Genesis 33:12]

72. [Obadiah 1:21. Esau had said to Jacob, "Travel on and let us go, and I shall go along with you." Jacob responded by asking Esau to go ahead, and that he would follow at a slower pace "until I come to my lord to Seir" (Genesis 33:14; see Rashi there). The fact that Jacob

D

XVIII.   The Torah was given in a desert, an owner-less place. This is to teach us that the Torah, too, does not have a distinct owner.[73] It is related to every Jew. Whoever studies Torah makes it his possession.

Why, however, was the Torah given in a desolate place, "a dry and weary land without water"—a place without garments, food and even water? When the Jews were in the desert, their garments were from the clothes they had and which, miraculously, kept adjusting to their sizes.[74] For food they had the mannah,[75] and G-d supplied them with water from rocks.[76] Why, then, was the Torah given in so desolate a wilderness?

In a *mashal* (analogy; simile) of Torah all its details correspond precisely to the *nimshal* (point to be made, or moral to be derived).[77] Thus it follows that all the details of the desert are relevant to *matan Torah*. The explanation given above, however, relates only to the desert being an ownerless place, and not to its other details.

XIX.   With regards to the obligation to study Torah, people refer to all kinds of obstacles. They present different kinds of arguments and strange excuses.

---

never went to Seir does not mean that he deceived Esau: he *will* go to Seir in the Messianic time when "saviors shall go up.. ;" *Bereishit Rabba* 78:14; Rashi on Genesis 33:14.]

73. [*Mechilta*, Yitro, Bachodesh:ch. 1, and *Mechilta deRashby* on Exodus 19:22. Cf. *Bamidbar Rabba* 1:7.]

74. [*Pesikta deR. Kahana*, ed. Buber, ch. X, p. 92a; Rashi on Deuteronomy 8:4.]

75. [Exodus 16:35; Deuteronomy 8:3 and 16.]

76. [Deuteronomy 8:15; Psalms 78:15f. Note *Tossefta, Sukah* 3:11ff. that the well of Miriam, which accompanied Israel in the wilderness, was a sieve-like rock from which the water gushed as from a spout.]

77. [See *Torah Or*, Miketz, p. 42b-c. *Sefer Halikkutim-Tzemach Tzedek, s.v.* mashal. *Likkutei Sichot*, vol. XI, p. 259. See also *L.S.- Vayikra, Pesach*, p. 107.]

For example, when asking a businessman to set aside times for Torah-study, he argues that this is not relevant to him. He claims that he is a businessman, and his spiritual concern is the area of charity and not the study of Torah.

He is aware that a businessman must pull himself aside in the midst of his preoccupations in order to recite the *minchah*-prayer. For, as known, this is the special aspect of the *minchah*-prayer,[78] to the point that even Elijah "was heard favorably only when offering the *minchah*-prayer."[79] Thus he already has a very significant task. Why, then, push him specifically to a study of Torah?

When asking him to study the weekly Torah-portion with the commentary of Rashi, let alone the daily lesson in *Tanya*, he argues: "Chassidut demands that man's *avodah* be orderly and gradual. Priority must thus be given to perfecting all of the current tasks, up to and including the *minchah*-prayer, as it was with the prophet Elijah. Thereafter one can proceed to higher planes." He does not reject, Heaven forbid, the learning of *Chumash* with Rashi, or of *Tanya*. He merely wants to leave everything to its 'due time,' when he will be free from his preoccupations, thus following a well-ordered pattern.

It is likewise with a *yoshev ohel* (one "who sits in the tent" of Torah[80]). When he is asked to develop an attitude of "my whole being declares.."[81] and "he did not depart [from the tent],"[82] and so forth, he does not reject this. He

---

78. [See "The Dynamics of Prayer," *Deep Calling Unto Deep* (Kehot 1990), p. 31. *Cf.* below, Shlach, sect. VII.]

79. *Berachot* 6b

80. [Term derived from Genesis 25:27, denoting devotion to Torah-study. See Targumim and Rashi on this verse; *Bereishit Rabba* 63:10; *Eliyahu Rabba*, ch. (5) 6.]

81. [Psalms 35:10, signifying total involvement with full concentration and energy. See *Tzava'at Harivash*, sect. 33 and the notes there.]

82. [Exodus 33:11, signifying total devotion to Torah. See *Sifre*, Pinchas, par. 141; *Menachot* 99b.]

merely argues that this requires proper preparations: first he needs sufficient rest in order to have a clear head; then he must concentrate on eating refined edibles etc.—

[it is stated in *Alsheich*[83] (and similarly in a responsum of Rambam[84]) that refined edibles refine the mind]—

and after all that he will devote himself to learning."

XX.   In truth, however, the fact that the Torah was given in a desert, in "a dry and weary land without water," teaches us that with Torah we must rely completely on G-d.

The Jewish people left Egypt and went to a wilderness, an uncultivated land, for the sake of *matan Torah*. They did not know how they will manage. Ultimately they obtained the mannah by virtue of Moses, the column of the cloud by virtue of Aaron, and water by virtue of Miriam.[85] They had to rely on the merit of three saints, and by virtue of that alone they were ready for receiving the Torah.

This serves as a moral for us as well. One must study Torah and rely on the Almighty. The Almighty will then provide all that is needed materially and spiritually.

E

XXI.   Our sages state:[86] "When you scatter your leg on behalf of the poor and on behalf of a *mitzvah*, you will

---

83. *Chavatzelet Hasharon* on Daniel 1:5. [See also *Shenei Luchot Haberit*, Sha'ar Ha'otiot:Kof-Kedushah, *s.v.* birchot hashulchan, par. 5 (p. 85b).]

84. [See citation in *Keter Shem Tov*, sect. 381 (and my notes there). On the negative effects of crude or forbidden foods, see the sources cited in *Torah Shelemah*, Shemini 11:43, notes 266 and 273; and *Likkutei Sichot*, vol. XIII, p. 260*f.*, and notes 28-31 there.]

85. *Ta'anit* 9a

86. *Derech Eretz Zutta*, ch. 9.

have fulfilled in you 'You are blessed in your coming, and you are blessed in your going'.[87]"

The choice of words in statements of our sages is subject to explanation:

a) The phrase "for the sake of the poor" obviously refers to *tzedakah* (charity). Why, then, refer to both "the poor" and "a *mitzvah*"? *Tzedakah* is an integral part of the *mitzvot*! In fact, throughout the *Yerushalmi* (Jerusalem Talmud) we find that *tzedakah* is referred to simply as '*mitzvah*'![88]

Offhand it may be suggested that our statement wants to allude that *tzedakah* is like all the *mitzvot*, that is, "equivalent to all the *mitzvot* together." But this is stated already explicitly in the Talmud;[89] why, then, an allusion to this here?

b) Instead of referring to 'legs' it would seem more appropriate to use an expression like 'walking' or 'running.'[90] What is the significance of the term 'scattering'?

XXII.   The human body is generally divided into three parts: head, body, and legs. More precisely, it divides into 248 organs.[91] The commandments of the Torah, too, contain 248 positive precepts.

[*Sefer Charedim* divides the various *mitzvot* into groups corresponding to the bodily organs, indicating for each *mitzvah* the particular organ relating to it.]

The 248 commandments generally divide into three categories:

---

87. [Deuteronomy 28:6]

88. *Tanya*, ch. 37. [See *Yerushalmi, Pe'ah* 8:8 "*maflig bemitzvah.*" Cf. Rashi on *Shabbat* 156a, *s.v.* tzadkan bemitzvot; Chida, *Devash Lefi, s.v.* tzadik, par. 37.]

89. [*Baba Batra* 9a]

90. [See, e.g., *Avot* 5:14 and *Bereishit Rabba*, end of ch. 55, for the term 'walking' in context of *mitzvot*; and *Avot* 4:2 and *Berachot* 6b, for the term 'running' in context of *mitzvot*.]

91. [*Oholot* 1:8]

a) There are *mitzvot* related to the mind, such as knowledge of the greatness of the Creator, study of Torah etc. These belong to the category of "head."

b) There are *mitzvot* related to the feelings of the heart, such as love of G-d, fear of G-d, love of Israel etc. These belong to the category of "body."

c) There are *mitzvot* that involve action. These are essentially related to *kabalat ol* (acceptance of the yoke [of Heaven]; submission to the Divine Will), the category of "leg."[92]

Mind and feelings are limited. Even *kabalat ol* based on mind or feeling (i.e., on understanding or feeling the need for accepting the "yoke of the Kingdom of Heaven"), too, is limited. The very principle of *kabalat ol*, however, is unrestricted.

This is the meaning of "scatter your leg." 'Scattering' has the connotation of being without limit. When and where can there be unrestricted scattering? In "your leg," the aspect of *kabalat ol*; in 'leg' in the pure sense, as it is on its own, independent of mind and heart. When the 'leg' is connected with the mind or the heart, this can result in walking and, at best, running. When the 'leg' is on its own, however, there is 'scattering'—without any limitation.

XXIII.   How can a rational being surrender his mind and feelings and adopt an attitude of "scatter your leg"?

The answer is provided by the next words in our proof-text: "on behalf of the poor." Man must contemplate his own status and condition. He will then discover that he himself is 'poor', i.e., "poor in mind."[93] His mind,

---

92. [See also *Tanya*, Igeret Hakodesh, sect. I; *Torah Or*, Mishpatim, p. 77b; and *L.S.-Bereishit*, Vayechi; on the meaning of these categories.]

93. [*Nedarim* 41a: "No one is poor except for him who lacks knowledge" (i.e., the poor in mind).]

therefore, is not something to go by. The same applies also
to the sentiments of his heart. This realization allows man
to effect within himself an attitude of "scatter your leg"
for any *mitzvah* in general, and for *"mitzvah* unqualified—
i.e., the *mitzvah* of *tzedakah"* in particular. He will use his
feet to run, without any calculations, to help out another
Jew with material *tzedakah* as well as with spiritual
tzedakah.[94]

XXIV. The reward resulting from this is, "You are
blessed in your coming and you are blessed in your
going." "Your coming" refers to *it'aruta dile'eyla* (stimulus
from Above) which *precedes* man's *avodah* and confers the
ability to proceed with it. "Your going" refers to the
it'aruta dile'eyla that follows as a response upon an *it'aruta
diletata* (initiative from below, by man).[95]

Both of these are coupled with the word "blessed."
This means that the *it'aruta dile'eyla* will be far greater than
normally, when it is proportionate to man's *avodah*. In
other words, an effort in a mode of "scatter your leg," that
is, without restriction, elicits a reward which exceeds by
far the actual effort exerted. For the Holy One, blessed is
He, dwells only in a place of wholeness[96] (i.e., wholeness
of *avodah*).

XXV. Even so, our statement of the sages does not
lose its literal meaning. Thus it applies also to all those
who fulfilled the "scatter your leg" by partaking in the
tahaluchah[97] which extended to a distance of several hours.

---

94. [On the concept of spiritual *tzedakah*, i.e., to tend to the spiritual needs of others, see *L.S.-Vayikra*, Kedoshim-C; and "The
Philosophy of Lubavitch Activism," *Chassidic Dimensions*, especially
ch. II.]

95. See *Likkutei Torah*, Shir, p. 24a, on the varying levels and
aspects of *it'aruta dile'eyla*.

96. [*Zohar* I:216b. See also *ibid*. III:90b.]

97. [*Tahaluchah*—procession. It is customary for Lubavitch

During that selfsame time they could have busied themselves peacefully with their own affairs. Nonetheless they
went along in a way of "scatter your leg," for the sake of
influencing those who are poor in the spiritual sense. May
they thus find fulfilled in them the "blessed you are in
your coming, and blessed you are in your going": your
coming and going of every day, of every week, of every
month and of every year. May there also be the "blessed
you are in your coming, and blessed you are in your
going" with regards to their *avodah*: a blessing 'in your
coming,' i.e., a supernal bestowal of ability to succeed in
their work to carry out their mission wherever they go;
and a blessing 'in your going,' i.e., that when concluding
the *avodah* of their mission they will see good fruits from
their efforts, the concept of "may you see your 'world' in
your lifetime."[98]

May they succeed in all their personal affairs: in the
study of Torah, in the fulfillment of *mitzvot* with *hidur*,[99]
and in the *avodah* of prayer—which is the 'spinal cord' of
everything,[100] as well as being blessed with all their material needs.

Chassidim to visit every festival (in procession and individually) synagogues within walking distance, to address the congregants on topical
themes and to inspire them with the joy and spirit of the festival.]

98. *Berachot* 17a [referring to future manifestations vouchsafed as
a reward for present efforts.]

99. [*Hidur*—adornment. *Shabbat* 133b: "'This is my G-d and I will
adorn Him' (Exodus 15:2)—this means, adorn yourself before Him in
the observance of *mitzvot*: make a beautiful *sukah* in His honor, a beautiful *lulav*.. " *Hidur mitzvah* means to go beyond minimal requirements
for the observance of a *mitzvah*. One is to add at least a third beyond
the ordinary expenses for the Halachic minimum of a *mitzvah* (*Baba
Kama* 9b). See *L.S.-Bereishit*, p. 180.]

100. *Likkutei Torah*, Balak, p. 70cff. [See "The Dynamics of
Prayer," *Deep Calling Unto Deep*, p. 38.]

F*

XXVI. *Matan Torah* signifies the joining of the higher and lower spheres, so that the light of Torah illuminate and penetrate all mundane matters, without distinction.[101]

This explains the statement of the *Gemara*, "all agree that with respect to Shavu'ot we require it to be *lachem* (for you) too."[102] On Pesach and Sukkot it may be sufficient to have either a purely physical or a purely spiritual celebration. With respect to Shavu'ot, however, all agree that we require *lachem*: it must be in a mode of inwardness, penetrating all one's affairs. The aspect of Shavu'ot is not to remain just for the day of that festival alone. It must affect the whole year, and not just the Sabbaths and festivals but also the everyday life.

XXVII. The *Rebbe*, my father-in-law, once said at a *farbrengen* that the daily hour of studying Chassidut must be distributed over every one of the twenty-four hours of the day. That is, in each of the twenty-four hours it should be notable that there is a person who learns Chassidut.

Just as this applies specifically to the teachings of Chassidut, so it does with respect to all of Torah. Torah must encompass all aspects throughout the whole day. Rambam thus states that a sage must be recognizable through his behavior, and he proceeds to enumerate ten aspects of behavior which encompass the totality of human life.[103]

This, indeed, is the order of the Torah. For the Torah was vested in a physical reality. It was given specifically to

---

101. [See below, Massey, note 31.]

102. *Pesachim* 68b [i.e., to enjoy the festival of Shavu'ot "with food and drink, to show that this day is pleasing and welcome to Israel by virtue of the Torah having been given on this day;" Rashi there.]

103. *Hilchot De'ot*, ch. 5.

souls that are vested in bodies, down here on earth.[104] The
Torah demands a sublimation of 'all physical matters. First
one is to refine one's own body and animal soul, and
thereafter his part of the world.[105] This goal must be
achieved, not by way of repelling or breaking, but specifically by way of refining, as the *Baal Shem Tov* said in comment on the verse "you shall surely help him."[106]

G*

XXVIII.   "Should a person tell you that there is wisdom among the nations, believe it .. but if he tells you that
there is Torah among the nations, do not believe it."[107] This

104. [See *Shabbat* 88bf.; *Midrash Tehilim* 8:2.]

105. [See *Tanya*, ch. 37. *Cf*. above, Bamidbar, note 100.]

106. ["When you see the *chamor* (donkey) of your enemy lying
under its burden, you might want to refrain from helping him, but
you must surely help him" (Exodus 23:5). The Baal Shem Tov interpreted: "When you see the *chamor*," that is, when you consider your
chomer, your material reality (the letters of *chamor* and *chomer* are the
same, rendering these two words interchangeable; see R. Judah Loewe,
Gevurot Hashem, ch. 29; *Torah Shelemah* on Exodus 4:20, note 109;
Tzava'at Harivash, sect. 100)—i.e., your body, you will note that it is
"your enemy;" for it has enmity towards the soul which craves G-dliness and spirituality. Moreover, you will also note that it is "lying
under its burden," i.e., the yoke of Torah and *mitzvot*. For the Holy
One, blessed be He, placed the yoke of Torah and *mitzvot* upon the
body so that it become purified and sublimated by it, but the body
regards this as an unwanted burden. Thus one may think to "refrain
from helping him;" that is, one might consider that the way to fulfill
our mission is to adopt fasts and self-mortifications to crush the body
and break its matter. The verse therefore concludes that this is not the
way to cause the light of Torah to dwell; rather, "you must surely help
him": purify and refine the body, and do not crush it by mortification.
Keter Shem Tov, Hossafot, par. 16. See "To Be One With The One," *The
Mystical Tradition* (Kehot 1990), ch. XV.] *Hayom Yom*, *s.v.* Shevat 28.

107. *Eichah Rabba* 2:13

statement of our sages indicates the difference between wisdom and Torah.

Comprehension of rational insights presupposes initial familiarity with axiomatic premises and the basic rules of scientific method. In philosophical terminology these are called the principles of logic. The rules of logic and axiomatic premises compel the conclusions of the intellect.

These rules and premises do indeed lead to conclusions, but they themselves are not based on any preceding principles that would compel their adoption. They depend on a person's 'good will': if he agrees with them, if he is prepared to accept them, then he will also accept the rational conclusions that follow from them. If one is not prepared to accept them, one has the option to reject them, and therefore will also reject any conclusions following from them.

This is one way of demonstrating that the intellect itself is dependent on something transcending intellect. The intellect itself senses that its own source of origin is not the intellect. For the initial point underlying the whole intellect [i.e., the axiomatic premise] is not compelling from a purely rational point of view. Axioms are adopted because they appeal to man. Their adoption, therefore, is an act of faith and psychological supposition.

Here lies the difference between wisdom and Torah. Acceptance of wisdom depends on a person's 'good will.' If the rational principles appeal to him, he will use them to draw various conclusions, even if these principles themselves are not compelling on their own. It is not so with Torah. For Torah, as this term is interpreted in the *Zohar*,[108] means *hora'ah* (instruction): Torah teaches man what is obligatory, what is permitted, and what is prohibited, i.e.,

---

108. *Zohar* III:53b. [See above, Bamidbar, note 91.]

the three categories of *issur* (the forbidden), *reshut* (the optional), and *mitzvah* (the Divinely ordained and sanctified); and Torah demands that one is to convert the realm of *reshut* into one of *mitzvah*.

The Torah does not make these instructions subject to man's approval. Torah teaches and demands that man must follow them regardless of his own opinions and desires.

This then is the meaning of "wisdom among the nations, believe .. Torah among the nations, do not believe." The concept of wisdom, something that is subject to man's good will and approval, exists among the nations as well. If and when they approve of the premises and principles of reasoning, they are prepared to accept also the conclusions. The concept of Torah, however, which is to be accepted even without prior approval, ·i.e., regardless of whether it is to his liking or not, that does not exist among the nations.

XXIX.   Acceptance of Torah, independent of subjective appeal and approval, is only with Jews. For every Jew has a soul bound up with the Almighty, as we say, "The soul which You have given within me;"[109] and all Jews stood at Mount Sinai for the giving of the Torah, including the souls yet to be, and even the souls from before that time.[110]

Thus every Jew heard G-d say to him, to each one individually, "*Anochi*—I am G-d, *your* G-d..;"[111] that is, "*Anochi*—I," the One that cannot be alluded to by any let-

---

109. *Sidur*, Morning Blessings. [*Cf. Tanya*, ch. 2.]

110. *Pirkei deR. Eliezer*, ch. 41 [see there *Bi'ur Haradal*, notes 65-66]; and *cf. Zohar* I:91a.

111. [Exodus 20:2. "Your G-d" is said here in singular tense, to emphasize that each one is addressed individually; see *Lekach Tov*, and Ramban, on this verse. *Cf.* also *Eliyahu Rabba*, ch. (25)23.]

ter or tittle,[112] "am your energy and your life-force."[113] Speech of the Holy One, blessed be He, is tantamount to action,[114] thus making the aforesaid a reality: the aspect of *Anochi*—which is an acrostic for "I Myself have written (and) given,"[115] signifying that He "wrote Himself into the Torah[116]—is the Jew's energy and vitality.

Thus it follows that faith in G-d is most deeply and absolutely ingrained in the very core of every Jew's soul. In fact, there is far more than faith: a Jew does not even need faith, because the reality of G-d is his very being, his very energy and life-force.[117]

To be sure, it is possible for all kinds of obstructions to accrue and conceal that ingrained awareness of Divinity. Nonetheless, Torah [instruction] is present in the very core of every Jew's soul. He has the whole Torah; and he has it not because of some personal approval or reason which extends only so far and is limited, but because "Torah means instruction," the Torah being his guide and mentor even in matters that he does not understand. The Torah penetrates to the very core of all his affairs, notwithstanding the fact that this is beyond his reason, because his very being is the "*Anochi Hashem*, I am G-d.."

XXX.   This teaches the following:

When setting out to bring others to *Yiddishkeit* and

---

112. *Likkutei Torah*, Pinchas, p. 80b. *Cf. Zohar* III:11a. [See *L.S.-Shemot*, Yitro, sect. III, note *g*.]

113. [*Shulchan Aruch*, Orach Chayim, sect. 5, defining the meaning of the Divine Name *Elokim*. The root-word of this Name is *El*, which means strength; see *Yevamot* 21a, and *Zohar* III:132a. Thus when uttering this Name one is to have in mind the idea that G-d is our strength, our vitality or life-force, without which we cannot endure.]

114. [*Bereishit Rabba* 44:22] *Cf. Shabbat* 119b.

115. *Shabbat* 105a

116. [See note 32; and above, Bamidbar, note 47.]

117. [See *Tanya*, ch. 18-19.]

meeting someone who is still far removed from this ideal, one is not to worry and despair. One must know that deeply ingrained and absorbed in the very core of that person's soul is the full awareness of all that a Jew must believe in. This awareness is there without any restrictions, for it is his very being. One must merely remove the obstructions, and the inner nature will then manifest itself.

When the inner reality works from within, and someone also rouses him from without, then these two factors together will also fully penetrate that which stands between these (i.e., the nature or character presently standing between his own inner self and the prompter without).

It is incumbent upon every Jew to go out and remove the obstacles that obstruct the inner core. The *Alter Rebbe* used to say that the order of sequence in Torah is itself also Torah (instruction).[118] Thus the very first commandment in the Torah is "be fruitful and multiply,"[119] which means that the very first commandment is that one Jew must make another Jew.[120]

H*

XXXI.   The *Alter Rebbe* once interpreted the verse[121] "You shall make the festival of Shavu'ot.." as follows: *shavu'ot* means *vochen* (weeks) and *vochedigkeit* (the aspect of weekdays, thus secular or profane); and this must be converted into a *festival*.[122]

---

118. See *L. S.- Shemot*, Shemot, sect. VIII. [See *Pesachim* 6b, and *Shenei Luchot Haberit*, Torah shebe'al peh, *s.v.* ot ha'alef (p. 402b; ed. Jerusalem, IV:p. 10d). *Cf.* Ramban on Numbers 16:1.]

119. [Genesis 1:28]

120. See *Likkutei Diburim*, vol. IV, p. 746a. [See *L.S.-Shemot, ibid.*]

121. [Deuteronomy 16:10]

122. [There is a play on words here: the Yiddish word *vochedigkeit* derives from the Yiddish *vochen*.]

The difference between Shabbat and a festival is that all work is forbidden on Shabbat.[123] Not only work itself is forbidden, but also all acts associated with weekdays. The very fact that it is identified with weekdays, with the secular or profane, renders it forbidden on Shabbat.[124]

Shabbat transcends the secular. Just as the Almighty rests on Shabbat from the work of creation, so must a Jew. For Jews are referred to as *adam* (man),[125] an idiom of *edameh leElyon* (I am compared to the One Above).[126] On Shabbat, therefore, he must desist from speech, i.e., "your speaking on Shabbat is not to be like your speaking during the week;"[127] for the universe was created by means of speech,[128] and speech of the Holy One, blessed is He, is tantamount to an action.[129]

This is in terms of the strict law. Texts dealing with the pursuit of piety, i.e., with behavior beyond the requirements of the law, state that even meditation on secular matters is forbidden on Shabbat.[130] For Above there was a

---

123. [On Shabbat all work is forbidden. On a *yom tov* (festival) one is permitted most types of work related to the preparation of food that is needed for that festival. *Betza* 36b; *Shulchan Aruch*, Orach Chayim, sect. 495.]

124. [See *Shabbat* 113a-b; *Tanchuma*, Bereishit:12. Cf. *Mechilta* and Rashi on Exodus 20:9, cited in *Shulchan Aruch [Harav]*, Orach Chayim 306:21. (See below, notes 127 and 130.)]

125. [*Yevamot* 61a]

126. *Shenei Luchot Haberit*, Toldot Adam [p. 3, s.v. achar kach]; also *ibid.*, Torah Shebiktav, Tzon Yosef [p. 301b; ed. Jerusalem, p. 29a]; and *Assarah Ma'amarot*, Em Kol Chai II:33; and other sources.

127. *Shabbat* 113b

128. [*Avot* 5:1]

129. [*Bereishit Rabba* 44:22. Cf. *Shabbat* 119b. The Almighty's resting from the Divine speech by means of which the universe was created must therefore be reflected in our faculty of speech as well; see *Yerushalmi,Shabbat* 15:3, cited in *Tanya*, Kuntres Acharon, sect. IX.]

130. See *Shulchan Aruch [Harav]*, Orach Chayim 306:21. [See above, note 124.]

rest from meditation as well, because Divine thought, too, has an effect.[131] The only difference is that the Supernal speech brought about the manifest world, while the Supernal thought brought about the concealed world.[132]

All this in terms of Shabbat. It is different, though, with *yom tov*, a festival. Work *per se* is prohibited on a *yom tov* as well, but for the purpose of preparing food it is permitted.[133] For on *yom tov* there are to be physical things as well, and one is to infuse holiness into the material needs: into the food and into secular activities (for the preparation of food).

With respect to Shabbat it is said, "they shall prepare on the sixth day."[134] For Shabbat is beyond *vochedigkeit* (the profane). *Yom tov*, on the other hand , is referred to as *mikra kodesh*.[135] The term *mikra*, as the *Zohar* interprets,[136] has the connotation of summoning, calling forth the *kodesh* (holiness) into the profane and elevating the profane into the holy. Thus "there cannot be joy save with meat .. and there cannot be joy save with wine,"[137] which, according to the ruling of the *Alter Rebbe* in his *Shulchan Aruch*,[138] is even nowadays a Biblical obligation. For as *yom tov* signifies *mikra kodesh*—to sanctify the profane, it is tied in with material substances, with meat and wine.

---

131. [See *Zohar* II:20a; *Zohar Chadash*, Bereishit 3a.]

132. [See *Tanya*, Sha'ar Hayichud, ch. 11.]

133. [See above, note 123.]

134. [Exodus 16:5]

135. [*Mikra kodesh*, a convocation of holiness, is a term used for each of the *yamim tovim*: Leviticus 23:2, 7, 21, 24, 27, 35, 36, 37. For the practical implications of this term see *Nedarim* 78b, and *Yerushalmi, Pesachim* 10:5.]

136. [*Zohar* III:93b, and *ibid.* 176b. See also *Sefer Halikkutim-Tzemach Tzedek, s.v.* Yom Tov, p. 486.]

137. *Pesachim* 109a

138. Orach Chayim 529:7

Scripture thus speaks of "'the dung of your festivals,'[139] and not of 'the dung of your Sabbaths.'"[140] For
Shabbat is altogether beyond physicality. The physical
aspects of Shabbat are sublimated. They lose their materialism, and thus have no dung.[141] On *yom tov*, however, it is
man's task to convert the profane into holy. When there is
a failure in this *avodah*, therefore, there is the 'dung of your
festivals.'

This then is the meaning of the *Alter Rebbe*'s teaching
that "You shall make the festival of *Shavu'ot*" implies to
change *vochedigkeit* (the profane) into *yom tov*. For the
whole purpose of Torah is to sanctify the profane.

I*

XXXII.   The first commandment ordained after
matan Torah is: "You shall not make with Me gods of silver
and gods of gold .. You shall make unto Me an altar of
earth, and you shall sacrifice on it your *olot* (burnt-offer-
ings) and your *shelamim* (peace-offerings)."[142] The *Alter
Rebbe* comments on this: The first thing (after *matan Torah*)
is something negative—"you shall not make..," because
negation (non-being) precedes being. This is followed by
the positive precept of "you shall make unto Me an altar
of earth," that is, an altar of self-negation—[indicated by
the term 'earth,' something that all step upon]—"and you
shall sacrifice on it your *olot* and your *shelamim*," i.e., all
your ascents and all your perfections.[143]

---

139. [Malachi 2:3]
140. *Zohar* II:88b. See *Sefer Hasichot 5703*, pp. 142 and 145.
141. [See *Eitz Chayim* 50:6; *Tanya*, Igeret Hakodesh, sect. XXVI (p.
143b).]
142. Exodus 20:20-21
143. [The term *olot* is from the root-word *alah* (to ascend), for "it

This deeper interpretation of *olot* and *shelamim* does not refer to aspects of pride, but to authentic ascents and perfections, recognized as such by the Torah. Even so there is the precept to sacrifice these on the altar. For *matan Torah* demands that one do not consider anything, not even silver and gold which signify the love and fear of G-d.[144]

This is analogous to the earlier discussion (about the nature of Jewish souls) that the Torah demands a goal of simply observing the Divine will without consideration of anything else. For by virtue of *matan Torah*, when the Almighty said "*Anochi*—I am G-d, your G-d"—i.e., that the "I, G-d" became your strength and your life-force, nothing else is of any significance.[145]

The *Baal Shem Tov* thus interpreted[146] the verse "*Shiviti*—I have set G-d before me always":[147] as G-d is before me, therefore all things are equal.[148] This equanimity applies even to spiritual aspects, to the very highest level, for one is not to desire anything but to carry out the Divine will.

---

ascends wholly to the Holy One, blessed be He" (*Tanchuma*, Tzav:1; *Zohar* III:26a). The term *shelamim* is of the root *shalem*—whole; perfect (*Sifra* and *Lekach Tov* on Leviticus 3:1). These two terms thus lend themselves to the interpretation of signifying spiritual aspirations and achievements of "ascents and perfections."]

144. [See *Zohar* II:148a; *Zohar Chadash*, Chukat 51a. *Cf. Tanya*, ch. 50.]

145. [See above, sect. XXIX-XXX.]

146. *Tzava'at Harivash*, sect. 2. For an explanatory discussion of this interpretation, see *Bi'urim Betzava'at Harivash* (2nd ed.; Kehot 1985) p. 22*ff.*

147. Psalms 16:8

148. [The Baal Shem Tov reads the word *shiviti* (I have set) as an idiom of *shaveh* (equal), thus rendering the concept of equanimity that "everything is equal to me"—whether people praise him or insult him, whether it is tasty food or not, and so forth. See also the sources cited in my notes on *Tzava'at Harivash*.]

That is why the very first precept after *matan Torah* states, "You shall not make .. and you shall sacrifice on it your *olot* and your *shelamim*." For this is the purpose of *matan Torah*, as explained above at length.

J*

XXXIII. "A Scriptural verse does not lose its plain meaning."[149] The same principle applies also to expressions of the sages. The expression *matan Torah*—the 'giving of the Torah' thus means that we are speaking of something that is continuously ongoing, even as suggested by the text of the blessings recited every morning—"who *gives* the Torah," in present tense.[150] This implies that there must be a daily study of Torah. Every single day there must be a set time for the study of Torah.

Torah-study must occur literally every day, because the Torah is "our life,"[151] and with life there must not be any interruption. A person's health may sometimes be stronger and at other times weaker. With life itself, however, any interruption, Heaven forbid, means total cessation. It is likewise with Torah, which requires daily study.

The *Gemara* states, "He who says that he has naught but Torah, he has not even Torah,"[152] for Torah must be supplemented with *gemilut chassadim* (practice of loving deeds; acts of kindness).[153] It is necessary, therefore, that

---

149. *Shabbat* 63a

150. [See above, Bamidbar, note 50.]

151. [Evening Prayers, blessing preceding the *Shema*: "For they are our life and the length of our days, and we will meditate on them day and night." See Deuteronomy 32:47; *Midrash Tana'im* and *Midrash Hagadol* on this verse.]

152. *Yevamot* 109b

153. This latter phrase is not part of the quotation in *Yevamot* 109b, but note *Likkutei Torah*, Re'ey, p. 23c: "Our sages said, 'He who

there be also the *avodah* of prayer; for prayer is included in *gemilut chassadim*, as explained by Rashi,[154] citing "He who deals kindly with his soul is a man of *chessed*."[155] Moreover, before the actual prayer there must be an act of *gemilut chassadim* in the literal sense, as it is said, "He gave a coin to the poor and then prayed."[156] The *avodah* of prayer, in turn, effects that the study of Torah will be as it should be.

The fixed study of Torah every day is subject to the Scriptural assurance, "If you will go in my ordinances"[157] —i.e., if you will exert yourselves in the study of Torah[158] —"I will give your rains in their season."[159] For this is the ring of betrothal of *matan Torah*,[160] and the Almighty surely keeps His promise.

If this applies to every individual, it does so no less to a comprehensive body. In other words, as of Shavu'ot teachers must make every effort that a greater part of the hours of instruction in educational institutions should be

---

says he has naught but Torah..' The simple meaning is that it is necessary for man to occupy himself with Torah and *gemilut chassadim* and not just Torah alone. Torah by itself is a light without a vessel, thus unable to endure except through *gemilut chassadim* which is the comprehensive principle of *mitzvot*." Cf. *Yevamot* 105a. *Tanya*, Igeret Hakodesh, sect. V (p. 108b*f*. [See R. Judah Loewe, *Netivot Olam*, Gemilut Chassadim, ch. 2; and my notes on Igeret Hakodesh *ad loc cit.*]

154. Rashi on *Shabbat* 127b, *s.v.* hanei nami.
155. [Proverbs 11:17]
156. *Baba Batra* 10a. [See *Shulchan Aruch*, Orach Chayim, end of sect. 92; *Tanya*, Igeret Hakodesh, sect. VIII and XII.]
157. [Leviticus 26:3]
158. *Sifra* on this verse, cited there by Rashi.
159. [Leviticus 26:4. See Ramban on this verse.]
160. [*Hayom Yom, s.v.* Tishrei 28, commenting on our prooftexts of Leviticus 26:3-4: "Torah-study and observance of *mitzvot* are the wedding-ring with which the Holy One, blessed be He, betrothed Israel with the obligation to sustain them and to provide them with livelihood." See also *Sefer Hasichot 5696*, p. 151b.]

devoted to Torah-studies. There must be a continuous expansion in Torah-study, in the sense of "I will walk in an expansion."[161] There must be reliance on the Almighty, and one should not hinder or twist the channels [of the Divine effluence]. One is to go about this expansively, with respect to the material as well as the spiritual, both quantitatively as well as qualitatively. Torah is to be increased and strengthened: increased quantitatively, and strengthened qualitatively.

Thus will come about the blessing expressed by the *Rebbe* ten years ago, that "the one shall become *revavah* (ten-thousand)."[162] This is meant in the literal sense of quantity as well as in the qualitative sense of each of these ten-thousand students being on the level of *revavah*—which is an aspect of *keter*.[163]

K*

XXXIV. Twenty years ago, at the *farbrengen* of Shavu'ot, the *Rebbe*, my father-in-law, said that each one should have a schedule for in-depth study of *Gemara*. As he discussed this on Shavu'ot, it follows that in-depth study is related to *matan Torah*.

The need for in-depth study is actually decreed by an explicit *Mishnah*:[164] "A rich person who brought the offering of a poor person has not fulfilled his duty;"[165] and we

---

161. [Psalms 119:45]

162. [*Sefer Hasichot 5705*, p. 107b.]

163. *Torat Chayim*, Chayeh Sarah, p. 126d. [See also *Sefer Halikkutim-Tzemach Tzedek, s.v.* misparim, p. 961*ff*.]

164. *Nega'im* 14:12

165. [The requirements for some sin-offerings are relative to a person's material means, thus more expensive for the wealthy than for the poor.]

have it on tradition that "no one is poor save he who lacks in knowledge," and in reverse, no one is rich save he who has knowledge.[166]

He who is "rich in knowledge," thus able to study in depth, cannot discharge his obligation by the offering of a 'poor person', that is, by cursory study. To do so would be to prevent all those things which the offering is to effect. Just as an offering is to induce certain effects, so, too, the study of Torah. If then he has not fulfilled his duty, those effects are not achieved.[167]

A person like that would not only miss out on the ultimate effects of Torah but also be remiss in his personal obligation to study Torah.

The law of Torah-study stipulates that he who has the time to study but fails to do so, falls into the category of "He has despised the word of G-d,"[168] as stated in the Gemara[169] cited by the *Alter Rebbe* in the first chapter of *Tanya*. The fact that he may be learning all the rest of the time is irrelevant: failure to use any opportunity to study is tantamount to despising the word of G-d.

This applies not only to the aspect of time, but also to one's soul-powers.

Failure to utilize all abilities with respect to Torah, notwithstanding the fact one may be studying all the time, is—in a subtle way—tantamount to *bitul Torah* (neglect of Torah-study) and subject to the aforementioned verse, may Heaven save us.

---

166. *Nedarim* 41a. ["No one is poor except for him who lacks knowledge.. He who has this, has everything (Rashi: 'he who has knowledge is as one who has everything, for he lacks nothing'). He who lacks this, what does he have? He who has acquired this, what does he lack? He who has not acquired this, what does he possess?"]

167. [Cf. *Zohar* I:12b.]

168. [Numbers 15:31]

169. *Sanhedrin* 99a. [*Hilchot Talmud Torah* [Harav] 3:6f.]

In cursory study one uses the faculty of speech (the concept of "to him who utters them with the mouth"[170]), the external aspect of thought and the external aspect of the intellect. The faculties of interpretation, scrutiny and inventiveness, which reflect the soul-faculties of *chochmah*, *binah* and *da'at*, are not utilized. In a subtle way, then, this would be tantamount to *bitul Torah*. For in effect only half the person is studying, while the other half is not. Moreover, only the external half is involved with the study, but not the principal part.

Each individual, therefore, must evaluate his potential for involvement with Torah-study, and then exert himself to use it to the fullest extent. There may be sincere effort; but when not exerting *all* abilities—and especially when neglecting the principal ones—this would mean that "you have not labored," and "if someone says, I have not labored but still have found (i.e., succeeded), do not believe him."[171]

Some are blessed with special abilities. They are able to do in a short time, and easily, that which would take others a great amount of time and much effort. Even so, when there is no exerted effort in terms of *all* abilities, it is a case of "you have not labored," thus precluding also the "you have found."

This applies not only to the study of Torah but to everything for which one is to exert oneself, as, for example, the fear and love of G-d (which are also subject to 'laboring'[172]), as well as to the effort required for the obser-

---

170. ["'For (the words of Torah) are life *lemotze'eihem* (to those that find them..'" (Proverbs 4:22); do not read *lemotze'eihem* but *lemotzi'eihem*, to the one that brings them out (i.e., utters them) with his mouth;" *Eruvin* 54a. See also *Hilchot Talmud Torah* [Harav] 2:12 that Torah-study requires the actual articulation of the words of Torah.]

171. *Megilah* 6b

172. [See *Tanya*, Igeret Hakodesh, sect. XVIII, and sources cited

vance of *mitzvot*.[173] The sphere of *kelipah* and *sitra achara* gives gratuitously, for free,[174] as it is written, "The fish we ate in Egypt *chinam* (for naught)."[175] In the realm of *kedushah* (holiness), however, there is need for effort.[176] In all those matters mentioned above, therefore, there must be an exerted effort with all one's soul-powers, for without this it would be of the category of "do not believe a claim of 'I have not labored yet have found'."

On the other hand, even he who has but average abilities yet exerts himself with proper efforts is assured that his effort will be blessed with success.

XXXV.   This provides also an answer to those who object to the demand that they learn Chassidut by arguing: "I am not yet perfect in my studies of Talmud and the codes. I wish that I would complete my knowledge of *nigleh*. Any involvement with *nistar*, therefore, is not for us!"[177]

In truth, however, the revealed part of Torah and *pnimiyut haTorah* together constitute the singular Torah[178]

---

there in my notes.] For an explanatory discussion see *Kuntres Ha'avodah*, ch. 3.

173. *Zohar* II:128a

174. [*Ibid.*: "The spirit of impurity is always accessible for free and naught, sold without a price.. "]

175. [Numbers 11:5. See *Zohar* III:108a: "We ate in Egypt *chinam*—without blessing, because the yoke of Above was not upon us..;" see there at length.]

176. [*Zohar* II:128a: "He who wishes to make an effort for the sake of a *mitzvah* and G-d must not do so empty and for free. Rather, man must exert himself properly, commensurate to his ability.. The spirit of holiness is not like (the spirit of impurity): it requires full compensation and immensely great effort, purification of one's dwelling and willingness of heart and soul.." See there also *Nitzutzei Orot*, note 2.]

177. [*Cf. L.S.-Shemot*, Yitro, sect. IV.]

178. [See above, note 3.]

given to every Jew at *matan Torah*. Thus it is written, "I am
G-d, *your* G-d,"[179] in the singular tense. This means that
the whole Torah—with all its components of *peshat, remez,
derush* and *sod*[180]—was given to every individual Jew.[181]
Thus it is ruled explicitly in *Hilchot Talmud Torah* that
every Jew is obligated to study all the parts of the Torah.[182]

As for the argument about inability to understand
nistar, the esoteric dimension of the Torah, one could raise
a much more serious question: how can man relate to
Torah altogether? After all, the Torah is G-d's wisdom,
thus infinite. How, then, can a finite human being grasp
Torah? The answer, however, is that G-d gave the Torah to
Israel in such a way that they are able to take it. Thus one
is able to take the mystical component of Torah as well, for
it, too, was given by G-d to every Jew.

The fact of the matter is that the *nigleh*-part is referred
to by our sages as "*gufei Torah*—the body of the Torah."[183]
It joins the revealed aspect of the soul with the revealed
aspect of the Holy One, blessed is He. The *nistar*-part of
the Torah is referred to as the "soul of the Torah," as

---

179. [Exodus 20:2]

180. [In context of the Talmudic passage of the "Four who
entered the *pardes* (orchard)"—*Chagigah* 14b—the *Zohar* reads the word
pardes as an acronym for *peshat* (simple meaning), *remez* (allusion),
derush (hermeneutical interpretation), and *sod* (esoterics; mystical
meaning), which are the four levels of meaning and interpretation of
the Torah; see *Zohar Chadash*, Tikunim 107c; also *ibid.* 102b; and *Zohar*
1:26b, III:110a and 202a.]

181. [See above, note 111.]

182. *Hilchot Talmud Torah [Harav]* 1:4. [See *L.S.-Bereishit*, Vayeitze,
sect. XIII; *ibid.* Miketz, sect. V; *L.S.-Shemot*, Yitro, sect. IV-VIII. *Cf.* "Let
Your Wellsprings Be Dispersed Abroad," *The Mystical Tradition*, ch.
II*ff.*]

183. [*Zohar* III:152a]

explained in the *Zohar*;[184] and it joins the concealed aspect of the soul to the concealed aspect of the Holy One, blessed is He.[185]

By studying *nigleh* alone, without Chassidut, one fails to utilize the concealed part of the soul, as it would not be bound up with Torah. In context of the distinction made above, this would be analogous to a cursory study as opposed to studying in depth.

True Torah-study exists only when the total person—his external reality together with his internal one—is involved and bound up with the totality of the Torah, that is, with its external—revealed—part *and* its internal part and Chassidut.

There must be a study of Chassidut, even if at first one may not sense its value and think that *nistar* does not relate to us. In fact, the learning of Chassidut will enhance the study of *nigleh*. It will infuse that study with the light of the *En Sof*, the "concealed aspect" of the Holy One, blessed is He, who "reads and studies opposite him."[186]

At the time of *matan Torah* there was a perception of the Divine Essence in the Torah;[187] and so now, too, he will draw forth the Divine Essence into his Torah-study, wherever and whenever it may be.

L*

XXXVI.　The Talmud states that King David died on

---

184. *Ibid.* [This passage of the Zohar is quoted in full in "To Be One With The One," *The Mystical Tradition*, ch. I, and see there also ch. II*ff.*]

185. [See *Zohar* III:73a; *Likkutei Sichot*, vol. V, p. 302. *Cf.* "To Be One With The One," ch. V, note 52.]

186. [*Eliyahu Rabba* ch. 18. See *Tanya*, end of ch. 37.]

187. [See *Tanya*, end of ch. 36.]

Shavu'ot.[188] *Tevu'ot Shor* and *Binyan Ari'el* note the following: It is said[189] that "The Holy One, blessed is He, com-
pletes the years of the righteous from day to day." Thus it
follows that David was born on Shavu'ot.[190] Shavu'ot is
then both the *hilula* and the birthday of King David.

The *Zohar*[191] notes that the verse, "[I have to proclaim,
G-d said to me:] 'You are My son, *Ani* (I) have begotten
you this day',"[192] was said by David on the day of his *bar
mitzvah*, when he entered his fourteenth year. A holy soul
was infused into him from the level of *Ani tefilah*.[193]

To be sure, the *nefesh elokit* (Divine soul) is infused at
the time of circumcision, as stated by the *Alter Rebbe* at the
beginning of *Shulchan Aruch*.[194] However, this refers merely to the aspect of *nefesh-ruach-neshamah*. Thereafter, when
properly living up to one's *avodah*, one merits higher levels, and at the time of *bar mitzvah* one is also infused with
the levels of *Atzilut*.[195]

---

188. [*Yerushalmi, Betza* 2:4; *ibid., Chagigah* 2:3; see also *Ruth Rabba*
3:2.] See above, note 64.

189. [*Rosh Hashanah* 11a]

190. [See *Sha'arei Teshuvah* on *Shulchan Aruch*, Orach Chayim
494:note 6.]

191. *Zohar* II:98a. See there the commentary of R. Chaim Vital
cited in *Or Hachamah*; and *Tehillim Yahel Or* on Psalms 2:7.

192. [Psalms 2:7]

193. [Psalms 109:4—"*Ani Tefilah*, lit. I am prayer": "*Tefilah* signifies *Knesset Yisrael* (lit. Assembly of Israel; in Zoharic and Kabbalistic
writings this term denotes the *Shechinah* and the *Sefirah* of *Malchut*), as
it is written, '*vaAni Tefilah*' (*Ani* is *Tefilah*);" *Zohar* III:49b. The deduction
is based on the principle that the term *Ani* denotes *Knesset Yisrael*
(*Shechinah*), as stated in *Zohar* I:260b and III:276a. The soul infused into
King David on the day of his *bar mitzvah*, therefore, was from the
Shechinah. See also below, note 195.]

194. Orach Chayim 4:2 (revised edition).

195. [See at length in the commentary of R. Chaim Vital cited
above, note 191. Cf. *Zohar* II:94b; and *Eitz Chayim* 39:5, and *ibid.*, 50:ch.
3 and 9.]

This is the reason why R. Shimon bar Yochai prepared a great feast and joyous celebration, just as for a
wedding, on the day of his son's *bar mitzvah*. When R.
Shimon was asked for the reason of that celebration, he
explained that it is to mark the *bar mitzvah* of his son, R.
Eleazar, as all this is related in *Zohar Chadash*.[196]

In context of Shavu'ot being the birthday of David, it
follows that King David said this verse on Shavu'ot.

XXXVII.   King David inserted this verse into the
Book of *Tehillim*. *Tehillim* is recited by all Jews, each one
according to his own level and condition. [My father-in-
law, the *Rebbe*, instituted that everyone should recite every
day the appropriate section of *Tehillim* according to its
division corresponding to the days of the month. This
applies equally to all. Some people have a custom to recite
Tehillim according to different divisions of its contents;
even so, they should also recite the daily portion of the
monthly cycle.]

All that King David said in *Tehillim* on behalf of the
community of Israel,[197] therefore, will become realized in a
manifest way to each Jew according to his level and condition. This applies also to the aspect and contents of the
verses, "You are My son, I have begotten you this day. Ask
of Me, and I will make the peoples your inheritance and
the ends of the earth your possession."[198]

These words imply that G-d will fulfill the wishes of
every Jew's heart in all that is asked from Him.

XXXVIII.   Of David it is said, "David, King of Israel,
is living and enduring,"[199] and "My servant David shall be
prince over them"[200]—which refers to the Messianic age.

---

196. *Zohar Chadash*, Bereishit:15d.
197. [See *Pesachim* 117a; and *Midrash Tehilim* 18:1.]
198. [Psalms 2:7-8]
199. *Rosh Hashanah* 25a. *Zohar* I:192b.
200. Ezekiel 37:25

Our text thus relates to both David and Mashiach. The coming of Mashiach is the heartfelt desire of every Jew. In context of the above, therefore, it is within the power of every Jew to realize this.

The fulfillment of wishes can be realized through the study of Torah and the observance of *mitzvot*. This includes also the practice of reciting *Tehillim*, i.e., to recite the daily portion of *Tehillim* at the conclusion of the morning-prayers.[201]

In *Levush*[202] there is reference to a custom to recite *Tehillim* before prayer. This, however, is something altogether different, distinct from the practice of everyone reciting *after* the prayers the daily portion of *Tehillim* as it is divided according to the days of the month.

XXXIX. The *Zohar*[203] states that David is called the "jester of the King," because he would effect Supernal joy. This characteristic of his applies to all times. He causes joy all year round. But it applies especially to the day of his birth and *hilula*.

Shavu'ot is then a time to undertake with joy a strengthening of the practice to recite the daily portion of *Tehillim*, according to its monthly division, and to bring this to the attention of all those who are as yet unfamiliar with it—thus to acquire the privilege that "the merit of the many is attributed to him."

---

201. [The recital of Tehillim qualifies as Torah-study like the recital of any Scriptural passages (see *Hilchot Talmud Torah [Harav]* 2:12-13). Furthermore, King David prayed that the recital of Tehillim be equal to the study of the Talmudic tractates of *Nega'im* and *Oholot* (dealing with some of the most abstruse laws); *Midrash Tehilim* 1:8. By the same token, to observe the daily recital of Tehillim as instituted by the *Rebbe* is tantamount to observing *mitzvot*—not only the *mitzvah* of Torah-study, but also the *mitzvot* related to the principle of obeying the instructions of sages (Deuteronomy 17:11; *Sifre*, Shoftim, sect. 154.]

202. *Levush Hatechelet* 1:9

203. *Zohar* II:107a

This will also lead to a fulfillment of that which my father-in-law, the *Rebbe,* related twenty years ago on Shavu'ot: one of the *Rebbes* was shown in a vision that the word *chitat* in the verse "*Chitat* (the dread of) G-d was upon the cities"[204] is an acronym for C*Humash-Tehillim-Tanya.*[205]

Every day one is to learn in *Chumash* part of the weekly *parshah* with the commentary of Rashi: on Sunday up to *sheni;* on Monday up to *shelishi;* and so forth. Every day one is to study *Tanya,* the daily lesson of this text according to the order that the *Tanya* was divided by my father-in-law, the *Rebbe,* for all the days of the year. Every day one is to recite in *Tehillim* the daily portion as it is divided according to the days of the month. This will then bring about that "*chitat* (the dread of) G-d was upon the cities"—so that—"they traveled,"[206] i.e., that we shall travel in peace to the Land of Israel through the complete and true redemption. For thus it was said to our father Jacob: "Travel on and let us go,"[207] which will be in the future to come when "Saviors shall go up on Mount Zion to judge the mount of Esau."[208]

Torah-study and the observance of *mitzvot,* including the practice of those daily *she'urim* (lessons and portions), will bring about our righteous Mashiach in the literal sense, speedily in our very own days.

M*

XL. The *Rebbe,* my father-in-law, said that the festival

---

204. [Exodus 35:5]
205. [See above, sect. XVII, and note 68.]
206. [See above, note 70.]
207. [Genesis 33:12]
208. [Obadiah 1:21. See above, note 72.]

of Shavu'ot is unique. All festivals are "festivals for rejoicing."[209] Shavu'ot, however, has additional rejoicing, a joy
related to a *mitzvah*, by virtue of the fact that the Jewish
people received the Torah on that day. It is analogous to
the initiation of a child to *cheder* (primary school) to learn
Torah, an event celebrated with joy: on Shavu'ot the
Jewish people were initiated to *cheder* to receive the Torah.
Thus it is an occasion for special rejoicing, beyond the normative joy of the festivals.[210]

Moreover, the extra joy is warranted by reading the
term *Shavu'ot*—a term related to *matan Torah*—as an idiom
of *shavu'ah* (oath). In this context, the plural tense of
shavu'ot signifies two oaths: a) the oath on the part of G-d
to Israel not to exchange them, Heaven forbid, for another
nation;[211] and b) the oath of every one being adjured "Be
righteous..,"[212] and that every Jew is "under a perpetual
oath from Mount Sinai" to remain a faithful Jew.[213] Every
Jew, regardless of his status and condition, is and forever
remains an Israelite even if he sinned.[214] Every Jew,
regardless of his condition, bears not only the name
'Jacob,' but also that of 'Israel' which denotes excellence.[215]

All this was effected by *matan Torah* which established both these oaths: the bond of G-d to the Jewish people and the bond of the Jewish people to G-d. Both of
these bonds are altogether intrinsic, totally independent of
the Jew's status and condition.

---

209. [Every festival there is a *mitzvah* to rejoice. *Pesachim* 109a;
Shulchan Aruch, Orach Chayim sect. 529.]

210. [See *Sefer Hasichot 5703*, p. 143f.]

211. [*Eliyahu Rabba*, end of ch. 24; *Eliyahu Zutta*, end of ch. 10;
Gitin 57b; Rashi on Deuteronomy 29:12.] *Ruth Rabba*, Petichta:3.
Pesachim 87a. See *Kidushin* 36a (and Responsa of Rashba, no. 194).

212. *Nidah* 30b [see *Tanya*, ch. 1 and 14].

213. [See *Nedarim* 8a.]

214. *Sanhedrin* 44a

215. [Rashi on *Sanhedrin* 44a, *s.v.* chata Yisrael.]

The rejoicing of Shavu'ot, therefore, is extraordinarily great. For the joy generated by *matan Torah* relates to every Jew, any time and any place. Moreover, this rejoicing effects that the inspiration of Shavu'ot endure throughout the year, for joy breaches all fences and obstacles.[216] Thus it will breach all fences or restraints of time and space, causing a receiving of Torah at all times and in all places.

XLI.   The Midrash relates: when the Almighty gave the Torah to Israel, He demanded a surety that they would keep it. The Jews responded, "Our patriarchs will be our surety," and "Our prophets will be our surety," but this was not found to be acceptable. Then they said, "Our children shall be our surety," and that was acceptable. G-d thus gave the Torah to all Jews, from the small to the great, by virtue of the children.[217]

We refer to G-d as "He who *gives* the Torah," in the present tense. For *matan Torah* is something ongoing, happening every day.[218] Thus every day we must teach Torah to our children and guide them according to the Torah.

As already stated, when a child is initiated to *cheder*, this is done with rejoicing. Thus when sending a child to *cheder* every day, this must also be done with joy.

There is no reason to worry about the future, to worry how this child will eventually earn a living. One must realize that by sending the child to learn Torah one bonds it with the "Life of all worlds," and "He who provides life also provides sustenance."[219] Thus there will surely be sufficient for the eventual needs of the child's material upkeep: "I will give your rains in their season,

---

216. [See *L.S.-Vayikra*, Tazri'a, sect. II, and notes 5-7 there.]
217. See above, note 50.
218. [See above, sect. XXXIII and note 150.]
219. [See *Ta'anit* 8b.]

and the land shall yield its produce,"[220] all the blessings which parents wish for their children.[221]

All this is achieved specifically by virtue of Torah-study. "If you will walk in My ordinances,"[222] and offer unto G-d the "first of *arisotechem* (your dough)"[223]—in the sense of reading this word as an idiom of *arisah* (cradle)[224] —so that the first thing when awakening is a recitation of *Modeh ani..*,[225] the child will be blessed with material success as well.

Thus when sending off the child to learn Torah, this is to be done with the greatest joy, in the full consciousness that this is the only way for its happiness, not only spiritual happiness but also material happiness.

N*

XLII.   The Midrash relates: When G-d gave the Torah to Israel, He demanded a surety that they would keep it. The Jewish people responded, "Our fathers will be our surety;" but this was not accepted. Then they offered, "Our prophets will be our surety," but this, too, was not accepted. But when they said, "Our children will be our surety," this was acceptable to G-d and He gave them the Torah.[226]

Americans have a special fondness for *derush* (homilies). Everybody preaches, from small to great. In view of the principle that "When you go into a city, act according

---

220. [Leviticus 26:4]
221. [See Ramban on this verse. *Cf.* above, sect. XXXIII.]
222. [Leviticus 26:3]
223. [Numbers 15:20]
224. *Sefer Hama'amarim-Kuntreisim*, vol. I, pp. 128a and 165a.
225. [See below, Korach, sect. II.]
226. [See above, notes 50 and 217.]

to its customs,"[227] I will interpret this Midrash in the local style of homiletics.

XLIII.   The Jewish people is the Chosen People, and they love to learn Torah. Of Torah it is said, "It is your wisdom and your understanding (even) in the eyes of the peoples."[228] Even so, for whatever reason it may be that someone will not study Torah nor observe *mitzvot*, notwithstanding the inherent goodness and pleasure of Torah and *mitzvot*.

Thus when G-d gave the Torah, He first wanted to be assured that the Jewish people will study Torah and observe its *mitzvot*. That is why He asked for a surety.

The Jews responded, "Our fathers will be our surety," *they* will study Torah: the elderly father in an old-age home, free of any worries, will learn Torah. We will support the father, and the father will enroll in a study-group of Mishnah or Talmud and learn. After all, he has nothing else to do and thus is free to learn.

Moreover, this will bring happiness to the father. For as he joins a group, its members meet once or twice a year for a social gathering, thus providing opportunities for enjoyment.

XLIV.   The Jewish people also offered its prophets as surety. 'Prophets' means 'speakers'; for the Hebrew word for prophets, *nevi'im*, is derived from *niv sefatayim*, speech of the lips.[229] The implication is that our 'speakers,' i.e, the rabbis, will be our surety; they will study Torah. We will hire a rabbi and support him, so that the rabbi will study Torah while the laymen engage in business.

The Almighty, however, did not accept this surety. He is not satisfied with Torah-study limited to rabbis. He

---

227. [*Shemot Rabba* 47:5. See also -] *Bereishit Rabba* 48:14.
228. Deuteronomy 4:6
229. [Isaiah 57:19]

wants all Jews to study Torah and to observe its *mitzvot*. Thus He asked for another surety.

XLV.   In the end the Jews offered their children as surety: the children will learn Torah.

For as·long as children are young and unable to engage in business, one is prepared to send them to a Talmud Torah, and later to a Yeshivah. Thereafter, however, as the children grow older, the parent will take them out of the Yeshivah and put them into business.

Even so, the Almighty accepted this surety. For children sent to a Yeshivah at an early age will not want to leave the Yeshivah when they grow older, and thus remain learning Torah.[230]

Furthermore, such children will speak and reason with their parents to the point of persuading them that they (the parents), too, will start learning Torah and observing *mitzvot*.

XLVI.   All this was said by way of a homily. Torah on the level of *derush* ascends to the world of *Yetzirah* or the world of *Beriah*.[231] In practical terms, however, as far as this world is concerned, there must be every exerted effort to bring children into Talmud Torah-schools and Yeshivot. The children will then also influence their parents. Thus *all* Jews will merit *kabalat Hatorah*.

O*

XLVII. In context of *matan Torah*, and as a preparation to *kabalat Hatorah*, it is said: "Thus you shall say to the

---

230. [See Proverbs 22:6: "Educate the child according to its way, (then) even when it grows old it will not depart from it."]

231. [See *Peri Eitz Chayim*, Sha'ar Hanhagat Halimud (ed. Jerusalem 1980, p. 356). *Cf. Tanya*, ch. 40, and *ibid.*, Igeret Hakodesh, sect. XXVI.]

House of Jacob and tell the children of Israel."[232] Our sages
explain that "House of Jacob" denotes the women.[233] Thus
Moses was to transmit the message first to the women,
and only thereafter to the men. For observance of Torah
depends on the women: education of the children
depends on the women; it is in their hands. Initially a
child is home all day. Even later on, as the child grows
older and goes to *cheder*, most of its time at home is still
spent with the mother.[234]

The very disposition of the home, and thus also to a
great extent the personality and conduct of the husband, is
in the hands of the woman, the 'foundation of the
house.'[235]

With regards to addressing the women, the Torah
says, "Thus *tomar* (you shall say) to the House of Jacob."
The verb *tomar* denotes gentle speech.[236] However, this
refers to the *manner of speech*, that it be gentle, and not that
they were told something different. The contents of the
words addressed to the women was the same as that
given to the men, except that it was to be expressed gently.
In a similar vein, my father-in-law, the *Rebbe*, once said:
"One should not speak negatively (e.g., 'if, Heaven forbid,
you will *not* go in the way of the Torah..'), but positively."

Mothers must be made to understand that if they
wish their children to be healthy in the physical sense—
(and no doubt but that physical health is something
desired by all)—and happy both materially and spiritual-

232. [Exodus 19:3]

233. [*Targum Yehonatan* on Exodus 19:3] *Mechilta*, Yitro,
Bachodesh:ch. 2 (cited in Rashi on Exodus 19:3). See also *Shemot Rabba*
28:2.

234. [See *Shemot Rabba* 28:2; and R. Bachaya on Exodus 19:3.]

235. [See *Pirkei deR. Eliezer*, ch. 49.]

236. [*Mechilta*, Bachodesh:ch. 2, cited by Rashi on Exodus 19:3.]
Sifre, Beha'alotecha, sect. 99.

ly, this can be achieved only through the good health of the soul. As the soul is healthy, so is the body.[237]

Even the wise among the non-Jews agree that the health of the body depends on the health of the soul. For as the soul is healthy, so will be the nerves, and thus also the body. With Jews all this is possible only by means of an education and life-style based on Torah.

A mother may ask: "What bearing does Torah have on physical health? It would seem that the latter depends on nutrition, proper rest, and so forth. How is this related to *kashrut* (observance of the dietary laws), the reading of the *Shema*, the recitation of blessings, wearing *tzitzit*, having *pe'ot*, learning *aleph-bet*, and so forth?"

One must realize, however, that as the Almighty is the creator of the world, He is also the sovereign and master of the world, of both the soul and the body. Thus one must follow the order He established.

On our human level we recognize that the one who puts together the plans for building a factory is also the one who knows best how to run it. Certain things may appear insignificant and irrelevant to an outsider. The one who put it together, however, knows differently. He knows that everything is quite relevant to the totality of the factory. It is likewise with the housewife: she does not rely on anyone else, and wants everything to follow her ideas. For she is the one who knows exactly the needs of her husband, her children, and the household.

If this applies to the running of private concerns, how much more so to a child. For all that happens to the child will affect not only itself, but also its children and grandchildren for generations to come. An outsider, therefore, should not interfere in the authority over it, and one must

---

237. [Cf. *Tzava'at Harivash*, sect. 106, and the sources cited there in my notes.]

follow the order determined by the Almighty, the Supreme Authority over the world. For we are dealing here with something that has implications for generations to come.

One must keep in mind that the Almighty is the sovereign not only for the heavens, but also for the United States or any other country. If one wishes the child to be healthy one-hundred percent, then the upbringing must also be a full one-hundred percent, i.e., one-hundred percent in accordance with Torah.

Parents would never agree that their child be, Heaven forbid, 'fifty-fifty,' that is, healthy for half a day but not so for the other half of the day. Parents stake everything for their children to have complete physical health, without any compromise. The Divine design, however, relates this to their upbringing being complete as well, thus without compromise, without any 'fifty-fifty'-deals of giving half to G-d and half to the mundane. The whole one hundred percent must be to G-d.

Furthermore, it is essential that every child have words of Torah engraved in its memory, proportionate to its age: the *Shema*, the *Modeh ani*, blessings, prayers, verses of *Chumash*, a number of paragraphs of *Mishnah*. This will have an impact even when the child is not learning or reviewing its studies, as explained in Chassidut.[238] Of late, medical practitioners, too, agree with this principle.

XLVIII.   For a brief summary of the above:

We see from the Torah, and this follows also from common sense, that to follow the directives of the Sovereign of the world is the *only* way to truly succeed in the world. When seeking true success, without any compromise, then it is necessary that one's conduct, too, be without compromise.

This applies especially with respect to children:

---

238. See *Likkutei Torah*, Kedoshim, p. 30d.

Children must be a hundred-percent healthy. Thus one must raise and submit them to G-d a full hundred percent. The Almighty will then also give the children, and their parents, a full one hundred percent for both their spiritual and material aspects. Scripture thus says: "If you will walk in My ordinances .. the land shall yield its produce .. and I shall multiply you and establish My covenant with you."[239]

P*

XLIX.   At *matan Torah* the women are mentioned before the men, as it is said: "'Thus you shall say to the House of Jacob'—this denotes the women, 'and tell the children of Israel'—this denotes the men."[240] The Jewish woman is the "foundation of the home." Achievement of the desired effect with the men, therefore, depends on the women.[241]

A Jewish daughter must know that the conduct of the home depends on her. It is up to her to exert the right influence upon the husband. To be sure, a wife must honor her husband, but with the proper resolve, used in pleasant and peaceful ways, she can achieve everything.

It follows, then, that her personal conduct must itself be proper. To achieve this, in turn, is up to the fathers and husbands. They must explain in a gentle way what is to be done and what is not to be done, so that everything conform to the Torah.

This includes also acts of *hidur mitzvah* and behavior

---

239. [Leviticus 26:3, 4, 9.]
240. [See sources cited above, notes 232-235; and *Tanchuma*, Metzora:9.]
241. [See above, note 235.]

"beyond the requirements of the law."[242] A Jewish daughter raised in a Chassidic home must know that one is to act also beyond the requirements of the law and with extraordinary piety. The *Rebbe* thus wished that women, too, should be instructed in the teachings of Chassidism. That is why he wrote various themes of Chassidut in the vernacular Yiddish. The principles of Chassidut, therefore, apply to women as well.[243]

This is especially pertinent when wishing for G-d to deal with us beyond the strictures of the law. In seeking this, one must conduct oneself likewise.[244] This will effect that the Almighty will grant, from His "full and generous hand," children, life and sustenance in abundance, to the full extent. As they say in America, "things will be alright."

L.   (Before leaving, the *Rebbe shalita* said:)

The day of *issru chag*[245] is called *"brey demo'ada*—son of the festival."[246] It is also said that "a son's power exceeds that of the father."[247] The *yom tov* itself, therefore, should be drawn into *issru chag*, and from *issru chag* into

---

242. [See above, note 99.]

243. [*Cf. Likkutei Sichot*, vol. VII, p. 268, and vol. VIII, pp. 289 and 355.]

244. ["All the measures taken by the Holy One, blessed be He, are 'measure for measure'" (i.e., commensurate to the human deeds and behavior); *Sanhedrin* 90a. Thus "in the measure with which man measures, it is meted out to him;" *Sotah* 8bff. Cf. *Keter Shem Tov*, Hossafot, sect. 60; *Tzava'at Harivash*, sect. 142; and *L.S.-Bereishit*, Mikeitz, sect. XVII.]

245. [The day immediately following a festival is called *issru chag* (bound up with the festival) and has a semi-festive character; *Sukah* 45b; *Shulchan Aruch [Harav]*, Orach Chayim 429:17. This applies especially (with greater stringency) to the day following Shavu'ot; *Chagigah* 18a; *Shulchan Aruch*, Orach Chayim 494:3.]

246. [*Yerushalmi, Avodah Zara* 1:end of 1. See *Bet Yossef* on *Tur*, Orach Chayim 494.]

247. *Shevu'ot* 48a

the whole year, so that it will be a blessed year in the study of Torah.

Q*

LI.   You all know that we are now in the month of Sivan. The Torah was given on a specific day of this month, namely the sixth of Sivan. The *Gemara*, however, relates the whole month to *matan Torah* by referring to it as the '*third* month' (i.e., the third month when starting with Nissan, the "first of the months"[248]): "the Merciful One gave the '*threefold* Torah' (as it divides into the three parts of *Torah, Nevi'im, Ketuvim*) to the '*threefold* people' (which divides into *Kohanim, Levi'im, Yisraelim*).. in the *third* month."[249] The *Gemara* thus indicates that not only the sixth day of the month is related to G-d giving the Torah and Israel's acceptance of the Torah on Shavu'ot, but the *whole* month, every one of its days. In this month, therefore, every day is to be a reminder that the Almighty gave us the Torah. At the same time He gave us also the ability to receive the Torah and to conduct ourselves throughout the whole year according to its instructions in all particulars of the day-to-day life.

LII.   In *Mechilta* and Midrashim we are told the detailed events of the giving of the Torah: G-d told Moses to inform the Jewish people that He will give them the Torah so that they could prepare for its acceptance. He

---

*) In view of the special relationship between the women and daughters of Israel and *kabalat Hatorah*, the following are a selection of talks delivered by the *Rebbe shalita* to the students of Bet Rivkah Schools and *Neshei Ubenot Chabad* (the organization of women and girls of Chabad), dealing with the role of the Jewish woman.

248. [Exodus 12:2]

249. *Shabbat* 88a. [See above, sect. I.]

instructed him to speak first to the women, young and old, and only thereafter to the men. Moses was told to follow this order, because it would assure that the Jewish people would overcome any delusions and temptations of the *yetzer hara* that the study of Torah and the observance of *mitzvot* involve grave difficulties; thus they would accept the Torah and keep all that is written in it.[250]

LIII.   All this offers a lesson even to our generation, even in the United States and in New York: we must be aware and remember that with *matan Torah* G-d gave us not only the Torah. Prior to this He endowed us with the ability to receive and observe it, to fulfill it in our day-to-day life,[251] and He said that this is to begin with the daughters of Israel. Thus even now, every year, and especially in the month of Sivan, the Torah must be accepted by the women and girls. This will also strengthen the men to receive the Torah with an undertaking of observing all year that which it prescribes.

LIV.   You are about to graduate. It is surely superfluous to stress that when Jews graduate from a school where they study Torah, this does not mean, Heaven forbid, that one may now forsake those studies, or to think that it marks an end. On the contrary: it is only a preparation and beginning to understand Torah and to observe its instructions with greater and deeper strength, with greater insight and greater vitality.

---

250. [See above, sect. XLVII-XLVIII.]

251. [It is axiomatic that G-d does not impose burdensome or unreasonable precepts upon his creatures; "He comes to man according to his own strength.. according to the ability of each individual." (*Avodah Zara* 3a; *Shemot Rabba* 34:1; Rambam, *Shemonah Perakim*, ch. 2, and also ch. 8. Cf. *Sefer Hama'amarim-Yiddish*, p. 1*ff.*; and "The Dynamics of Teshuvah," *Deep Calling Unto Deep*, ch. I.) Thus as G-d gave us the Torah with all its precepts and ordinances, it follows that He endowed us with all the necessary abilities to observe and fulfill it.]

Just as there was a directive then, that everything was to begin with the daughters of Israel, so too now: the Almighty expects from each of you not only to continue achieving knowledge of the contents of Torah and an observance of its instructions, but that you will do so with greater and more profound abilities, strength and vitality. Moreover, you are also to offer guidance in this to your friends, your relatives, and the whole environment.

May the Almighty grant you to do so in good health, with excitement, vitality, fresh and renewed strength. This will bring upon you the Almighty's blessings in all your endeavors, whether they be material or spiritual.

LV.   Have a healthy summer and success in all your endeavors. May you grow in *Yiddishkeit*, in Torah and *mitzvot*, and do so in a way that will bring true joy and satisfaction to your parents and teachers.

May the administration of *Bet Rivkah* be able to pride itself with you, and say: "See what students we have reared *this* year!"

May this also give renewed strength to the administration, that the standard of learning and the education of the students will grow from year to year, in quantity and quality.

Be well and successful, materially and spiritually.

R*

LVI.   Of the present moment* it can be said that we are standing on the threshold of the new year with respect to the practical conduct in the day-to-day life. For nearly the whole month of Tishrei one is busy with preparations

---

*) This *sichah* was delivered on *Shabbat Bereishit*, the last Shabbat in the month of Tishrei.

for the festivals and then the festivals themselves. As the festive days of Tishrei are now finished, we are entering the mundane days of the whole year. As of now begins the order which the *Rebbes,* our saintly leaders, of blessed memory, termed *"And Jacob* (denoting every Jew, man and woman) *went on his way"*[252]—to carry out the Divine mission that *everyone* has in his day-to-day life.[253]

This is a time of consideration for Jewish women in general, and in particular for the women and daughters of *Chabad*—a term which, after all, is an acronym for Chochmah-Binah-Da'at (Wisdom-Understanding—Knowledge): to consider and reflect on their unique responsibility with respect to their household.

They must know that it is incumbent upon them to infuse their household with warmth, light and joy—*true* warmth, light and joy.

The goal of the home to be a truly Jewish home—which will of itself make it a warm, radiant and joyful home—depends in very great measure on the woman, more so than on the man. For the man is preoccupied for the greater part of the day with concerns of livelihood outside the home. The woman is the *akeret habayit,* the principal foundation of the home. The conduct of the home, and the education of the children, are mainly her responsibility.

LVII.   The duties of the Jewish woman, and her

---

252. [Genesis 32:2]

253. ["Right after *Simchat Torah* (and *Shabbat Bereishit*) begins the order of *"VeYa'akov halach ledarko*—And Jacob went on his way", i.e., that a Jew moves on to his way (and order of *avodah*) of the whole year." *Likkutei Sichot,* vol. XV, p. 259, and see the sources cited there, as well as the sequel explaining this statement. For a further, detailed discussion of this principle, see *Likkutei Sichot,* vol. XX, pp. 264, 266*ff.,* 281*ff.,* and 301*ff.* Note also *Torah Or,* Vayeitze, p. 24b, that *darko* (his way) refers to Torah and *mitzvot.*]

responsibilities, are indicated and emphasized in the three *mitzvot* that were given specifically to Jewish women:

a) The kindling of lights on the eves of Shabbat and *Yom-Tov*;

b) the setting aside of *challah*; and

c) *taharat hamishpachah*.

Following are some of the allusions in these three *mitzvot*:

a) *Candle-lighting* — the kindling of lights for Shabbat and *Yom-Tov*. Shabbat and *Yom-Tov* are the days from which we draw strength for the weekdays.[255] Their lights further peace and harmony in the home,[256] make the home radiant, also in the physical sense, by means of the light generated by *ner mitzvah* ('the *mitzvah*-lamp'). This indicates the woman's duty to infuse the home with peace and illumination from "*ner mitzvah veTorah or*—a *mitzvah* is a lamp, and the Torah is light."[257] This will bring about that G-d's light will dwell there as well.[258]

b) *Setting aside of* challah: "Of the first of your dough you shall give unto G-d."[259] *Challah* is a holy heave-offering which a Jew sets aside from his dough and bread—the principal nourishment of man[260]—prior to using it. Women merited that this *mitzvah* was given to them. It indicates their duty to set aside part of that which is first in rank and size from the income, to devote it specifically for *tzedakah* (charity) and for Torah and the Divine pre-

---

254. [*Shabbat* 31b; *Bereishit Rabba* 17:8]

255. *Zohar* II:63b. *Likkutei Torah*, Berachah, p. 98b.

256. *Shabbat* 23b

257. [Proverbs 6:23]

258. *Tanchuma*, ed. Buber, No'ach:1.

259. [Numbers 15:21]

260. *Sefer Hachinuch*, sect. 385. [See *Zohar* III:289b; *Bereishit Rabba* 48:11, cited in Rashi on Genesis 18:5.]

cepts in general. This will effect that all nourishments, and the income in general, will be used as intended, for health and blessing.[261] The whole income will be spent only for good and healthy things, and not, Heaven forbid, for doctors, medication and grievous things.[262]

c) *Taharat Hamishpachah* (Family-purity). By means of the *mitzvah* of *nidah*, the *mitzvah* of purity and ritual immersion given to the Jewish woman, she brings purity and holiness into the family-life. By means of this *mitzvah* one merits healthy and good children, whole in body and soul; children who will proceed to follow the path of Torah and *mitzvot*, and cause true happiness and joy to their parents.[263] This is achieved when the woman fulfills her obligation, the obligation of a Jewish mother to care for the pure and truly Jewish education of her sons and daughters, a proper education purely following our sacred tradition, so that the whole family be pure and holy.

LVIII. Women and daughters of *Chabad*, and Jewish women in general!

This is the beginning of a new year. Remember the great and pleasant duty and responsibility that is upon you with respect to your household!

You have the ability to make your house a Jewish home, a warm and radiant home!

You can bring G-d's blessing into your home, so that you and all the members of your family shall have a healthy year, a happy and successful year, materially and spiritually!

LIX. My father-in-law, the *Rebbe*, used to wish "a healthy winter." In line with this "expression of the mas-

---

261. Ezekiel 44:30. [See below, Shlach, sect. XXI.]
262. [Cf. *Bamidbar Rabba* 9:13; *Shir Rabba* 6:11.]
263. [See *Shevu'ot* 18b.] Cf. *Tanchuma*, Metzora:1; *Kalah Rabbaty*, beg. of ch. 2.

ter," I wish you, your husbands and children, a healthy, happy and successful winter, a good *tamid*.[264]

S*

LX. The *Gemara*[265] relates that both Abba Chilkiyah and his wife gave *tzedakah* (charity). Even so, when both prayed for rain, her prayer was answered before that of her husband.

The same source explains the reason: Abba Chilkiyah distributed money to the poor, which they then could use to purchase food and other necessities. His wife, however, would give them actual food, and not just a means toward it. Her prayer, therefore, was accepted before that of her husband.

The *Gemara*[266] states that the verse "He does *tzedakah* at all times,"[267] refers to one who maintains his young sons and daughters. This shows that the principle of *tzedakah* relates not only to strangers, but also to one's own children. Moreover, this applies not only to material charity, but also to spiritual charity.[268] To provide children with a proper education is also included in the principle of *tzedakah*.[269]

---

264. [*Tamid*—continuously.] "The good-hearted (or: the one of a merry heart) has a continual (*tamid*) feast" (Proverbs 15:1)5—(cited by Rema, *Shulchan Aruch*, Orach Chayim 679:1, the very conclusion of Orach Chayim; and *Sanhedrin* 100b that "this refers to him who has a good wife")—because of ("being happy and joyous at all times;" *Tanya*, Igeret Hakodesh, sect. XI) "I have set G-d before me *tamid*, continuously" (Psalms 16:8).

265. *Ta'anit* 23b

266. *Ketuvot* 50a. [See *Shulchan Aruch*, Yoreh De'ah 251:3, and *Siftei Kohen* there.]

267. [Psalms 106:3]

268. [See above, sect. XXIII, and note 94.]

269. [See sources cited above, note 267.]

With *tzedakah* in general we find that the man gives
the poor the means for his needs, while the woman gives
him food, the actual need. It is the same with the spiritual
tzedakah of the education of one's own children: the father
provides the means, while the mother provides the (spiritual) food itself.

To be sure, the father is obligated by the *mitzvah* of
"You shall teach them to your children."[270] In most cases,
however, he does not teach the child himself, but hires a
teacher.

In this context there is a well-known story about the
Alter Rebbe.[271] Once he summoned a *chassid* and said to
him: "I have the *mitzvah* of 'You shall teach them to your
children.' You have the *mitzvah* of sustaining and providing for your family. Let us trade: I will provide the expenses for your needs, and you teach my Berel." Thus he hired
him to become the teacher for his son, who later became
the *Mitteler Rebbe*.

The *tzedakah* given by the father to the child, therefore, is not the spiritual food itself, but merely the means
for it. He provides the funds for the teacher, while the
teacher is the one who learns with the child.

The mother, on the other hand, offers the child the
spiritual food itself. It is up to her to see to it that the child
wears a *talit katan*,[272] washes *negel-wasser*,[273] recites blessings, and so forth. The child may learn in a Yeshivah or
cheder, but it is still possible that everything absorbed
there may dissipate when at home. Thus it is up to the

---

270. [Deuteronomy 11:9; *Kidushin* 29b.]

271. *Hayom Yom, s.v.* Adar-I 8.

272. [*Talit katan*, a small, four-cornered garment with *tzitzit* to be
worn all day, and ideally at night as well; see *Sidur Admor Hazaken*,
Hilchot Tzitzit.]

273. [Ritual washing of hands immediately when rising in the
morning; see *Shulchan Aruch [Harav]*, Orach Chayim 1:7.]

mother to watch over the child and guide its proper conduct.

It is thus by virtue of the mother that the "rains of
blessing" for the whole household will come more speedily.[274]

That is why the Torah refers to the Jewish mother as
akeret habayit; for she is indeed the very foundation of the
House of Israel.

---

274. [As in the story of the wife of Abba Chilkiyah, cited above.]

NASSO   נשא

A

I.   In the *maamar* "*Bati Legani*,"[1] my father-in-law, the *Rebbe*, explains the concept of "folly of the opposing side."[2] He refers to the verse, "If his wife turn aside,"[3] as a prooftext. Everything in Chassidut, generally speaking, is meticulous. When verses are cited as prooftexts, this is not to demonstrate erudition but an indication that the particular verse is directly related to the subject-matter.

The relationship between the verse "If his wife turn aside" and the concept of "folly of the opposing side" would seem to be quite obvious. For our sages derive from this same verse the principle that "A person does not commit a transgression unless a spirit of folly has entered into him."[4]

This itself, however, needs further clarification. There

---

1. *Bati Legani 5710*, ch. 3.
2. ["G-d has made one thing opposite the other" (Ecclesiastes 7:14). Every aspect in the realm of holiness has a corresponding aspect in the "other side," in the realm of *kelipot* and impurity (*Sefer Habahir* 9(11); *Zohar* I:160a; *ibid*. III:282a. See sources cited in my notes on *Igeret Hakodesh*, sect. II, notes 16-17). Thus even as there is a concept of "folly of holiness" (supra-rational behavior in the service of G-d, motivated by consuming enthusiasm, which externally appears foolish; see *Ketuvot* 17a), so, too, there is a corresponding folly (sub-rational—or irrational—behavior) in the realm of impurity. See *L.S.-Shemot*, Terumah, note 18.]
3. Numbers 5:12
4. *Sotah* 3a

are numerous statements of our sages for which no proofs
are adduced from verses. If, then, in this case they do cite
this verse, there must be an inherent relationship between
the verse and the principle of "A person does not commit
a transgression unless.." What is this relationship?

Another question arises: There is a maxim that "the
sum of two-hundred includes the sum of one-hundred;
but one-hundred does not include two-hundred."[5] In
other words:

The principle that "A person does not commit a
transgression unless a spirit of folly has entered into him"
applies not only to major sins, such as those which incur
the penalty of *karet*,[6] but to all sins, including the violation
of minor enactments of the rabbis. It applies even to the
concept of "Sanctify yourself in that which is permitted to
you."[7] For, as explained in *Tanya*,[8] the idea underlying this
principle is the fact that sin means a violation of the
Divine Will. This relates equally to the obligation of
"Sanctify yourself in that which is permitted to you."[9]
Why, then, should we use as prooftext for our principle
the verse "If his wife will turn aside," which deals with a
major transgression? We cannot really deduce an argument from a major transgression for a minor one!

---

5. *Baba Kamma* 74a; *Baba Batra* 41b.

6. [*Karet* is the severe punishment of extirpation, i.e., "to be cut
off" (*Mechilta*, Bo, Pis'cha:ch. 10) from the Divine root of the soul (see
Tanya, end of ch. 24; and *ibid.*, Igeret Hateshuvah, ch. 5; *cf.* R. Chaim
Vital, *Likkutei Torah* on Isaiah 57), which includes premature death
(*Mo'ed Katan* 28a). See Rashi on Genesis 17:14, and on Leviticus 17:9
and 23:30; Ramban on Leviticus 18:29.]

7. *Yevamot* 20a; *Nidah* 12a.

8. *Tanya*, ch. 24.

9. [Note that some authorities regard the principle of "Sanctify
yourself.." as one of the 248 positive precepts of the Torah! See *L.S.-
Vayikra*, Acharei, sect. III, and Kedoshim, note 1.]

II. There is, however, a two-fold relationship
between the principle and the prooftext:

(a) The law of *sotah* applies only to a married woman.
Only a married woman becomes a *zonah* when committing
adultery.[10] (To be sure, R. Eleazar is of the opinion that a
relationship between a single man and a single woman
would also render her a *zonah*; but this is merely the opinion of a single authority, and it is not adopted as a
Halachic ruling.[11]) Thus it follows that the seriousness of
this transgression lies in the fact that she is married. It is
likewise with the principle that "A person does not commit a transgression..," which implies that the person has
become separated from Divinity: the seriousness of any
sin, even the minor ones, derives from the fact that Jews
are the 'spouse' of G-d, as explained further on.

The *Zohar*[12] relates that a philosopher asked R.
Eleazar: The Jewish people claims to be the "chosen people." How come, then, that they are weaker than all other
nations [as seen in the fact that they cannot eat impure
animals]? R. Eleazar responded that the answer lies in the
question itself. Jews are the "chosen people" and therefore
too delicate to tolerate refuse such as spiritual insects and
vermin; thus they are also unable to tolerate those things
on the physical level.[13]

---

10. *Likkutei Torah*, Korach, p. 53c. [*Zonah* is conventionally translated *harlot*. In the Halachic context of the women a *kohen* is forbidden
to marry (Leviticus 21:7), *zonah* is generally defined as a woman who
had a relationship with a man forbidden to her at the time, or a
woman subject to other disqualifications to the priesthood. See *Sifra*,
and Rashi, on Leviticus 21:7; Rambam, *Hilchot Issurei Bi'ah* 18:1-3.]

11. *Yevamot* 59b and 61b. Rambam, *Hilchot Issurei Bi'ah* 18:2.

12. [Cf. *Vayikra Rabba* 13:2-3; *Tanchuma*, Shemini:6, cited by Rashi
on Leviticus 11:2.]

13. *Zohar* III:end of 220b-221b.

[This is analogous to the theme discussed (in the *maa-mar*[14]), that the nations of the world are not regarded as rebels for referring to the Almighty as "G-d of gods."[15] It is altogether different, however, with Jews. As they are on a more sublime level, even the smallest transgression will separate them altogether from Divinity, even more so than *kelipah* and *sitra achara*.[16]]

The Jewish people is compared to the heart.[17] The heart, by virtue of it being the chosen of all organs, is too delicate to tolerate any base substance, even if it be of the most subtle kind. So, too, it is with the Jewish people.[18]

We can understand now the relationship between the prooftext of "If his wife turn aside.." and the principle of "A person does not commit a transgression.."

Israel is the 'spouse' of G-d: G-d is the 'husband' and the Israelites are the 'wife'.[19] This is a bond for all times, even the period of the *galut*. [The present time differs, in this context, from the Messianic future only in that presently the Almighty is referred to as *ba'al*, while in the future to come He will be referred to as *ish*.[20] Scripture

---

14. *Bati Legani 5713*, ch. 2-3.

15. [*Menachot* 110b.] *Rema* on *Shulchan Aruch*, Orach Chayim 156. See *Mayim Rabim 5717*, ch. 3 [*Sefer Hama'amarim-Melukat*, vol. I, p. 52f.] and the notes there.

16. [See *Tanya*, ch. 24.]

17. See *Zohar* III:221b [and *ibid.* 234a]; *Kuzary* II:[8-12 and] 36. *Tanya*, Igeret Hakodesh, sect. XXXI.

18. [*Zohar* III:221b]

19. [*Bamidbar Rabba* 9:45. See also *Or Hachayim* on Leviticus 12:2, and *Likkutei Torah*, Tazri'a, p. 20a (both cited in *L.S.-Vayikra*, Tazri'a, sect. VII and XV, and see there note 49).]

20. [Hosea 2:18. Both *ish* and *ba'al* mean *husband*; but *ish* has a connotation of love and tenderness, while *ba'al* has a connotation of master and fear. See Rashi on this verse, and *Likkutei Torah*, Matot, p. 84c-d.]

thus states (G-d's retort to Israel's allegation that He has 'divorced' them, and a man has no claims upon his former wife): "Where is the bill of your mother's divorcement whom I have put away..?!"[21] For He has already sworn that it is impossible to exchange them, Heaven forbid, for another nation.[22]

In context of the premise that "the becoming wife performs the will of her husband,"[23] any transgression assumes great significance. For even the violation of a minor wish—which would include the principle of "Sanctify yourself in that which is permitted to you"—is tantamount to neglecting the "will of the husband," thus implying that Israel fails to be a "becoming wife."

Any sin, therefore, separates man from Divinity. Even our attitude toward permissible things matters. That is why the verse "If his wife turn aside.." is cited as a proof-text. This verse is not simply a prooftext, but also an *explanation*: why is it that even minor transgressions matter so much? Because the compound of the *neshamah* (Divine soul) with the animal or natural soul and the body, are the 'spouse' of the Almighty, and a 'becoming wife' does the will of her husband. Thus even a minor wish is significant as well.

III.   (b) The subject of "If his wife turns aside.." does not deal with a woman who has surely been defiled. It deals with a woman who had secluded herself, and it is quite possible that she is innocent of infidelity. Nonetheless, the very fact that she had secluded herself is already referred to as *tisteh* (she turned aside), an idiom of *shtut* (folly). It is regarded as 'animal behavior,' and thus

---

21. Isaiah 50:1. *Sanhedrin* 105a.
22. [*Eliyahu Rabba*, end of ch. 24; and sources cited above, Shevu'ot, note 211.]
23. *Eliyahu Rabba*, ch. 9.

requires the offering of a substance that is used as animal fodder.[24]

This itself raises a question: It is not known whether this woman has actually been unfaithful. Thus there should be a presumption of innocence, for most daughters of Israel are moral and worthy. Why, then, must she bring an offering of animal fodder? The answer lies in the fact that she created a situation of becoming suspect, which is itself regarded as 'animal behavior.' For a Jew should never be in a situation that gives rise to suspicion.

Secluding herself is regarded as 'animal behavior,' and it causes her to be forbidden to her husband.[25] Even so, this is but a temporary condition, for a short while. For when it will be seen that she was not defiled, that she had merely secluded herself, she will again be permitted to her husband and "she is free and shall conceive children."[26]

It is likewise when a Jew commits a transgression, which is tantamount to an act of folly. This act does not render him impure and forbidden to the 'Husband,' Heaven forbid. For "My glory—(which refers to the spark of Divinity inherent in every Jew)—I shall not give to any other."[27] There was but a momentary act of animal behavior, and ultimately "she is free and shall bear children," for "none is rejected by Him."[28]

This offers an additional reason why the verse "If his wife turns aside.." is cited in context of the "folly of the opposing side." For this verse explains that the concept of "folly of the opposing side" is not, Heaven forbid, an aspect of defilement for the Jew. It is but a momentary act of animal behavior.

---

24. *Sotah* 14a [Rashi on Numbers 5:15].
25. [*Sotah* 2a]
26. Numbers 5:28. [See below, note 31.]
27. Isaiah 42:8
28. II Samuel 14:14. [See *Tanya*, end of ch. 39.]

IV.   Any assumption that there is another reality
beside Divinity is tantamount to a denial of the Divine
unity.[29] When realizing, therefore, that one has violated a
Rabbinic enactment or worse, thus having committed an
act of folly, one might think to be in the state referred to as
"Zion said, G-d has forsaken me, and G-d has forgotten
me."[30]

Thus reference is made to the verse of "If his wife
turns aside": The woman who secluded herself is forbidden to her husband for a short while; but in fact there was
no defilement, and thereafter she is again permitted to
him. Moreover, thereafter "she shall conceive," as the
Gemara[31] interprets: "If until then she gave birth to children in pain, from now on she shall bear them with ease;
if until then she bore only girls, she shall bear boys."
Indeed, the Gemara[32] even cites an opinion that if she had
been barren, from now on she shall bear children.

It is likewise in our context. Every one knows his own
"folly of the opposing side." Yet he is not to despair. He is
to know that in fact he has never really been defiled,
Heaven forbid; for "My glory—(the spark of Divinity
inherent in every Jew)—I will not give to another."[27] He
was momentarily involved with animal behavior, but
thereafter "she is free and shall conceive": he will merit to
be imbued with love and fear of G-d. Moreover, there will
be 'male children', i.e., a love and fear that result from his
own efforts.[33] 'Husband' and 'wife' will be united; that is,
the Shechinah will be manifest in his soul, a manifestation

---

29. [See Tanya, ch. 20-21; Derech Mitzvotecha, "Achdut Hashem."]

30. Isaiah 49:14

31. Sotah 26a [cited by Rashi on Numbers 5:28; and -] Rambam,
Hilchot Sotah 2:10 and 3:22.

32. [Ibid.]

33. [See L.S.-Vayikra, Tazri'a, sect. VII-VIII and XVII.]

of the very core of the soul. This is the individual Messianic redemption of each one, which, in turn, is a preparation for the general Messianic redemption for all.[34]

---

34. [The Baal Shem Tov taught that just as there is a physical *galut* of the people of Israel and its redemption therefrom, so, too, there is a spiritual *galut* of every individual's soul and its redemption therefrom. Before praying for the general redemption, therefore, one is to pray and make efforts for personal redemption, to bring "redemption to my soul" (Psalms 69:19), which will then bring about the physical redemption for all of Israel as well. *Sefer Baal Shem Tov*, Shemot, par. 5-6, and note 4. (See also below, Yud-Bet Yud-Gimel Tamuz, sect. XXII, on the Baal Shem Tov's teaching that every Jew has within him a part of the soul of Mashiach which must be brought out into the open.)]

BEHA'ALOTECHA   בהעלותך

A

I.   In the *haftorah* of *Beha'alotecha* it is said: "I looked,
and behold, there is a *menorah* all of gold."[1] This verse
refers to the community of Israel; for all Jews together are
a *"menorah* all of gold."[2]

The *menorah* had seven lamps. Among Jews, too,
there are seven kinds of approaches, as explained in detail
in Chassidut: there are those whose approach is by way of
chessed, others by way of *gevurah*, and so forth. These
seven ways reflect the seven lamps.[3]

Every one of these, however, share the common
denominator of being lamps. All of them illuminate the
Bet Hamikdash. Moreover, their light is not restricted to the
Bet Hamikdash: it radiates from there over the whole world.
That is why the windows in the *Bet Hamikdash* were "wide
and narrow."[4]

The windows of common buildings are made in a
way that as much as possible of the light from without
will *enter* the house. The *Bet Hamikdash*, however, was
built in a way that light would emanate from it to the

---

1. Zechariah 4:2
2. [*Pesikta Rabaty* 8:4. See also *Bamidbar Rabba* 13:8 and *Shir Rabba*
4:7.]
3. See *Likkutei Torah*, Beha'alotecha, p. 29c. [See also *ibid.*, p. 32d;
and *cf. Sefer Baal Shem Tov*, Behar, par. 3 and note 1.]
4. I Kings 6:4. See *Menachot* 86b ["'wide' without and 'narrow'
within, for I (G-d) am not in need of light], and Rashi there ["wide on
the outside to allow the light to go out, to the outside"].

whole world.[5] That is the whole purpose of the *Bet Hamikdash*.

Who brought about this illumination? The lamps, i.e., the souls of Israel.

To be sure, there are different kinds of Jews. Each one is to serve the Almighty with *his* or *her* unique abilities: "I was created solely to serve my Creator."[6] Every one, with all of his or her personal aptitudes, was created to serve the Almighty with *those* aptitudes Even so, all share the common denominator of being lamps, to generate light.

Whatever the differences, they are but with respect to the individual approach to *avodah* (service of G-d). Some have to serve by way of *chessed*, because it is suited to their aptitudes and dispositions. Others have to serve through *gevurah*, in terms of stringencies and by way of *dinim*, corresponding to their dispositions. This simply means that their *approach* is by means of *gevurah*, but the goal of their efforts is the same, namely to generate light.

The ultimate goal is the same for all. Nonetheless, there is a big difference in terms of approach, whether it be by way of *gevurah*, or whether one is to set out by way of *chessed*. In the latter case there is no need for too much pondering as its purpose is self-evident; for even on the empirical level it is the way of "Love your fellow like yourself."[7]

This was the way of Aaron the High Priest who lit the *menorah*.[8] Aaron "loved the *beriyot* (creatures) and brought them near to Torah."[9] The term *beriyot* denotes beings who

---

5. *Vayikra Rabba* 31:7; *Tanchuma*, Tetzave:6 and Beha'alotecha:2.
6. *Kidushin* 82a
7. [Leviticus 19:18]
8. [Numbers 8:3, and *Midrash Aggadah* there.]
9. *Avot* 1:12, and see the commentaries there. [See *Avot deR. Nathan* 12:3; and *Eliyahu Rabba* ch. 13.]

possess no advantages or virtues on their own, and manifest only deficiencies. Their sole virtue is in the fact that they were created by the Almighty, as explained by the *Alter Rebbe*.[10] Yet Aaron extended love to these as well.

This deportment of Aaron signified not only his intended objective, but also the *means* towards that end. In other words, even on the manifest level he used the approach of "loving *beriyot*" and "bringing them near to Torah" in order to turn them into Torah-Jews.

This was also the approach of the *Rebbes*, our leaders, up to and including my father-in-law, the *Rebbe*, whose work was also to light the lamps.[11]

Every Jew is possessed of the "lamp of G-d, which is the soul of man,"[12] but there are those who wait for someone to light it. This is the work of the leaders of Israel: to light the "lamp of G-d, which is the soul of man" and inherent in every Jew, of which there are seven types.

The approach of the leaders of *Chabad* in general, and of my father-in-law, the *Rebbe*, in particular, was by way of manifest love. 'Light' was not only the goal but also the means to achieve that goal. He kindled the "lamp of G-d, which is the soul of man" in every kind of Jew by relating to them with affinity and pleasantness.

B

II.   The wellsprings [of Chassidut] must be disseminated in the outside-world (*hafatzat hamayanot chutzah*).

---

10. *Tanya*, ch. 32.
11. [See "The Philosophy of Lubavitch Activism," *Chassidic Dimensions*, ch. IV and VII. *Cf. Bamidbar Rabba* 21:15; *Tanchuma*, Pinchas:11.]
12. [Proverbs 20:27. See *Tanya*, ch. 19.]

This does not mean to wait until those who as yet are 'outside' come to the wellsprings. Rather, "let your wellsprings *be dispersed* abroad":[13] one is to go to the outside and disseminate the wellsprings *there*.[14]

This approach started with Aaron the High Priest, who "loved peace and pursued peace, loved the creatures and brought them near to the Torah."[15] Aaron did not wait for people to come to him. He took the initiative and went to them.[16]

He went even to *beriyot*, i.e., people who have nothing to show for themselves except for the fact that they are *beriyot*, creatures of the Almighty. Aaron went even to those, and he brought them near to the Torah.[17]

There is, though, one qualification: he brought them near *to the Torah*, as opposed to bringing the Torah *to them*. Aaron did indeed go to *beriyot*, but he did not offer them the Torah in a way that would conform to their outlook. He did not offer compromises and permissiveness in matters of Torah. He did not bring the Torah down and near to the spirit of the *beriyot*, but raised them and brought them near to the Torah, to the reality of the Torah in its perfect state.

III.   This aspect of Aaron's *avodah* is alluded in this *parshah*: "When you light up the lamps."[18] The lamps denote the souls of Israel,[19] as it is written, "The lamp of G-d is the soul of man."[20] Generally speaking, there are

---

13. [Proverbs 5:16]
14. [See "Let Your Wellsprings Be Dispersed Abroad," *The Mystical Tradition*, p. 111ff.]
15. [*Avot* 1:12]
16. See above, note 9.
17. [See above, sect. I.]
18. [Numbers 8:2]
19. [See above, note 2.]
20. Proverbs 20:27

seven types of Jewish souls, as explained in *Likkutei Torah*, corresponding to the seven lamps of the *menorah*.[21] Aaron's *avodah* was to light and raise all these lamps. The Divine light is inherent in every Jew, but it may be in a state of latency. Thus it was Aaron's task to light these lamps, to make the latent manifest.

When Aaron manifested the soul in every Jew, he did so to the point that "the light-flame would ascend of itself."[22] For as long as there is a need for Aaron to light the Divine lamp in the *beriyot*, one has not achieved the intended goal. The lamp is to be kindled to the point that the flame rises by itself, that is, that there is no further need to light it because it burns and shines on its own.

IV.   The lighting of the *menorah* in the *Bet Hamikdash* involves three laws: a) a kindling of the *menorah* is acceptable even when done by a non-*kohen*; b) the setting up of the lamps is to be done only by a *kohen*; and c) the site for the lit *menorah* is specifically in the *hechal* of the *Bet Hamikdash*.[23] All this applies equally to the lighting of the spiritual *menorah*. In other words, the illumination of Jewish souls is subject to the same three conditions:

a) "Kindling the *menorah* is acceptable even if done by a non-*kohen*."

The task of influencing others, and of disseminating the wellsprings in the outside world, is not restricted to special individuals. It is a merit and obligation incumbent upon every Jew. The *Mishnah* clearly addresses *every* Jew when stating "Be of the disciples of Aaron.."[24] Every sin-

---

21. See above, note 3.

22. [*Shabbat* 21a; and Rashi on Numbers 8:2.]

23. [The *hechal* is the closed-off hall in front of the Holy of Holies.] See *Yoma* 24b; Rambam, *Hilchot Bi'at Hamikdash* 9:5 and 7. [See also *Sifra* on Leviticus 24:4. *Menachot* 98b; *Yoma* 33b; Rambam, *Hilchot Bet Habechirah* 1:7 and 3:17.]

24. *Avot* 1:12

gle Jew must follow the path of Aaron to bring *beriyot* near to the Torah. Nonetheless—

b) "The setting up of the lamps is to be done only by a *kohen*."

One might think to oneself: "The ultimate goal is to influence others. What difference, then, does it make what means I shall use to achieve this objective? I will explain to them subjects of the Torah as *I* understand them, in a way I feel suitable to their understanding. I will choose an approach to *mitzvot* suitable to myself and them, and so forth, and that way I will be able to make an impact upon them."

That is why there is the directive: "The setting up of the lamps," that is, putting in the oil and the wick—the things used for the lighting of the lamp—must be done only through a *kohen*. Not everyone is able and suitable to choose and prepare the things used for lighting the lamps of Jews. Only a *kohen* is able to do so.

A *kohen* is one who has no portion and inheritance of his own, as "G-d [alone] is his inheritance."[25] Rambam[26] defines it: "He whose spirit moves him .. to withdraw from the mundane, in order to stand before G-d to serve and minister to Him," i.e., he is completely devoted to attaching himself to G-d to serve Him. Only a person like that can prepare the things to light the lamp of the soul. Once the *kohen* has prepared the oil and wick, then it becomes incumbent upon every single individual to light them, to disseminate those wellsprings in the outside-world.

c) "The site for the lit *menorah* is specifically in the *hechal*."

"There are ten levels of holiness"[27] (the Holy of

25. [Deuteronomy 18:1-2; see there also 10:9.]
26. *Hilchot Shemitah Veyovel* 13:13.
27. *Kelim* 1:6

Holies; the *hechal*; and so forth). The levels enumerated after (and lower than) the *hechal* are also holy. Nonetheless, if the lit *menorah* is in any of the places whose sanctity is inferior to that of the *hechal*, the *mitzvah* has not been fulfilled. Every task has its own place, and that of the *menorah* is to give its light in the *hechal*.

V.   All this has the following implications for man's *avodah*:

One is not to say, "Indeed, I must light the lamp within me and the lamp within another; but who says that I must do so in a way of such sublime holiness? There are so many Jews who do not have such great demands placed upon them; why, then, must I do all that?" Thus follows the directive:

"Everyone has his task. If you are endowed with abilities and possibilities to bring light into a place that is more holy, this proves that this is your mission which the Almighty expects from you. By not pursuing it you will have failed to carry out your mission because you failed to carry out the will of the Creator."

Ratzon (will; desire) is not divisible.[28] Here lies the difference between 'intellect' and 'will'. In terms of intellect and reason it is possible to understand a mere part of the insight. In terms of will, however, he who fails to execute it in all its details cannot claim to have fulfilled 'at least half of the will.' That will has not been fulfilled at all. In fact, one has violated it, one has done its very opposite.

People differ one from another.[29] Each one has a unique task which may not be relevant to another.[30] The

---

28. [See *Sefer Hama'amarim-Kuntresim*, vol. II, p. 312a.] *Cf. Likkutei Diburim*, vol. IV, p. 1540.

29. [*Berachot* 58a. Rambam, *Hilchot De'ot* 1:1; and *Moreh Nevuchim* II:40.]

30. [See *Tanya*, Igeret Hakodesh, sect. VII, in explanation of

same applies to generations.[31] In earlier generations there were many G-d-fearing and accomplished people who did not study *pnimiyut haTorah*. In these latter generations, however, now that *pnimiyut haTorah* has become revealed and manifest, the very fact that there is this revelation proves of itself that the study of *pnimiyut haTorah* is one of the obligations of our times and generation. Thus it follows that there is no alternative, for *ratzon* is not subject to division.

The kindling of the *menorah* teaches us, in essence, that there must be an involvement with *pnimiyut haTorah*. In context of the concept of fire,[32] we must know that it is not enough to have the 'dark fire,' i.e., the *galya* (the revealed or manifest part) of Torah; there must also be the 'bright fire,' i.e., *pnimiyut haTorah*.[33] The study of *pnimiyut haTorah* infuses the ability and strength to overcome any obstacles, and also adds vitality to the study of the manifest part of the Torah and the observance of the *mitzvot*.

৯

Shabbat 118b; and below, Pinchas, sect. VII*ff.*, and the sources cited there.]

31. [See *Tanya*, Igeret Hakodesh, end of sect. VII.]

32. In a flame there are two kinds (colors) of fire: a dark fire (which is close to the wick), and a bright ('white') fire. [See *Zohar* I:51a; and *cf. Berachot* 52b. See *Derech Mitzvotecha*, "Tzitzit," ch. 3: "The 'white' (bright) fire is the essential color of fire; the 'dark' fire is close to the wick, where the (essential) color of the fire changes because another substance is mixed with it."]

This applies also to the Torah which is compared to fire [*Mechilta*, Yitro, Bachodesh:ch. 4; *Sifre*, Berachah, end of par. 343; *Tanchuma*, Yitro:12; and *cf. Berachot* 22a. See also next note.]

33. [*Cf. Zohar* I:23b and 252b (*Zohar Chadash*, Tikunim:115a), and *Tikunei Zohar* 56:90b, that in the Torah there is a dark fire and a bright fire, "the bright one *within* (inner part) and the dark one *without* (external part)."]

VI.   One of the principal aspects in the conduct of
Jewish women, greatly influencing their sons and daughters, is the concept of *tzeniyut* (modesty; chastity): "The
honor of a king's daughter is within (in privacy)."[34] The
Gemara[35] thus informs us about the extraordinary *tzeniyut*
of Kimchit, that the walls of her house never saw the hairs
on her head; by virtue thereof she merited that seven of
her sons served in the *Bet Hamikdash* as *kohanim gedolim*
(High Priests).

One is not to think, "Why should I conduct myself
with extraordinary *tzeniyut* just so that my children will be
High-Priests? I shall be quite content with them being
ordinary priests. After all, all Jews are holy!"

The kindling of the *menorah* thus teaches us that the
menorah must burn specifically in the *hechal*. This implies,
as stated above, that one must utilize an opportunity to
kindle in a place of greater sanctity. In our context: if a
woman has the opportunity to raise her children to be
kohanim gedolim, that itself proves that it is her obligation
to do so. Not to do so means failing altogether to fulfill her
obligation; she will have failed to carry out G-d's will.

VII.   We can now understand why it says, "Say to
Aaron .. When you set up the lamps," which implies that
Aaron is to light the *menorah*. This verse raises a question:
the *menorah* may be lit even by a non-*kohen*. Furthermore,
the preparation of the *menorah* can be done by an ordinary
kohen and does not require a *kohen gadol* (High Priest).
Why, then, was *Aaron* told to do so? Our text implies that
all this was to be done specifically by Aaron the High
Priest!

As stated above, however, it is incumbent upon all to

---

34. Psalms 45:14
35. *Yoma* 47a

see to it that everyone kindle the Divine lamp—the *neshamah*—within him. Also, for the kindling to effect this in another, it must be rooted in the holiness of a *kohen gadol*. It is not sufficient to effect this in another by means of a lower grade of holiness; it must be done with the holiness of a *kohen gadol*.

The significance of a *kohen gadol* is that one day in the year he would enter the innermost chamber, the Holy of Holies. The Holy of Holies contained but the *aron* (the holy ark) with the *luchot* (the Tablets engraved with the Ten Commandments). This means that the concept of *kohen gadol* signifies that he has nothing but Torah.

Moreover: the *luchot* in the Holy of Holies had the Torah *engraved*. Written letters (as opposed to engraved letters) are an addition, supplementary to the parchment on which they are recorded. Engraved letters, on the other hand, are carved *into* the tablets; thus they are an integral part thereof.[36] This is the significance of a *kohen gadol*: his very being is Torah.

This then is the meaning of "Say to Aaron .. when you set up the lamps." It is the merit and duty of every Jew to kindle the lamp of G-d within him and within another with the power—and in the manner—of Aaron the High Priest, to the point that his whole being will be but Torah. This is incumbent upon *every single* Jew, for kindling can be done even by a non-*kohen*.

This applies especially to Jewish women, because the education of their sons and daughters depends essentially on them. They must realize that their own conduct must be in a manner and measure that would make it possible for their children to grow up to be *kohanim gedolim*.

Of the *kohen gadol* it is said, "*gadlehu*—raise him,

---

36. *Likkutei Torah*, Bechukotay, p. 45a. [See *L.S.-Bereishit*, Chaye Sarah, sect. X.]

make him great."[37] To follow the procedures stated above will negate all and any hindrances and obstacles in the lives of sons and daughters, and there will be a blessed abundance of children, life and sustenance in the literal sense.

---

37. *Yoma* 18a [I.e., he must be made great, endowed, to the point of being the greatest and most elevated among his brethren (fellow-*kohanim*) both spiritually and materially.]

SHLACH.   שלח

A

I.   In this *parshah* it is said that "Moses called Hoshea
the son of Nun, Yehoshua."[1] The *Gemara* explains that
Moses prayed, "May *Yod-He* (G-d) save you from the (evil)
counsel of the spies."[2]

This raises a difficulty: When the spies were appointed they were worthy men.[3] This must have been the case,
for otherwise Moses would not have agreed to send them.
(Their appointment and mission, after all, was left completely to Moses, as it is said, "'Send for *you*'—i.e., according to *your* judgment."[4]) Why, then, did he pray, "May G-d
save you from the counsel of the spies?"

It may be suggested that the spies were indeed worthy men. Nonetheless, Moses considered all kinds of even-
tualities and thus prayed for Joshua. But why would he
pray only for Joshua and not also for all the others?

II.   The *Gemara* states: "Such are the wiles of the *yetzer hara*: today he says to man, 'Do this,'; tomorrow he tells
him, 'Do that;' until he tells him, 'Go and serve idols'.."[5]
This *Gemara* explains how it is possible for a Jew to commit a sin. For a Jew is the offspring of Abraham, Isaac and
Jacob, and is possessed of a soul of which it is said, "The

---

1. [Numbers 13:16]
2. *Sotah* 34b [By prefixing a *yod* to Hosheah, the name is changed
to *Yehoshua* which means "G-d saves."]
3. [*Zohar* III:158a. *Bamidbar Rabba* 16:5. Rashi on Numbers 13:3.]
4. [Numbers 13:2, and Rashi there. *Sotah* 34b.]
5. *Shabbat* 105b

soul which You have given within me is pure; You have
created it, You have formed it, You have breathed it into
me, and You preserve it within me."[6] How then is it possible for a Jew to violate a command of his Creator? The
Gemara thus answers that "Such are the wiles of the *yetzer
hara*..": a sinful act is not something that happens instantaneously, just like that, but develops gradually; it is the
result of a gradual process.

In the observance of *mitzvot* there is a degree of *hidur
mitzvah*.[7] On the other hand, it is also possible to perform a
mitzvah yet failing to fulfill one's obligation. The *yetzer
hara* argues initially, "Why must you observe the *mitzvah*
with *hidur*? It is quite enough to do it simply as stipulated." The next time around the *yetzer hara* argues to
observe a *mitzvah* according to minimal requirements that
suffice in a state of emergency. Thus gradually he gets an
ever greater hold on the person to the point of telling him
to violate a prohibition.

A lenient approach to the fulfillment of *mitzvot* sets a
trend that may lead to the commitment of sin. This applies
to any particular *mitzvah*, and thus surely to the comprehensive *mitzvah* of *ahavat Yisrael*. For *ahavat Yisrael* is the
very foundation of all the *mitzvot*, as stated in *Yerushalmi*:[8]
"Rabbi Akiva said, 'Love your fellow like yourself'[9]—this
is the great principle of the Torah." A lenient approach to

---

6. [*Sidur*, Morning Blessings.]

7. [*Hidur mitzvah* is the adorning of a *mitzvah*: "This is my G-d
and I will adorn Him' (Exodus 15:2)—this means, adorn yourself
before Him in the observance of *mitzvot*: make a beautiful *sukah* in His
honor, a beautiful *lulav*..;" *Shabbat* 133b. *Hidur mitzvah* thus means to
go beyond the legal minimum of an obligation. One is to add up to a
third beyond the ordinary expenses for a minimal observance (*Baba
Kama* 9b). See also *L.S.-Bereishit*, p. 180.]

8. *Nedarim* 9:4

9. [Leviticus 19:18]

ahavat Yisrael, therefore, may cause the very opposite of this *mitzvah*, Heaven forbid.

III.   With respect to *ahavat Yisrael*, the *Gemara*[10] relates that a would-be convert came to Shammai and said to him: "Teach me the whole Torah while I stand on one foot." Shammai repulsed him with a builder's gauge. That man then asked the same of Hillel, and he responded: "What is hateful to you, do not do to your fellow. That is the whole Torah, while the rest is commentary.. ." This incident raises a question: the fact that Hillel gave this reply indicates that it is absolutely true and correct; why, then, did Shammai not respond likewise?

In the *avodah* and conduct of *tzadikim*, however, there are two approaches. One approach relates to the *tzadik's* personal conduct which is bound up with his personal status. This is a form of conduct by way of *gevurot* (strictness; with the full severity of the law). It concentrates on *hala'ah* (elevation; sublimation), with detachment from the mundane, from the physical reality of the world. Thus it is said in *Likkutei Torah*[11] that their observance of *mitzvot* is essentially spiritual, as was the case with R. Shimon bar Yochai when he lived in a cave.[12]

This is not, however, an *avodah* applicable to every one. It is appropriate for *tzadikim* who are here below (in their physical existence) even as they are above, in their spiritual reality, but it is inappropriate for the reality of this world. For example, R. Shimon bar Yochai said: "If a man will plough and sow.. what is to become of Torah?"[13] —yet the *Gemara*[14] concludes that many tried to follow the way of R. Shimon bar Yochai but were unable to do so.

10. *Shabbat* 31a
11. *Likkutei Torah*, Shemini, p. 18a.
12. [See *Shabbat* 33b]
13. *Berachot* 35b
14. [*Ibid.*]

Thus it was with Bet Shammai (the school of
Shammai). Their *avodah* and conduct was based on
gevurot.[15] Indeed, as explained in *Likkutei Torah*,[16] the very
name *Shammai* is an idiom of *"ha-sham* (he who *appraises*)
his ways."[17] This, however, was an approach appropriate
to themselves, but not for the world at large. That is why
the law is not determined according to the view of Bet
Shammai and, moreover, when the opinion of Bet
Shammai conflicts with that of Bet Hillel it is not considered at all.[18]

Thus when the convert came to Shammai and said
"Teach me the whole Torah while I stand on one foot," he
repulsed him with a builder's gauge. For that request was
inconsistent with the approach of Shammai—an approach
based on *gevurot*, detached from the world. A builder's
gauge is a measure. In terms of the measures and restrictions of Shammai's building, the convert's request was out
of place and repulsed. *Hillel,* on the other hand, signifies
"behillo nero—His light *shone,"*[19] the aspect of *chessed* (kind-

---

15. [The souls of Bet Shammai are rooted in *gevurah*, and that is
why—generally—their Halachic rulings are more stringent. See *Zohar*
III:245a; *Sha'ar Hagilgulim,* ch. 36; *Tanya,* Igeret Hakodesh, sect. XIII.]

16. *Likkutei Torah,* Shir Hashirim, p. 48c.

17. [Names are not merely conventional signs for purposes of
identification but signify the very nature of the person or object named
(see the Maggid's *Or Torah,* sect. 14; *Tanya,* Sha'ar Hayichud, ch. 1.)
This is especially evident with saints, for "surely their names indicate
their actual qualities and level;" R. Judah Loewe, *Gevurot Hashem,* ch.
41. (For a fuller discussion of this principle see the Rebbe's responsum
in *Teshuvot U'Biurim,* no. 1) In this context, Shammai is interpreted as
an idiom of *shuma* (appraisement), as in *"'ve-sam*—and orders his way'
(Psalms 50:23), do not read *ve-sam* but *ve-sham*—and appraises his
way..;" *Mo'ed Katan* 5a.]

18. *Berachot* 36b; *Betza* 11b; *Yevamot* 9a.

19. Job 29:3. See *Likkutei Torah,* Shir Hashirim, p. 48c.

ness; love) and *hamshachah* (drawing forth).[20] Thus when the convert came to Hillel he found a place for him as well, and said that by way of *ahavat Yisrael* one has the whole Torah.

IV. The *Zohar*[21] contrasts three *tzadikim*, each of which lived in a generation that was not as it should have been: Noah, Abraham, and Moses. In the generation of Noah, when the flood was about to happen, Noah prayed but for himself and the members of his household. He did not concern himself with the rest of his generation. To be sure, when people came and asked him why he builds the ark, he would tell them that the Almighty is about to bring a deluge upon the world and rebuked them for their evil ways. He did so, however, only when they approached him. He did not approach them. The *Zohar* sharply criticizes this conduct most severely.

Abraham did not wait for people to come to him: "He proclaimed there the Name of G-d, G-d of the universe."[22] He went out to everyone and propagated G-dliness in the world. Even so, his goal was to make everyone into a *tzadik*. He did not pray for those who were not *tzadikim*. With the impending decree upon Sodom he beseeched G-d: "Perhaps there are .. *tzadikim* in the midst of the city,"[23] and if so, the city should not be destroyed in their merit. When he was told that there are not even ten

---

20. [The souls of Bet Hillel are rooted in *chessed*, and that is why—generally—their rulings are more lenient; see sources cited above, note 15. For a further discussion of principles underlying the disputes between Bet Hillel and Bet Shammai, see *L.S.-Shemot*, Beshalach, section XV*ff*.]

21. *Zohar* I:106a; and see also *ibid*. 67b.

22. Genesis 21:33; and see *Bati Legani 5711*, ch. 8. [See *L.S.-Bereishit*, Vayera, sect. X; and *ibid.*, Toldot, sect. VI.]

23. [Genesis 18:24-32]

tzadikim, "Abraham returned to his place"[24] and made no further demands.

The approach of Moses, the Faithful Shepherd,[25] was altogether different. When the Jewish people sinned, Moses demanded that G-d forgive *all* the Jews, even the wicked ones. Thus he differed from Noah who prayed but for himself and his household. Indeed, he went so far as to say, "Forgive their sin; and if not, please erase me from the book which You have written!"[26]

Moses put himself out in behalf of all Jews. From a rational point of view it makes no sense to pray for those who sinned with the golden calf, especially when that sin was committed wittingly. Nonetheless, Moses interceded even for them, with a powerful devotion and self-sacrifice that transcended reason and intellect. The *Zohar*, the 'soul of the Torah,' refers to this approach alone as "perfect, the way it should be."[27] This is the approach that follows after *matan Torah*, and it is the very mark of a faithful shepherd.

The leader of a generation, especially after *matan Torah*, submits himself on behalf of *all* Jews, without exception. He does so regardless whether it makes sense or not. He does not withdraw to lock himself up in an ark along with "his sons, and his wife, and his sons' wives with him,"[28] without interceding on behalf of the others because they, after all, are ... For an attitude like that, the "waters of the flood are referred to by that person's name."[29]

A faithful shepherd exposes himself to risks on behalf

---

24. Genesis 18:33
25. [*Zohar* II:21a. *Cf. Esther Rabba* 7:18.]
26. Exodus 32:32
27. [*Zohar* I:106a]
28. [The procedure followed by Noah; see Genesis 7:7.]
29. *Zohar* I:67b

of his charges to the point of literal self-sacrifice. He will do so even if they be a 'generation of the wilderness' of which R. Akiva—[notwithstanding the fact that he loved Israel and taught that "'Love your fellow like yourself' is the great principle of the Torah"[30]]—said, that they do not have a share in the world to come.[31] Moses, the faithful shepherd, risked himself even for them. Indeed, he remained in the wilderness because of them. The Midrash thus comments on the verse, "He performed the righteousness of G-d and His ordinances together with Israel,"[32] that Moses remained in the wilderness in order to bring that generation with himself.[33]

V.   Now we can understand why Moses prayed only for Joshua, that G-d may save him from the advice of the spies, and did not do so for the others as well.

Chassidut[34] discusses the reason why the spies did not wish to enter the Land of Israel: they did not want to become involved with the materialism of the world. For the duration of the Jewish people's stay in the desert, they were free from mundane involvements: their bread came from heaven (the manna); they had water from the well of Miriam; and even their garments were cleaned and pressed by the clouds of glory.[35] Thus they did not wish to leave the wilderness to enter the Land of Israel. In the Land of Israel they would have to become involved with ploughing, sowing, and so forth.

For the spies themselves this kind of life might have

30. See above, note 8.
31. *Sanhedrin* 108a
32. [Deuteronomy 33:21]
33. *Bamidbar Rabba* 19:13
34. *Likkutei Torah*, Shlach, pp. 36d*f.* and 37b.
35. Rashi on Deuteronomy 8:4. [*Pesikta deR. Kahana*, ed. Buber, ch. X, p. 92a; and see there note 209.]

been fine. For, as stated above, there are *tzadikim* whose conduct is based on *gevurot*. The shepherd and leader of a generation, however, he whose task it is to achieve the Divine intent of having a *dirah betachtonim*, an abode for G-dliness in this lowly world,[36] he must effect within himself the negation of all personal aspects and devote himself to his people.

That is why Caleb disagreed with the spies, for he negated himself fully before Moses, the head of the generation. Thus it is said, "Caleb stilled the people towards Moses"[37] who signifies the level of *venachnu mah*,[38] i.e., self-negation to the point of non-being.[39] Caleb, therefore, "had another spirit with him."[40]

This, then, explains why Moses prayed only for Joshua. Moses knew that Joshua would succeed him as leader of the generation, for "'Eldad and Medad prophesied in the camp': Moses will die and Joshua will bring Israel into the Land."[41] Moses thus prayed for him, "May G-d save you from the advice of the spies"—notwithstanding the fact that they may be worthy; for the leader must be bound up with everyone, with all the people.

---

36. [*Tanchuma*, Nasso:16. See *Tanya*, ch. 36; and *cf. L.S.-Vayikra*, Vayikra, note 54.]

37. Numbers 13:30

38. [Exodus 16:7-8; see Rashi there.]

39. [The word *mah* (lit. 'what', as in the expression of Exodus 16:7-8, or in the question 'what is it', signifies total self-negation to the point of realizing that there is no true reality but G-d alone. See *L.S.-Bereishit*, Vayechi, sect. IV; and *L.S.-Vayikra*, Shemini, note 34.]

40. [Numbers 14:24] See *Torah Or*, Yitro, p. 68c; *Likkutei Torah*, Vayikra, p. 2a.

41. Numbers 11:27. *Sanhedrin* 17a. [Rashi on Numbers 11:28.]

B

VI.   The Midrash states that Moses questioned G-d about the efficacy of having given Israel the Torah and *mitzvot*. After all, as they live in this physical and materialistic world they are liable to forget their obligations. The Almighty answered that He will give them the *mitzvah* of *tzitzit* to remind them of all the *mitzvot*.[42] For the *gimatriya* (numerical value) of *tzitzit* is 600; when adding 8 for the number of threads, and 5 for the number of knots, there is the sum-total of 613 — the number of all the *mitzvot* in the Torah.[43] *Tzitzit* thus remind man of all the *mitzvot*, as it is written, "And you shall see it and remember all the commandments of G-d."[44]

Offhand, though, this begs for further clarification. The significance of the *tzitzit* is that they remind us of the *mitzvot*, yet they must be attached to a garment. If the whole idea is to have *tzitzit* to serve as a reminder for the 613 *mitzvot*, it should be sufficient to have just *tzitzit* on their own. Why, then, the need for a *talit* (garment)? However:

A *talit* is *makif*: it encompasses a person. It is not some kind of food that is taken internally, but a garment that encompasses externally, from without. A *talit* thus signifies a reality beyond comprehension. The implication is that one must know that the 613 *mitzvot*, alluded in the *tzitzit*, come from a *talit*, from something that transcends the intellect.

There is no *mitzvah* at all in taking *tzitzit* on their own, without a *talit*. To do so would not remind us of any-

---

42. [See *Midrash Aggadah*, Shlach. See also *Yalkut Shimoni*, Shlach, par. 750, citing *Eliyahu Rabba* (26)24.]
43. [*Tanchuma*, Korach:12; *Bamidbar Rabba* 18:21.]
44. Numbers 15:39, and Rashi there.

thing. There is a *mitzvah* only when the *tzitzit* are taken suspended from a *talit*, that is, when man recognizes that all of Torah and *mitzvot* derives from a source beyond his own comprehension.

VII.   At the conclusion of the section on *tzitzit* it is said,"I am G-d, your G-d, who has brought you out of the land of Egypt."[45] When considering the way of the Torah, one may think that it is inconsistent with the reality of the world. It demands observance of Shabbat and Yom Tov, and moreover to extend their holiness into the non-sacred time,[46] even when one must deal with competitors among gentiles [and even with Jews who do not observe the Shabbat]. One must also pray first thing in the morning,[47] then study some Torah,[48] and only thereafter engage in business. Even when already in the business, there is a further demand that in the middle of the day, in the very midst of involvement with the business, there is a further obligation to put everything aside and pray *minchah*. Indeed, this interruption signifies the special virtue of the *minchah*-prayer.[49] At night, again, one must recite the *ma'ariv*-prayer and the prayer before going to sleep. There are still further demands to abide by the prohibitions against theft, robbery, deceit and infringement—the observance of which often runs counter to the normative way of conducting business. Thus one begins to wonder: "How can I conduct myself according to the Torah when it is altogether inconsistent with the realities of the world?"

The passage of *tzitzit*, signifying the aspect of tran-

---

45. Numbers 15:41

46. *Shulchan Aruch [Harav]*, Orach Chayim 261:4 [and *ibid.* 293:1].

47. [*Berachot* 10b and 14a; *Shulchan Aruch*, Orach Chayim 89:2*ff.*]

48. [*Shulchan Aruch*, Orach Chayim 155:1]

49. [See my *Deep Calling Unto Deep* (Kehot: 1990), p. 31, and note 15 there.]

scending reason and intellect, thus concludes "I am G-d, your G-d, who has brought you out from the land of Egypt."[50] This tells us: If man will not concern himself with the calculations and restrictions of reason and mind, and observe the *mitzvot* with an attitude transcending his intellect, G-d, too, will relate to him in a way that transcends natural limitations.[51] For Egypt, our sages tell us,[52] was a country from which not even a single slave could escape in any natural way. At the time of the exodus, however, six hundred thousand adult males left there on foot together with all their women and children. Moreover, they took with them great substance: every Jew had no less than ninety donkeys loaded with silver and gold.[53] "A mixed multitude, too, went up with them,"[54] for even gentiles recognized that extraordinary event for what it was. All this, then, was altogether beyond all laws of nature.

Thus when a Jew conducts himself without consideration of natural restrictions, then "I am G-d, your G-d, who has brought you out from the land of Egypt": he will merit an effusion of blessings in children, life and sustenance, beyond natural norms.

C*

VIII. When the Jewish people were incited by the evil report of the spies, one of their complaints was, "Our

---

50. Numbers 15:41

51. [G-d relates to man in a reciprocal way: "in the measure that man measures it is meted out to him" (*Sotah* I:7-9; *Sanhedrin* 90a). See above, Shavu'ot, note 244.]

52. *Mechilta* on Exodus 18:11. Rashi on Exodus 18:9.

53. *Bechorot* 5a

54. [Exodus 12:38. See *Mechilta* on this verse.]

wives and *our little children* shall become prey."[55] The same
wording appears also in the Divine retort: "As for your *little children*, of whom you said they shall become prey ..
they shall possess it."[56]

This phrase needs explanation. After all, the spies
were thinking not only of the small children but of the
older ones as well: *all* will become prey. Why then did the
people refer specifically to 'taf—small children,' and not
simply to 'children,' which would include the younger
and the older ones?

Offhand it may be suggested that the spies tried to
throw the greatest possible scare upon the people: they
referred to small children because there is a more manifest
love and greater feelings of compassion for them. [Thus
we find that G-d's love for Israel is related to "For Israel is
a youth and"—therefore—"I loved him."[57]]

This answer, however, would only explain the use of
the term *taf* in the people's argument. Yet we find specific
use of this term also in the Divine retort: G-d speaks
specifically of the little children in saying "I will bring
them in,"[58] and "they shall possess it."[59] This indicates,
then, that the little children are more closely related to the
inheritance of, and entry into, the Land of Israel.

IX.   Our text can be understood in context of the saying of our sages that a child crumbles more than it eats.[60]
Joseph is thus praised for his insight to provide his
father's household "with bread according to their little
ones,"[61] because he realized that for little ones one must

---

55. [Numbers 14:3]
56. Deuteronomy 1:39
57. [Hosea 11:1]
58. [Numbers 14:31]
59. [Deuteronomy 1:39]
60. *Lekach Tov* on Genesis 47:12
61. [Genesis 47:12, and see *Midrash Hagadol* there.]

give more food than they actually eat to make up for the amount they will crumble.

Bread, in the spiritual sense, generally symbolizes Torah.[62] The Torah and *mitzvot* are referred to as food and drink.[63] In this context there is a difference between those who are mature in mind and the little ones, i.e., those who are 'little in mind.' People of mature mentality spend most of their time and energy on Torah and *mitzvot*, and their Torah and *mitzvot* themselves are as they should be. It is otherwise with the 'little ones,' with those of immature mentality: most of their time and energy is wasted on other things, and their Torah and *mitzvot* are with ulterior motives.

"A child crumbles more than it eats." Of their practice of Torah and *mitzvot* more is crumbled than enters within them. For only Torah and *mitzvot* practiced *lishmah*, for its own sake, will reach the inwardness of a person and become food and a garment for the Divine soul.[64] With little ones (in mind) this is but an insignificant amount. Most of their Torah and *mitzvot* is based on ulterior motives.

X.   All this was implied in the counsel of the spies when they argued that it is better to remain in the desert than entering the Land of Israel. For, as stated earlier at length, in the wilderness everything was lofty and spiritual. In the Land of Israel, however, people will have to become involved with the physical reality of life. Most of their time will thus be spent on mundane matters. Even of the little time devoted to Torah and *mitzvot*, a great part will be self-centered, crumbled.

The Almighty thus retorted, "As for your *taf*, of

---

62. [*Bamidbar Rabba*, end of ch. 8; *Tikunei Zohar* Intr.:1b. See also *Shabbat* 120a; and *Bereishit Rabba* 43:6.]

63. *Kohelet Rabba* 2:24

64. See *Tanya*, end of ch. 39f.

whom you said they shall become prey"—it is *they* that "I will bring in" and *"they* shall·possess it." This refers to the 'little ones,' precisely those involved with physical reality, *they*, and not the "generation of the desert—the generation of knowledge."[65] With those who force themselves to observe Torah and *mitzvot* in the face of mundane entanglements, this very need of having to force themselves makes the little bit that they do more precious than the sublime *avodah* of the 'generation of the desert.'[66] The 'generation of the desert' lacked the virtue of *itkafya*, of having to subdue themselves, the advantage of which is explained in context of the *avodah* of *birurim*.

XI.   Even so, "Scripture does not lose its plain meaning."[67] All explanations of *sod, derush* and *remez* ultimately converge for the plain meaning. The plain meaning of *taf* is children in the literal sense.

The study of Torah by children—school-children in the literal sense—has an advantage over the study by adults, analogous to the advantage of *taf* in the spiritual sense discussed above. The actual level and degree of their study is of a low grade, yet in many respects it is more precious to G-d than the study of adults.

The Midrash[68] comments on the verse[69] "*Vediglo* (and His banner) upon me is love": "'*Vedilugo* (and his mistake; his omission; his skipping over) upon Me is love'—even if a child skips the Name of G-d" it still evokes G-d's love. For as the child's action is based on love, its love for G-d, it evokes a Heavenly love in kind.

---

65. [*Zohar* II:62b. See *Vayikra Rabba* 9:1, and parallel passages.]
66. [See *Avot deR. Nathan* ch. 3; *Shir Rabba* 8:10. See also *Sha'ar Hagilgulim*, ch. 38.]
67. [*Shabbat* 63a]
68. *Shir Rabba* 2:4
69. [Song 2:4]

Indeed, in view of the Heavenly love for school-children, G-d gave the Torah to *all* of Israel only by virtue of the children—"our children are our guarantors."[70]

That is why the law states that "One is not to make school-children neglect their studies even for the building of the *Bet Hamikdash*."[71] Building the *Bet Hamikdash* is extremely important, because it allows for the attainment of the highest levels. Nonetheless, the study of school-children is yet more sublime.

XII.   Today is *Shabbat mevarchim* for the month of Tamuz. From this day are blessed all aspects of that month, and especially the blessed aspects in it—[such as the auspicious date of the twelfth of Tamuz].

The concept discussed above is one of the principal aspects related to the twelfth of Tamuz, the day of the liberation of my father-in-law, the *Rebbe*:

He sacrificed himself for strengthening and spreading *Yiddishkeit*. He stood up, full force, against all those who would do battle against G-d and His anointed. Education of school-children in particular was one of the principal causes for which the *Rebbe* exerted himself. In those days the *Rebbe* enunciated *several* times[72] the explanation of the verse,[73] "Out of the mouth of babes and sucklings You have established strength .. to silence foe and avenger": it is only by virtue of the babes and sucklings, the school-children learning Torah, that the strength is found to destroy and nullify all enemies that would obstruct Jews and *Yiddishkeit*. The rescue for the totality of Israel comes specifically from the school-children.

---

70. [*Shir Rabba* 1:4. See above, Bamidbar, note 111.]

71. *Shabbat* 119b. *Shulchan Aruch*, Yoreh De'ah 245:13; *Hilchot Talmud Torah [Harav]* 1:10.

72. See *Vekibel Hayehudim-5687*, published in *Sefer Hama'amarim 5711*, p. 180.

73. [Psalms 8:3]

It is even now just as in the days of Mordechai and Esther:[74] when the Almighty heard the voice of the little ones, the voice of the school-children, this effected the stirring of great compassion Above and brought about the rescue and redemption for *all* of Israel.[75]

D*

XIII.*   The *mitzvah* of *challah* consists of setting aside a certain amount of one's dough and to give it to a *kohen*. The remaining dough remains profane. The piece set aside becomes holy, must be eaten in purity, and *kohanim* alone may consume it.[76]

Offhand this begs for clarification. Of the Torah it is said, "Its ways are the ways of pleasantness, and all its paths are peace."[77] Moreover, Rambam states that the whole purpose of the giving of the Torah is to establish peace in the world.[78] Why, then, does the Torah bring

---

74. [See *Esther Rabba*, end of ch. 9.]

75. In context of the above, there is a special emphasis in the Scriptural phrase (Deut. 1:39) that the *taf* "shall *inherit* it." This expression clearly relates even to those who were *taf* even when they entered the Holy Land or after the land was conquered and divided among the tribes: one inherits fully at any stage of life, regardless of age. The *taf* would thus inherit even if they had not been born in the time of the spies. This emphasis cannot be read into the earlier verse (Numbers 14:31) "As for your little ones, of whom you said they shall become prey .. they shall *know* the land.."

* An excerpt of this *sichah* appears in the earlier volume, *L.S.-Vayikra*, Acharei, with some variations; see there pp. 124-128.

76. [Numbers 15:17-21. For the detailed laws relating to *challah*, see Rambam, *Hilchot Bikurim*, ch. 5*ff.*; *Shulchan Aruch*, Yoreh De'ah, 322*ff.*]

77. Proverbs 3:17
78. *Hilchot Chanukah* 4:13

about a situation of divisiveness, ordaining that a piece of dough must be separated, leaving the whole dough profane while making that piece holy?

The Midrash states that the *mitzvah* of *challah* was given to women to rectify the sin with the Tree of Knowledge which came about through Eve, the first woman: she corrupted the *challah* (dough) of the world—[for Adam is referred to as the *challah* of the world]—thus she rectifies that sin by means of the *mitzvah* of *challah*.[79]

XIV.   The transgression with the Tree of Knowledge was instigated by the snake who envied the glory of Adam.[80] The sin itself became possible by man adding something which had not been ordained by G-d. G-d had said only not to *eat* from the Tree of Knowledge.[81] Man's adding the supplementary restriction that the tree is also not to be *touched*[82] brought about the subsequent sin.[83]

Offhand this is difficult to understand. The Torah itself ordains, "Provide a guard for the guarding of My (word),"[84] which is the principle of "Make a fence around the Torah."[85] This refers to all the restraints and fences instituted by the rabbis. Rambam[86] says of these that their observance is a Biblical precept, because the Torah states,[87] "You shall not turn [from the word they shall tell you..]."

---

79. [*Bereishit Rabba* 17:8. *Yerushalmi, Shabbat* 2:6.]

80. [*Sanhedrin* 59b]

81. [Genesis 2:17]

82. [*Ibid.* 3:3]

83. See *Sanhedrin* 29a.

84. [Leviticus 18:30.] *Yevamot* 21a.

85. *Avot* 1:1

86. *Hilchot Mamrim*, ch. 1. [See also Rambam's introductions to his commentary on the *Mishnah* and his *Mishneh Torah*.]

87. [Deuteronomy 17:11; and see *Sifre*, Shoftim, sect. 154. *Cf. L.S.- Vayikra*, Acharei, p. 124, and the notes there.]

[To be sure, on the practical level there are differences between Biblical *(de'orayta)* and Rabbinic *(derabanan)* precepts. These distinctions, however, are themselves based on the premise established *by the Torah* that in the case of a doubt relating to a Biblical law we side with the stringent view, while in the case of a doubt relating to a Rabbinic law we side with the lenient view.[88]]

Texts dealing with *mussar* (ethical behavior) state that it takes restrictive measures in one hundred areas of the permissible in order to avoid trespassing the boundaries of a single area of the prohibited.[89]

What then was wrong with adding a restriction of "you shall not touch it," when this is to be standard procedure?

XV.   Man must always consider the conditions of a situation. All depends on *who* imposes the restriction, and *where* this is done.

Adam was in *Gan Eden* (Garden of Eden), a place that does not tolerate any form of evil at all.[90] Thus after the sin was committed, he was expelled from *Gan Eden*.[91]

For as long as he was in *Gan Eden*, Adam had no

88. [*Betza* 3b; *Avodah Zara* 7a. Cf. L.S.-*Vayikra*, p. 126.]

89. [See *Chovot Halevovot*, Sha'ar Hateshuvah, ch. 5. *Or Hachayim* on Numbers 26:23.]

90. [To be in *Gan Eden* is to be in the presence of G-d, of which it is said, "No evil can sojourn with You" (Psalms 5:5); "You do not dwell with evil, nor does evil dwell with You;" Midrash Tehilim 5:7. See also *Shabbat* 149b: "G-d, You are righteous, therefore evil will not sojourn in Your habitation."]

91. ["Before Adam sinned, he ascended and stood in the supreme wisdom, and he was not separated from the Tree of Life.. He separated from the Tree of Life and knew evil, and forsook the good. Thus it is written, 'For You are not a god who desires wickedness, no evil sojourns with You.'(Psalms 5:5) He who is drawn after evil cannot abide with the Tree of Life." *Zohar* I:52a, and II:193b.]

association whatsoever with evil.[92] He was a 'chariot unto Divinity,'[93] in the same sense that it is said of the patriarchs that they were a 'chariot' because all their aspects were in holiness.[94] The significance of a chariot is that all its doings are totally subject to the will of the charioteer.[95]

In the Garden of Eden there is no apprehension of going astray. Precautions and 'fences', therefore, are not necessary there. Moreover, such measures in *Gan Eden* are not only superfluous but would in fact constitute a defect.

To be a 'chariot unto Divinity' implies that all his doings reflect holiness. He sublimates everything that he is involved with. To withdraw from anything, therefore, would mean in effect to withhold its sublimation.

In this context the *Yerushalmi* (Jerusalem Talmud) quotes an *amora* to the effect that man will be held accountable for things he could have consumed but did not do so.[96]

There is then no contradiction between the admonition of "Provide a guard for the guarding of My word" on the one hand, and the impropriety of claiming "you shall not touch it" about the Tree of Knowledge on the other hand.

When 'fences and restrictions' are needed, they are a virtue. When they are not needed, they may be detrimental. Our sages thus said about the insertion of "you shall not touch it": "He who adds, *subtracts*!"[97]

---

92. [See above, note 91; and see *Likkutei Torah*, Matot, p. 84b;*Maamarei Admur Hazaken-Al Hatorah Vehamo'adim*, vol. I, p. 244.]

93. [*Ma'amarei Admur Hazaken-Et'halech*, pp. 58-9.]

94. *Bereishit Rabba* 47:6. See *Torah Or*, Vayetze, p. 24a.

95. [To be compared to a chariot, therefore, implies total submission to the Divine Will, with "all organs completely holy and detached from mundane matters, serving as a 'vehicle' solely for the Supreme Will alone;" *Tanya*, ch. 23, and see there also beg. of ch. 34.]

96. *Kidushin* 4:end of 12.

97. [*Sanhedrin* 29a]

XVI. The *mitzvah* of *challah* was given to rectify the sin with the Tree of Knowledge which came about through the inappropriate application of something.

Challah means to separate one piece of dough from another: the dough as a whole is profane, while the piece separated is holy and is to be eaten only by *kohanim* in a state of purity.

To be sure, the Torah signifies peace and unity.

[The *Alter Rebbe*, in *Tanya*, chapter 32, elaborates emphatically on the significance of *ahavat Yisrael*. He explains at length how it is the very foundation of the whole Torah. In *Ma'amar Hechaltzu*,[97*] too, there is an elaborate emphasis on the harm of divisiveness and how it is the very source for all evil character-traits.]

Nonetheless, when someone comes and proclaims "Never mind the *Shulchan Aruch*! We must strive for unity!"—the response is, "Do not say 'alliance' [with regards to all that this people refers to as an alliance]."[98]

There are situations when true unity is established only by separation. The division of the Jewish people into *Kohanim*, *Leviyim* and *Yisra'elim*, does not mean divisiveness, Heaven forbid. On the contrary: it signifies true unity. The division of ten degrees of holiness,[99] too, signifies unity. It is likewise with the *mitzvah* of *challah*.

This, then, is the relationship between the *mitzvah* of *challah* and the sin with the Tree of Knowledge, that is, how the former rectifies the latter. The sin with the Tree of Knowledge started from the inappropriate application of a principle. Its rectification, therefore, is the *mitzvah* of *challah*: division and separation can sometimes be a *mitzvah*.

97*. [*Likkutei Torah*, Matot, p. 85d*ff*. See also *Ma'amar Hechaltzu 5659*. Cf. below, Massey, note 39.]

98. [Isaiah 8:12. See below, note 108.]

99. *Kelim* 1:6

Indeed, it may be a *mitzvah* so unique that it alone can rectify a comprehensive sin.

XVII.   *Kohanim* are separated from regular Jews. Among *kohanim* themselves, the *kohen gadol* (High Priest) is separated from all other *kohanim*.

The *kohen gadol* entered the Holy of Holies on *Yom Kippur*, while all other *kohanim* had to remain without. Other Jews *(Yisra'elim)* would not enter even the *Ezrat Kohanim*.[100]

Of the *Kohanim*, and the Tribe of Levi in general, it is said, "They shall teach Your laws to Jacob and Your Torah to Israel."[101] Nowadays this applies to rabbis and those appointed to determine Torah-law.

Rabbis, therefore, are distinct and separate. Not everyone is able to be a rabbi, because this position is subject to various qualifications.

XVIII.   When we speak of Jews *qua* Jews, we must befriend and bring close *every one*. But when dealing with the rabbinate—the authority and title of a rabbi—not everyone is fit to be a rabbi.

He who wishes to be a rabbi must first be examined thoroughly (for his knowledge of Torah). Most important is his status as a G-d-fearing person. For if he is not meritorious, his Torah "becomes for him.."[102]

He who does not admit the Divine authority and authenticity of the *whole* Torah is unfit to render decisions even in matters of laws that he agrees with and personally observes. He may not act as a *dayan* (religious judge) at all.

The laws relating to *dayanim*, codified in *Choshen.*

---

100. [The *ezrat kohanim* was a section within the sanctuary, entry to which was prohibited for *Yisra'elim* except for specific rituals; *Kelim* 1:8; Rambam, *Hilchot Bet Habechirah* 7:19.]

101. Deuteronomy 33:10

102. *Yoma* 72b [i.e., it becomes for him the very opposite of an elixir of life].

Mishpat, determine who is fit to be a *dayan.* Anyone who says, "This ruling is a fine one, but this ruling is not a fine one,"[103] is disqualified from rendering decisions even with respect to the ruling that he agrees with. He is subject to the law discussed in the last sections of *Choshen Mishpat,* and as ruled by Rambam: to reject even one word of the Torah is tantamount to denying the whole Torah.[104]

As for those who grant rabbinical ordination to such people, allowing them to determine Torah-law, the collar of responsibility rests on their shoulders.

Those who present themselves as legitimate rabbis and representatives of the Jewish faith even while they are of those who deny the Torah, as defined by Rambam, reduce the Torah to a forgery, Heaven forbid.

XIX.   Some may argue: "*Ahavat Yisrael* is a fundamental principle of the whole Torah! The whole Torah is to establish peace and unity, and the *Alter Rebbe* elaborates on the importance of unity. Why, then, do you cause controversy and divisiveness?"

That selfsame 32nd chapter of *Tanya,* however, cites the words of the *Mishnah:* "Loving creatures, and bringing them close to Torah."[105] The emphasis in that expression is "*bringing them close* to Torah," that is, to bring the creatures to the Torah.

This is altogether different from, Heaven forbid, taking the Torah out of the *Shulchan Aruch,* from cutting up the Torah to suit the measures of the creatures so that they themselves assume the authority to determine "this ruling is a fine one, and this ruling is not a fine one."

To plead "Love your fellow like yourself"[106] for the

103. [*Eruvin* 64a]

104. *Hilchot Teshuvah* 3:8

105. *Avot* 1:12 [See *L.S.-Vayikra,* Shemini, sect. VII; and above, Beha'alotecha-B.]

106. [Leviticus 19:18]

sake of defending the cause of certain individuals in a context that would violate the command of G-d, will not further the cause of peace and unity. On the contrary: to do so will bring about ruin, may the Merciful save us.

XX.   Those who use the argument of unity to remove any professional partition between *rabbanim* (legitimate rabbis) who observe the whole Torah and the so-called 'rabbis' who declare "this ruling is a fine one [and this ruling is not a fine one]," in effect dismantle all partitions in the life of Jews that observe Torah and *mitzvot*. They remove the partition in the synagogue between the male and female sections; and so onwards to breaking the partitions between kosher and non-kosher meat, purity and impurity, all the way down to removing the partition between Jews and non-Jews, may the Merciful One save us, to the point of, Heaven forbid, "your sons and your daughters shall be given to another people."[107]

"Do not say 'alliance' with regards to all that this people refers to as an alliance," even if Shebna himself is right there with them![108]

---

107. [Deuteronomy 29:32]

108. [Shebna was the high-priest (according to others, a steward in the Temple or of the royal palace) in the days of King Hezekiah (Isaiah 22:15 and commentaries there; *Vayikra Rabba* 5:5). When Sennacherib of Assyria invaded the Kingdom of Judah, Shebna betrayed Hezekiah and plotted against him. Hezekiah was concerned about the fact that the students and followers of Shebna outnumbered his own. The prophet Isaiah thus reassured him: "Do not say 'alliance' with regards to all that this people refers to as an alliance,"—i.e., though the faction of Hezekiah was smaller, when the majority consists of wicked people we do not apply the principle of following the majority (Isaiah 8:12; Rashi there). Shebna's faction is an alliance of the wicked, and as such has no bearing and cannot be counted for anything, regardless of its numbers. *Sanhedrin* 26a; and see *Vayikra Rabba* 5:5.]

We must fortify the partitions of *Yerushalayim* (Jerusalem), of *yira-shalem*,[109] counter to the opinion of Shebna and his followers. That alone will save the children educated by Hezekiah from Sennacherib, King of Assyria.[110] Then there will be "no breach and no bad tidings, and no outcry in our streets"[111]—i.e., there will not be any pupils who disgrace their education in public,[112] but—

"Fortunate is the people whose lot is thus, fortunate is the people for whom G-d is its G-d."[113] This verse refers to the future redemption, as our sages note that the word *hoy* (woe) appears twenty times [in the Book of Isaiah] with reference to the *galut*, and corresponding to these there are twenty occurrences [in the Book of Psalms] of the word *ashrei* (fortunate) with reference to the future redemption.[114]

XXI.   This, then, is the significance of the *mitzvah* of *challah*. There are times when one must make a separation, a partition, and set aside the argument of unity. True unity of the Jewish people is established only when there are clear distinctions between *Kohanim* and *Leviyim* and *Yisraelim*; between rabbis and Jews in general; and so forth.

---

109. [*Bereishit Rabba* 56:10; *Midrash Tehilim* 76:3.] This concept is explained in *Likkutei Torah*, Pekudei, p. 4a; and *ibid.*, Re'ey, p. 29d; etc. Cf. *Tossafot, Ta'anit* 16a, *s.v.* har, based on *Bereishit Rabba* 56.

110. [Hezekiah assured universal education in his time, so that in all his land there could not be found a single boy or girl, man or woman, who was not thoroughly versed even in the complex laws of purity and impurity. By virtue thereof, the yoke of Sennacherib was destroyed and his threat removed. *Sanhedrin* 94b.]

111. [Psalms 144:14]

112. [*Berachot* 17b]

113. [Psalms 144:15]

114. *Midrash Tehilim* 1:8 [see there the editor's notes 113-114]; explained in *Or Hatorah-Nach*, vol. II, p. 911*f*.

This does not mean divisiveness. On the contrary: it signifies true and ultimate unity.

In the Book of Ezekiel[115] it is said of the *mitzvah* of *challah* that specifically that *mitzvah* causes blessings to rest upon your house.

To be sure, it is said that the Holy One, blessed be He, found no instrument to contain blessing save for peace.[116] Nonetheless, there are situations when only the distinction of partitions will achieve true unity and peace. This, in turn, will cause "blessing to rest upon your house," a blessing without any restrictive qualifications whatsoever for all spiritual and physical matters.

---

115. Ezekiel 44:30
116. *Uktzin* 3:12

KORACH   קרח

A

I.   The *sidrah* begins, "And Korach .. betook himself,"[1] relating Korach's quarrel against the priesthood of
Aaron. Then we are told about the staff of Aaron which
proved the authenticity of Aaron's priesthood.[2] This is followed by the enumeration of the "gifts of the
priesthood,"[3] which relates to the preceding.[4]

"Gifts of the priesthood" refers to the obligation that
one must give to the *kohanim* (priests) part of all one's possessions, from both *or pnimi* and *or makif*:[5] from *or pnimi*
such as *terumah* and *bikurim*;[6] from *or makif* such as the first
of the fleece,[7] which is related to garments.[8]

---

1. [Numbers 16:1]
2. [Numbers 17:16*ff.*]
3. [Numbers 18:8*ff.*]
4. [*Sifre*, Korach, sect. 117. Rashi on Numbers 18:8.]
5. ["*Or pnimi*—inner light," relating to inwardness. "*Or makif*—
encompassing light," relating to transcendence, covering. See below,
notes 6, 8, and 15.]
6. [*Terumah* is the heave-offering for the *kohanim*; Numbers 18:24,
and Rashi there; Deuteronomy 18:4. *Bikurim* are the first fruits to be
given to the *kohanim*; Exodus 23:19, and Rashi there; Deuteronomy
26:2-3, and Rashi there; *Bikurim* 3:12. *Terumah* and *bikurim* are related to
or pnimi because they are edibles, thus entering the inwardness of man;
cf. below, note 15.]
7. [Deuteronomy 18:4]
8. [Garments are worn upon the body, encompassing it, thus
related to *or makif*. See below, note 15.]

Scripture explains the principle of the "gifts of the priesthood": the first of everything must be given to G-d. Of the *kohanim* it is said that G-d is their inheritance:[9] they were not involved with material affairs; G-d is their inheritance. The gifts, then, are really given unto G-d, and the *kohanim* are entitled to them as gifts "from the table of the Most High."[10]

This principle applies even nowadays, as stated by Rambam:[11] when feeding the poor, one should give them of the best and sweetest of his table; when clothing the naked—"when you see the naked, clothe him"[12]—one must give them of the finest of his garments; when building a house of prayer, one must build it nicer than his own dwelling. Thus Scripture says, "All the *fat* is for G-d."[13]

[Rambam's Code (*Mishneh Torah*) is generally regarded as a purely legal text (thus exoteric);[14] even so, he inserted in many passages allusions of *pnimiyut Hatorah*. In this passage, too, Rambam touches upon the three concepts of 'food, clothing, and shelter.'[15]]

---

9. [Joshua 13:33. *Cf.* Deuteronomy 10:9 and 18:1-2.]
10. *Betza* 21a
11. *Hilchot Issurei Mizbe'ach* 7:11
12. [Isaiah 58:7]
13. [Leviticus 3:16. 'Fat' signifies the best and finest part; see Targumim on Numbers 18:12; and sources cited in *Torah Shelemah* on Leviticus 3:16, note 47*.]
14. [Rambam states so explicitly in the introduction to his code, when defining its goal and scope; see there.]
15. [Food, clothing and shelter (or house) are the three essentials for human life on earth (alluded in Genesis 28:20- 21). They correspond to the three essentials for the spiritual life of the soul: food relates to Torah, while clothing and shelter relate to *mitzvot*. *Mitzvot* divide into two categories: those which depend on the conscious assent of man to do them, and those which are beyond conscious assent (*Tossefta, Pe'ah* 3:13; *Midrash Tannaim* on Deuteronomy 24:19);

This ruling means that from all his possessions—
food, clothing, and shelter—man must give the first and
best part to "the *kohen* in the soul within," i.e., for holy
purposes. In this context, the 'poor' in terms of 'food' and
'clothing' refers to the *nefesh elokit* (Divine soul) of the
benoni (the average person).[16] As for 'shelter,' Rambam
refers explicitly to a 'house of prayer,' which is self-evidently for G-d.

For man's conduct to conform to this principle in all
details, there must first be the comprehensive preparation
stated in Rambam's conclusion: "When consecrating
something to G-d, one ought to give of the best of his possessions, as it is said, 'All the fat is for G-d.'" There must
be a general approach of all things being first and foremost "*la-Hashem*—for G-d; for the sake of G-d." In turn,
this will cause man to relate to his food, clothing and shelter in a way of giving the best parts thereof to the "*kohen*
in his soul within."

This kind of approach affects also man's material
reality. For as we are dealing with the gifts of the priesthood, there is the instructive moral derived from an inci-

---

the first are analogous to 'garments' (*makif*), and the latter to 'shelter'
(*makif* of *makif*). For a detailed discussion of these concepts and their
significance in the *avodah* of man, see *Sidur im Dach*, p. 19*ff.* See also]
sources cited in the index on *Likkutei Torah, s.v.* mazon-levush-bayit.
[*Cf.* also *L.S.-Bereishit*, Toldot, sect. XIX.]

16. As opposed to Hillel who "performed an act of kindness to
the lowly and poor creature" [by nourishing the body; *Vayikra Rabba*
34:3]; *Tanya*, ch. 29. See *Likkutei Torah*, Bechukotai, p. 49a.

[Both the *benoni* and the *tzadik* have a body and a Divine soul.
With the *benoni*, the body and natural ('animal') soul are his very being
to which the Divine soul is an addition. His Divine soul is the '*kohen* in
his soul,' the 'poor' who needs support. A *tzadik*, however, like Hillel,
is identified with his Divine soul, while his body and natural soul are
the 'poor' in need of sustenance.]

dent related by our sages: a certain individual once tithed less than his obligation, and the next year his total produce was only as much as he was supposed to have given the *kohen*.[17]

II.   This principle applies equally to the aspect of time. In the life of man there are times when one is not involved with mundane affairs. Generally speaking these are man's first years. Then there are times that one is involved with mundane affairs. In the course of any year, too, there are the (profane) weekdays, during which one is preoccupied; and there are the Sabbaths and Festivals when one is not preoccupied, and especially *Rosh Hashanah* and the Ten Days of *Teshuvah*—when "the Luminary is close to the spark."[18]

In this context of time, too, one must know that "All the fat is for G-d": the first and best time must be offered unto G-d. Man's best and quietest time each day is immediately after rising, for then his mind is calm. That time he must offer up to G-d, as it is said, "The first of *arisotechem* you shall offer *challah* as a heave-offering."[19] My father-in-law, the *Rebbe*, interpreted this verse as follows: the first of *arisotechem* means that as soon as a Jew rises from his bed,[20] "you shall give a heave-offering unto G-d"—i.e., he must offer that time to G-d.[21]

17. *Tanchuma*, Re'ey:10. *Tossafot, Ta'anit, s.v.* asser. [*Pesikta deR. Kahana*, ed. Buber, ch. 11, p. 96a; Rashi on Numbers 5:10.]

18. *Kuntres Ho'avodah*, end of ch. 5. *Sefer Hama'amarim-Kuntresim*, vol. I, p. 11a. [I.e., there is a greater Divine manifestation to the soul, which is a spark of G-dliness.]

19. Numbers 15:20

20. [The word *arisah* means dough, but may also mean a cradle or bed.]

21. *Sefer Hama'amarim-Kuntresim*, vol. I, pp. 128a and 165a.

Some years ago there was a discussion about the scheduling of studies in Yeshivot here in America. For the reason just stated, the *Rebbe* was emphatic in his demands that the mornings be devoted to sacred studies, while the secular studies should be left for the afternoon. For the morning, when the mind is rested, is that best time of which Rambam rules that "all the fat is for G-d." Later in the day one may become involved in those things of which it is said, "G-d, your G-d, will bless you in all you do."[22]

The same principle applies also to businessmen. They are preoccupied with mundane matters. Nonetheless, they must realize that Torah and *mitzvot* are primary, and the first and best time of the day must be offered unto G-d. Before anything else one must pray. Next one must study Torah, in line with the ruling that from the *bet haknesset* (synagogue) one is to go to the *bet hamidrash* (House of Study);[23] and only thereafter is the time for breakfast. The *Tzemach Tzedek* rules[24] that the time for breakfast is after the morning-prayer; but as one must go from the *bet haknesset* to the *bet hamidrash*, it follows that the time for breakfast is after learning. Any involvement with the mundane, therefore, is only after all this.

One must realize that Torah and *tefillah* (prayer) are primary. Business is not to be man's priority, reducing Torah-study to "one chapter in the morning and another chapter in the evening"[25] to conform to the minimal obligation stated in *Shulchan Aruch*,[26] let alone to just mum-

22. [Deuteronomy 15:18. See *L.S.-Shemot*, Vayakhel, sect. II.]
23. *Shulchan Aruch—Harav*, Orach Chayim 155:1. [See *Berachot* 64a.]
24. *Piskei Dinim*, Orach Chayim, sect. 89.
25. [*Menachot* 99b]
26. [*Hilchot Talmud Torah* [Harav] 3:4]

bling the words without hearing what he says or concentrating on what he hears. The very best time, the very best of one's energy and abilities, mental effort and even physical effort, must be offered to Torah and *tefillah*.

To be sure, of *terumah* it is said that it must be "first fruit in such a way that whatever remains (after setting aside the *terumah*) shall be distinguishable from it."[27] The amount of *ma'aser* (the tithe) must be one tenth, and there is the enactment of Usha that one should not disperse more than a fifth.[28] All this, however, does not contradict the above. For one thing, the *Alter Rebbe* states[29] in the context of rescuing life that "healing the soul is surely not inferior [to healing the body where money does not count], 'And all that man has he will give for the sake of his life.'[30]" Moreover, above we are not discussing the principle of *tzedakah* (charity). Thus even if the greater part of the day is spent on mundane things, and only a minor part on Torah and *tefillah*, since that smaller amount of time is the primary part of the day—*it* must be the 'fat,' the best part.

The general way to attain this is by means of *kabalat ol*: immediately upon waking from his sleep, one must recite *Modeh ani*[31] with a sense of *kabalat ol*. There must be a realization and acknowledgment that "all the fat is for G-d." As stated earlier, this affects man's material reality as well.

---

27. *Eruvin* 37b; *Pesachim* 33b; *Chulin* 136b.

28. *Ketuvot* 50a

29. [*Tanya*, Igeret Hakodesh, end of sect. X. See also *ibid.* -] Igeret Hateshuvah, end of ch. 3.

30. [Job 2:4]

31. [*Shulchan Aruch [Harav]*, Orach Chayim (rev. ed.) 1:6. For a detailed discussion of the significance of this prayer, see *Inyanah shel Torat Hachasidut* (English ed. *On the Essence of Chassidus*), ch. IX-XI *et passim*.]

III.   Korach rebelled against Aaron's priesthood. He reasoned that there is no need to give 'all the fat' to the *kohen*, "For all the congregation are holy, every one of them, and G-d is in their midst; why then do you exalt yourselves.."[32] The implied argument is that "The Shechinah hovers over any assembly of ten Jews"[33]—even when they are not involved with Torah.[34] Moreover, any individual Jew has a *nefesh elokit*, a Divine soul. Even the very least among the worthless and the altogether wicked, too, has a *neshamah* (soul), except that with him it is by way of *makif*, encompassing him from without.[35] Thus wherever he goes, he goes with that *neshamah*, with G-d. Why, then, "do you exalt yourselves?"

Moreover, it would seem that for a Torah-scholar it is safe to act as he pleases, for "Torah protects and rescues": a transgression nullifies [the merit of] a *mitzvah* but not of Torah.[36] Thus he is free to talk .. and the Torah will protect him.

[There is a Chassidic discourse[37] which explains the argument and quarrel of Korach against Moses and Aaron as follows: When everybody is a soul from the sublime level of *Atzilut*, there is no reason for 'exalting yourselves.' In later generations, when only a few select individuals are souls of *Atzilut*, there is need for a Moses; but not so in the case of the *dor hamidbar* (the generation of the desert), which was a 'generation of knowledge.'[38] For of the seven-

<hr>

32. Numbers 16:3
33. [*Sanhedrin* 39a]
34. See *Tanya*, Igeret Hakodesh, sect. XXIII. *Korban Ha'edah* on *Yerushalmi, Eruvin* 1:10, *s.v.* vekamah; *Tossafot, Nedarim, s.v.* tzarich.
35. *Tanya*, end of ch. 11.
36. *Sotah* 21a; see there.
37. [See *Or Hatorah*, Korach, end of p. 696.]
38. [*Zohar* II:62b. See *Vayikra Rabba* 9:1, and parallel passages.]

ty elders it is said that "I shall confer from the spirit,"[39] and through them this was conferred upon the individual souls of all 600,000 Jews.[40] Thus they argued: as all are bound up with the level of *Atzilut*, why then do you "exalt yourselves," why reach out for still higher!]

Korach's argument appears nowadays as well (for all aspects related to the exodus from Egypt apply to later times as well[41]). There are those who claim that it is sufficient to be involved with Torah-study, and there is no need for anything else.

In response it is said that an altogether blue garment by itself is not sufficient.[42] There must be *tzitzit*, which signify *yirah* (fear; reverence) and self-negation.[43] Likewise, a

---

39. [Numbers 11:17]

40. [The individual souls of the nation receive from the comprehensive souls of the saints and sages, the leaders of their generation; see *Tanya*, ch. 2.]

41. [See *Tanya*, ch. 47; also *ibid.*, ch. 31.]

42. [Korach questioned the laws of *tzitzit*. *Tzitzit* remind us of G-d, as the *t'chelet* (blue thread) resembles the color of the Divine Throne of Glory (*Sotah* 17a; *Menachot* 43b). Korach thus asked: "If a garment is entirely blue, would it still need *tzitzit* with *t'chelet*?" When Moses answered in the affirmative, Korach mocked this answer as inconsistent and absurd. In the same vein Korach continued to question the laws of *mezuzah* (which likewise reminds us of G-d—*Zohar* III:263b): "Would a house full of Scriptural books need a *mezuzah*?" When Moses answered in the affirmative, Korach mocked again: "The whole Torah, which contains 275 sections cannot exempt the house, yet the two sections in the *mezuzah* exempt it?! These cannot be things that you have been commanded, but you invented them of your own mind!" See Rashi on Numbers 16:1;] *Yerushalmi, Sanhedrin* 10:1; *Tanchuma*, Korach:2; *Bamidbar Rabba* 18:3. [This was the pretext by analogy for his ultimate intent when he argued, "All the congregation are holy, every one of them.. why then do you (Moses and Aaron) exalt yourselves."]

43. [See *Zohar* II:152b and III:175a.]

house full of sacred texts, thus filled with Torah, still needs a *mezuzah*, that is, a scroll inscribed with the two sections of *'Shema'* and *'Vehayah'*: the *'Shema'* contains the precept of "You shall love G-d," while *'Vehayah'* signifies *yirah*.[44]

This is the significance of *mezuzah* which protects the house and everything in it.[45] Analogous, a "house full of sacred texts" signifies possession of Torah. A lack of *ahavah* and *yirah* (love and reverence), however, leaves that Torah defective, for "Torah without reverence and love will not soar upwards."[46] A "house full of sacred texts," therefore, needs a *mezuzah*. *Ahavah* and *yirah* protect the integrity of Torah, man's *"yirah* preceding his wisdom"— which is the only way for his wisdom to endure.[47] As for "whoever says that he has nothing but Torah.."[48]

IV.   Korach's punishment was that he and his followers "descended alive into the grave."[49] It is said that the emphasis here is in the combination of the terms "grave" and "alive": one may be in the "grave", i.e., the lowest abyss, in evil, indeed in the very depth of evil, yet still assume to be "alive." He argues that "every one of them is holy," for everyone has a *neshamah* and G-d is with him wherever he may be ("G-d is in their midst"[50]).

Korach's argument that everyone is holy is correct.

---

44. [The *Shema* (Deuteronomy 6:4-9) thus signifies *ahavah* (love of G-d); *Vehayah* (Deuteronomy 11:13-21), which contains a warning about retribution, signifies *yirah* (fear of G-d). See *Torah Or*, Vayechi, p. 45b.]

45. [See *Avodah Zara* 11a; *Yerushalmi, Pe'ah* 1:1; *Mechilta, Bo*: Pis'cha, end of ch. 11; *Zohar* II:36a, and *ibid.* III:263bf. and 265bff.; *Zohar Chadash*, Ruth:84d; Rashi, *Pesachim* 4a, *s.v.* chovat hadar.]

46. *Tikunei Zohar* X:25b. See *Tanya*, ch. 39. Cf. *Pesachim* 50b.

47. *Avot* 3:9

48. [-he does not have even Torah;"] *Yevamot* 109b.

49. [Numbers 16:33]

50. [Numbers 16:3]

Indeed, regardless of status, everyone has a *neshamah* and has Torah. Nonetheless, he could still be in the abyss. What use is the Torah when the Torah is in one place while he is somewhere else!

The *Alter Rebbe* states that improper study of Torah exiles the Torah among the *kelipot*.[51] This is comparable to the simile, cited in *Tanya*,[52] of seizing the king's head and dipping his face into a place full of vomit and filth. This offers another interpretation of the words "*chayim* (alive) into the grave": taking the Torah, which is *chayim* (life),[53] along with himself into the abyss.

One can avoid this through the 'gifts of the priest-hood': to put the best of his time and energy into Torah and *tefillah*. The first and best of one's food, clothing and shelter, is to be offered unto G-d. The general preparation for this is that immediately upon waking one utter the *Modeh Ani* with a sense of *kabalat ol*.

By the "gifts of the priesthood" one merits the bless-ing of the priests: "He shall bless you and He shall guard you"[54] with regards to children and the acquisition of wealth;[55] and so forth. Moreover, "The staff of Aaron flow-ered."[56] This signifies the aspect of "His word runs most swiftly,"[57] that the supernal blessing is not interrupted but descends all the way to this lowly world: "[it ripened into] *shekedim* (almonds),"[56] an idiom of *shakad* (to hasten), has-tening to bring goodness in everything desirable, in all and any material and spiritual needs.[58]

---

51. *Hilchot Talmud Torah* 4:end of 3; *Tanya*, end of ch. 39.
52. *Tanya*, end of ch. 24.
53. [*Avot deR. Nathan*, end of ch. 34; *Bamidbar Rabba* 5:8.]
54. [Numbers 6:24]
55. [*Tanchuma*, Nasso:10]
56. [Numbers 17:23]
57. [Psalms 147:15]
58. *Likkutei Torah*, Korach, p. 55c-d.

V.   It is customary to take along some themes to present in the synagogues. Thus: the underlying thought of this *parshah* is the theme of "Korach betook himself" to quarrel against the priesthood of Aaron with the argument that everyone is holy.

There are people who argue that everyone is holy, that everyone can determine the law as he sees fit, and that everyone is an authority in all matters of what is permitted or forbidden. That kind of argument, however, is the very attitude and approach of Korach. It will result in quarrels even among themselves, for "A quarrel that is not for the sake of Heaven—that is *the quarrel of Korach and all his faction.*"[59] There must be self-negation before the Torah-authorities, before those properly qualified to determine Torah-law; for their decisions affect reality as well, because the Torah governs reality.[60]

Another point to be taken from this *parshah* is the concept of the "gifts of the priesthood" discussed above. These gifts, as explained by Rambam,[61] signify the principle of "all the fat is for G-d": when providing the poor with their needs—which is really giving unto G-d, as it is written, "He who is gracious unto the poor, lends unto G-d"[62]—one must give of the finest; and the same applies to the House of Prayer.

This relates to the very best of one's time, the very best of one's energies, the very best of all that man has. The very best and most precious of man are his children. The children, therefore, must be devoted unto G-d, especially the very best of their time, i.e., their early years.

---

59. *Avot* 5:17
60. [*Yerushalmi, Nedarim* 6:end of 8, and parallel passages.]
61. See above, note 11.
62. [Proverbs 19:17. *Baba Batra* 10a; *Shemot Rabba* 31:12. See *Tanya*, Igeret Hakodesh, end of sect. XVI, and notes there.]

To do so will assure the blessing conferred by the priests: "G-d shall bless you" with children and wealth; "and He shall guard you" that any expenditures will be for healthy and joyous purposes. For wealth in itself offers no assurance: if the money needs to be spent on doctors, it is preferable to be healthy without the few dollars that go for doctors. Thus "He shall guard you" that any expenditures will be but for healthy and joyous purposes.[63]

The priestly blessing concludes, "He shall grant you peace,"[64] of which it is said that "the Holy One, blessed be He, found no other instrument to maintain blessings for Israel save peace."[65] Thus even when the facet of "all that you do"—which serves as the instrument and vessel for the Divine blessing[66]—is but small, there is still the aspect of peace which maintains the blessing.

All this is yet followed by "I shall bless them,"[67] signifying "the addition granted by the Holy One, blessed be He, which exceeds the principal blessing."[68] When offering the "gifts of the priesthood" to G-d—of whom the *Gemara*[69] says, "Your G-d is a *kohen*"—then "I shall bless them," beyond and exceeding the principal blessing.

The phrase "I shall bless them" has two interpretations: a)"them" refers to the *kohanim* (priests); and b)"them" refers to Israel.[70] In context of the above, this would mean: "I shall bless them"—the *kohanim* within the

---

63. [See *Tanchuma*, Nasso:10; *Bamidbar Rabba* 11:5; and Rashi on Numbers 7:24.]

64. [Numbers 7:26]

65. *Uktzin* 3:12

66. [See above, note 22.]

67. [Numbers 6:27]

68. *Bereishit Rabba* 61:4; *Tanchuma*, ed. Buber, Chaye Sarah:10. *Chanoch Le'na'ar*, p. 38.

69. Sanhedrin 39a. [*Cf. Zevachim* 102a; and *Zohar* III:17b.]

70. *Chulin* 49a [cited by Rashi on Numbers 6:27].

soul, referring to a blessing for the spiritual needs, i.e., to
have a sense of vitality and delight in the study of Torah
and the observance of *mitzvot*; as well as a blessing for
Israel, referring to a blessing "in all your ways"[71] and for
all and any material needs.

---

71. [Proverbs 3:6, referring to all of man's involvements, including all mundane preoccupations such as eating, sleeping, conducting
business, and so forth; see Rambam, *Hilchot De'ot* 3:2-3.]

CHUKAT   חוקת

A

I. In teachings of our sages on themes in *parshat Chukat*, we find "Clouds of Glory" attributed to the merit of Aaron, the "Well (of Water)" to the merit of Miriam, and the manna to the merit of Moses. The "Clouds of Glory" and the "Well" disappeared with the passing of Aaron and Miriam, but were then restored in the merit of Moses.[1]

The Torah signifies *chochmah* (wisdom), as it is said, "For it is your wisdom and understanding in the eyes of the nations."[2] Nonetheless, it is not referred to as *chochmah* (Wisdom), but as *Torah*, an expression of *hora'ah* (instruction; teaching).[3] For everything in the Torah is *hora'ah*, instruction for the day-to-day life, for any time and any place.

In other words, not only the *mitzvot* (the positive and negative precepts) in the Torah, but the narratives in the Torah, too, provide instructions for life.[4] Indeed, even the *mitzvot* themselves are not recorded in the Torah as direct commands but appear in narrative contexts: G-d spoke to Moses, and then Moses related this to the Jewish people. Thus just as the *mitzvot* are instructions (notwithstanding the fact that they are related in narrative form), so also the narratives in the Torah are instructions, for they, too, are an integral part of the Torah.

---

1. *Ta'anit* 9a
2. Deuteronomy 4:6
3. *Zohar* III:53b. [See above, Bamidbar, note 91.]
4. [See *Zohar* III:152a; and *ibid.* 149a-b.]

[Rambam thus writes[5]—and this is already alluded in the *Gemara*[6]—that there is no difference between a verse like "And Timna was concubine.."[7] and the verse "Hear, O Israel.."[8] The verse "Hear, O Israel.." does indeed teach one of the fundamental precepts [of the Torah], while the verse "And Timna was.." is merely a narrative; even so, both are narratives, both offer instructions, and both represent the Divine wisdom and will.]

As all narratives in the Torah offer instructions for life, this applies also to the narrative referred to above.

II.   The three concepts of "Clouds of Glory," the manna and the "Well," all of which are found in the Torah, are readily understood.

The "Clouds of Glory" offered protection against anything from without. They protected from all four directions, killed the snakes in the desert and leveled mountainous terrain.[9] Furthermore, they kept the Israelites' garments clean and neat, as it is said,[10] "Your garments did not wear out."[11] All these are aspects of protection from without.

The manna is something edible, and it assumed any

---

5. *Perush Hamishnah*, Introduction to *Sanhedrin*, ch. X, Principle 8 [in the standard editions, comparing the verse cited, along with Genesis 10:6 and 36:3 (as examples of verses seemingly irrelevant to Torah); ed. Kapach does not cite this verse.]

6. [*Sanhedrin* 99b; *Yerushalmi, Sanhedrin* 10:1; referring to the verse cited along with Genesis 36:12 "And Lotan's sister was Timna."]

7. Genesis 36:39

8. Deuteronomy 6:4

9. *Mechilta*, Beshalach:Petichta; *Bamidbar Rabba* 1:2; *Tanchuma*, Beshalach:2.

10. Deuteronomy 8:4

11. [*Pesikta deR. Kahana*, ch. 10 (ed. Buber, p. 92a-b); *Devarim Rabba* 7:11.]

taste desired by those who ate it.[12] Edibles are things that are taken in, something related to within.

The "Well" is water. Water *per se* is not a nutriment. That is why an *eruv* cannot be effected with water,[13] as Rambam explains,[14] because an *eruv* can be effected only with food, and water is not regarded as food. On the other hand, water moves the food to all parts of the body.

These three concepts apply to Torah as well: there is the concept of Torah being effective from within; the concept of Torah protecting from without; and the concept of the Torah carrying over these two aspects to all Jews.

III.   Torah, as stated, means instruction. The Torah teaches and instructs proper conduct in daily life. This is the concept of Torah being effective from within, just like the manna: one must understand and absorb it internally in order to determine the proper conduct for oneself, for the members of one's household, and for one's children thereafter.

In context of this analogy, comparing the Torah to the manna, there are differences from one Jew to the next. We speak here of *pnimiyut*, of internal absorption. This is something individual. The manna, too, was received in different ways, ranging from finished bread to something that had to be crushed in a mortar: the righteous received it fully prepared for immediate use, but for the wicked it

---

12. *Yoma* 75a
13. [On Shabbat one is not allowed to go beyond 2000 cubits from the boundaries of one's city or town. This limitation can be extended by means of an *eruv*, consisting of a certain quantity of food placed in a distinct location within the 2000 cubits, thus establishing a "residence" on that spot. This will allow a further 2000 cubits beyond that spot. One can effect this kind of *eruv* with any kind of edibles except for water and salt. *Eruvin* 26b.]
14. *Perush Hamishnah, Eruvin* 3:1

was different.[15] There were no such distinctions with the "Clouds of Glory" and the "Well." This was unique to the manna, because the manna relates to *pnimiyut*. It is likewise with Torah: some are compelled by circumstances to fulfill their duty of Torah-study with the mere recital of the *Shema*,[16] while others must study all day long.[17]

The same applies to *hidur mitzvah*.[18] Indeed, there are some forms of *hidur mitzvah* which have a bearing on, and are obligatory for, only those who have reached certain levels of accomplishment. Others, who lack this accomplishment, are not to undertake those extraordinary practices because it would appear presumptuous on their part.[19] The very same things that are forbidden to the average person, therefore, are obligatory for prominent people, to the point that if the latter would fail to practice them it would be tantamount to a *chilul Hashem*, Heaven forbid.[20]

IV.   Torah also has the quality analogous to the aspect of the "Clouds of Glory" to protect from without.

There are times when one has to go out into a wilderness. In a general sense this refers to this material world as a whole, which is called "the world of *kelipot* and *sitra achara*,"[21] a "great and terrible wilderness .. where there is no water" but only *kelipot*—"snakes, poisonous serpents and scorpions."[22] Protection against this is found in the

---

15. *Yoma* 75 a

16. *Menachot* 99b. See *Hilchot Talmud Torah [Harav]* 3:4.

17. See *Torah Or*, Esther, p. 98c.

18. [See above, Shlach, note 7.] See *Likkutei Torah*, Matot, 84d*f.*; and see also *Kuntres Ha'avodah*, ch. 7.

19. [See *Berachot* 17b (and Rashi, *s.v.* lo; *Tossafot, s.v.* Rav Shesha; *ad loc.*); *Ta'anit* 10b (Rashi, *s.v.* oseh, and *s.v.* R. Yossi); *Yerushalmi, Berachot* 2:9.]

20. See *Yoma* 86a. Rambam, *Hilchot Yessodei Hatorah* 5:11.

21. *Tanya*, end of ch. 6.

22. [Deuteronomy 8:15]

quality of *mesirat nefesh* inherent in *every* single Jew, without exception. This is seen in the fact that the term *Yisrael* (Israel) is an acronym for "*Yesh Shishim Ribo Oti'ot Latorah* (there are sixty myriads letters in the Torah),"[23] and the ritual fitness of a Torah-scroll depends on the presence of all its letters.[24] Every Jew, therefore, even the least worthy, has the power of *mesirat nefesh* to offer his life for the sake of *kidush Hashem* (the sanctification of G-d's Name).

This is the "Clouds of Glory"-aspect in the Torah. The "Clouds of Glory" encompassed and enclosed all Jews, from the time of *keri'at yam suf* (the splitting of the sea) until they entered the Land of Israel. They encompassed even those who took along a *pessel* (idolatrous statue).[25] It is likewise with the corresponding aspect of the Torah, which contains the full 600,000 letters: it encompasses all Jews, from the greatest to the least worthy, infusing all of them with the power and strength to go through the great

---

23. [R. Chaim Vital, *Eitz Hada'at Tov*, Yitro, on Exodus 20:1 (p. 12d)] *Megaleh Amukot*, ofan 186 (cited in *Yalkut Re'uveni*, beginning of Bereishit; *Yalkut Chadash, s.v.* Torah, par. 178; and other sources). Some refer to *Zohar Chadash*, Ruth:88c, as a source. [*Cf. Zohar Chadash*, Shir:74d, and *Nitzutzei Zohar* note 10 *ad loc.*] There are, of course, many more than 600,000 Jews (and may they multiply even more). The number 600,000, however, relates to the number of *root-souls*, "and each root subdivides into 600,000 sparks, each spark being one *neshamah;*" *Tanya*, ch. 37, see there.

[On the principle of the 600,000 letters in the Torah corresponding to the 600,000 root-souls of Israel, see *Likkutei Torah*, Behar, 41b and 43d; and *Likkutei Sichot*, vol. VII, p. 33, and vol. XX, p. 419.]

24. See *Zohar* III:71a; *Tikunei Zohar* 25:70a.

25. [Michah, one of those who partook in the exodus, had a *pessel* made while still in Egypt and carried it with him throughout the journeys in the desert. See *Mechilta*, Bo, Pis'cha:ch. 14; Rashi on *Sanhedrin* 103b, *s.v.* zeh pisslo.]

and terrible wilderness without being affected by the presence of snakes, serpents and scorpions, to be filled with a sense of *mesirat nefesh.*

The *Rebbe,* my father-in-law, related[26] that when bombs fell on Warsaw, people ran to hide. One time a large group was gathered together: the *Rebbe,* average people, simple folks, and some who had thought of themselves that they have nothing to do with *yiddishkeit.* When a bomb exploded close by, *all* of them together as one cried out *"Shema Yisrael.."*!

It is difficult to attain something that will touch the soul-aspect of *yechidah* and the very core of the soul. But when this does happen, whether under such dire circumstances or in a pleasant way, even the lowest and least worthy will cry out *Shema Yisrael* with the same intensity as the very leader of Israel.

Perhaps they cried out *Shema Yisrael* because they happened to be in close proximity to that all-comprehensive soul of which they are specific parts.[27] That proximity, however, could merely account for their *yechidah* being affected. The actual outcry itself came from their own *yechidah.*

V.   In order for a Jew to bring out the Torah-dimensions of the manna and the "Clouds of Glory," one needs to have the "Water"-aspect of Torah. Waters descend from a higher plane to a lower one.[28] It is likewise with the

---

26. *Sefer Hasichot 5700,* p. 12.

27. [The spiritual leaders of Israel have comprehensive "root-souls" which compound the individual souls of their charges (see *Zohar* II:47a and 198a; and *cf. Tanya,* ch. 2). For the "head of the generation" is the whole of that generation (*Zohar* II:47a; *Bamidbar Rabba* 19:28; and *Tanchuma,* Chukat:23). Thus they affect the souls compounded within their own to evoke a sense of *teshuvah.* See *Chassidic Dimensions,* p. 101-111, and the sources cited there.]

28. [*Ta'anit* 7a]

Torah:[29] it descended to, and became invested in, the lower world[30]—"beautiful wisdom in an ugly vessel."[31] By virtue of this lowering of the Torah, every Jew can bring out the Torah-dimensions of the manna and the "Clouds of Glory" when reciting *Torah shebik'tav* (even if he does not understand the meaning of the words),[32] or learning *Torah shebe'al peh* (even if he understands no more but its simple meaning).

Just as water transports the food to all parts of the body, so, too, the "'Water' of the Torah." As the Torah descended and became invested below, it carries the "manna of the Torah" and the "'Clouds of Glory' of the Torah" throughout the camp of Israel, to every Jewish man and woman,[33] with respect to all and any of their needs.

VI. We can now understand how the manna relates to Moses, the "Clouds of Glory" to Aaron, and the "Well" to Miriam.

Moses was the "shepherd of Israel." He took care of each one according to his individual needs. When he tended the sheep, he gave soft grass to the young and stubble to the older ones.[34] For pasture relates to the inner being and therefore must be suited to each one. That is why the manna, which relates to the internal and, therefore, must be apportioned accordingly, came by virtue of Moses.

Aaron "loved *beriyot* (creatures)":[35] he loved even

---

29. [Which, therefore, is compared to water; *Ta'anit* 7a.]
30. *Tanya*, ch. 4.
31. [See *Ta'anit* 7a]
32. [See *Hilchot Talmud Torah* [Harav] II:12-13.]
33. See *Hilchot Talmud Torah* [Harav] I:14.
34. See the sources cited in *Midrash Tehilim*, ed. Buber, 78:21, note 152. [Cf. *Zohar* II:21a; and *Shemot Rabba* 2:2.]
35. *Avot* 1:12

those people who had no other virtue but the fact that they are 'creatures [of G-d].'[36] Thus of him alone it is said that "the *entire House of Israel* mourned Aaron for thirty days."[37] His love extended toward all creatures, and in turn evoked in them a desire for *mitzvot* notwithstanding the fact that on their own they were not inclined that way at all.[38] That is why the "Clouds of Glory" came by virtue of Aaron, for everything follows the principle of "measure for measure":[39] as he loved all beings without any distinctions, he elicited the "Clouds of Glory" which encompassed all Jews equally.

Miriam is identified with Pu'ah[40] who took care of the little children in Egypt and helped raise them. She was named Miriam because she was born when the harshness of the *galut* became more severe,[41] yet she prophesied that the savior of Israel is about to be born.[42] Thus she negated not only the decree of Pharaoh but also that of Amram, notwithstanding the fact that the latter was well-founded.[43] She proceeded with *mesirat nefesh* to raise children

------

36. See above, Beha'alotecha, sect. I-II.

37. Numbers 20:29, and see *Yalkut Shimoni* on this verse [Chukat:par. 764, citing *Avot deR. Nathan* 12:4].

38. See *Avot deR. Nathan* 12:3.

39. *Sotah* 1:7 (8b). [See above, Shlach, note 51.]

40. *Sotah* 11b

41. [*Seder Olam Rabba*, ch. 3; *Tanchuma*, ed. Buber, Bo:7; *Pesikta Rabbati* 15:11.]

42. *Megilah* 14a; *Sotah* 11b and end of 12b.

43. [Amram, Miriam's father, was the greatest of his generation. When Pharaoh decreed the death of male children, Amram divorced his wife, and all Israelites followed his example. Miriam then rebuked him: "Your decree is worse than Pharaoh's; for Pharaoh decreed only against the males, while you have decreed against the males and the females.." Amram acknowledged the validity of Miriam's argument, remarried his wife, who then gave birth to Moses, the redeemer of Israel. *Sotah* 12a.]

who would say "This is my G-d, and I will praise Him,"[44] a whole generation that would receive the Torah. The "Well"—water—thus came by her virtue; for water signifies bringing the Torah to a lowly place,[45] i.e., to those who are at the very end of the camp.

VII. The 'Clouds of Glory' and the 'Well' were removed with the passing of Aaron and Miriam, but then were restored in the merit of Moses. This shows that Moses must have undertaken a new kind of *avodah*. The unique *avodah* of Moses was to shepherd Israel (the aspect of the manna); his new *avodah*, however, restored the "Clouds" and the "Well."

The true sign of a Shepherd of Israel is that he does not restrict himself to the *avodah* related to his own personality. When the need arises, he will forego himself, disregard himself, and sacrifices himself for the sake of Israel.

When there is a need to move the hearts of Israel to G-dliness, even the heart of the least worthy among them, the shepherd of Israel disregards all personal aspects and teaches them the *aleph-bet*—whether the *aleph-bet* of Torah and *mitzvot*, or *aleph-bet* in the literal sense.[46] He may be a *kohen*,[47] of whom one could ask, "What is a *kohen* doing in a cemetery?"[48] in the sense of "The wicked are called dead even while alive."[49] He may be an "'old man' -i.e., one who has acquired wisdom,"[50] of whom one could ask, "Why is this elder involved in restoring a lost object?"

44. [Exodus 15:2] See *Sotah* 11b.
45. [See above, sect. V, and notes 28-31.]
46. [See *Eliyahu Rabba*, ch. 13.]
47. See above, Beha'alotecha, sect. IV, and note 26.
48. [A rhetorical question (mentioned in *Lekach Tov* on Exodus 5:2; and similarly in *Tanchuma*, Va'eira:2) for someone in an inappropriate place.]
49. *Berachot* 18b
50. *Kidushin* 32b

when this is inconsistent with his dignity[51] and is not his function. An elder is to teach the leaders of Israel how to guide the people, and it is not for him to deal with unworthy individuals. Even so, when Aaron and Miriam have passed on and there is no one else to undertake this task, the head of all of Israel does so himself. He becomes personally involved in these matters notwithstanding the fact that it is inappropriate to his status.

VIII.   In *Tanya*[52] it is stated that every Jew contains within himself a 'spark' of Moses. The principle stated above, therefore, offers clear instructions for each Jew: Every individual has his or her personal function and mission. Nonetheless, if there is no "Well" (which had been by virtue of Miriam) nor the "Clouds of Glory" (which had been by virtue of Aaron), and there is a threat of "snakes, serpents and scorpions," it is then incumbent upon *each* individual to restore the "Well" and the "Clouds." It is altogether irrelevant whether this is one's normative function or not.

One could be of a status that personally he has nothing to fear from the "snakes, serpents or scorpions." The Divine likeness in man may be manifest upon him, thus precluding that anything will overpower him, as stated in the *Gemara*: "A wild beast has no dominion over man unless he appears to it as a brute animal."[53] Nonetheless, if another is threatened, and there is no Aaron or Miriam to avert that danger, this becomes a matter of *piku'ach nefesh*, of having to save life. For *piku'ach nefesh* one must dese-

----

51. [Every Jew is obligated to restore lost property to its owner (Deuteronomy 22:1-3). Under certain circumstances one is exempted from this *mitzvah*, as, for example, the case of "an elder for whom it would be inconsistent with his dignity;" *Berachot* 19b; *Baba Metzi'a* 30a.]

52. *Tanya*, ch. 42.

53. *Sanhedrin* 38b. [Note *Zohar* I:191a, and] see *Tanya*, ch. 24.

crate the Shabbat,[54] and *piku'ach nefesh* supersedes the whole Torah[55]—even in cases of various doubts,[56] and even when the person to be saved has but a short while to live.[57] *Everyone*, therefore, is obligated to become involved and to see to it that there be the manna as well as the "Clouds" and the "Well."

To disregard oneself, to put aside any considerations whether it is up to him to do *this* or to deal with more sublime matters, and to bring Jews closer to their Father in Heaven, will effect that G-d, too, will bring him and his family closer.[58] G-d will provide them with all their needs, and especially to fulfill the most important principle of "They shall make Me a sanctuary,"[59] for that is a *mitzvah* incumbent specifically upon the community as a whole,[60] both men and women,[61] and it will bring about that "I shall dwell in their midst,"[62] i.e., within each and every one of Israel.[63]

---

54. *Shabbat* 132a; *Yoma* 84b.

55. [All the *mitzvot* of the Torah must be violated to save life, except for the three cardinal sins of idolatry, prohibited sexual relationships, and murder; *Yerushalmi, Shevi'it* 4:2; *Sanhedrin* 71a. See Rambam, *Hilchot Yessodei Hatorah*, ch. 5.]

56. [See *Shabbat* 129a; *Yoma* 83a, 84b and 85a. *Shulchan Aruch*, Orach Chayim, ch. 328-330.]

57. [*Yoma* 85a; *Shulchan Aruch*, Orach Chayim 329:4. Note *Yoma* 84b, and Rambam, *Hilchot Shabbat* 2:3 and 16, that one is not to look for gentiles to desecrate the Shabbat to save life, but this is to be done by "*gedolei Yisrael*—the great of Israel and their sages;" the more speedily one acts the more praiseworthy he is, and there is no need to obtain any permission from a *bet din. Cf.* below, Pinchas, note 26.]

58. [See above, note 39.]

59. [Exodus 25:8]

60. *Sefer Hachinuch*, end of sect, 95.

61. Rambam, *Hilchot Bet Habechirah* 1:12.

62. [Concluding phrase of Exodus 25:8.]

63. [See above, Bamidbar, note 35.]

BALAK   בלק

A

I. In *parshat Balak* it is said: "He couches, he lies down like a lion."[1] One Midrashic interpretation[2] states that this verse applies to the period from King Zedekiah until Mashiach, for the generation of Zedekiah saw the beginning of the *churban* (destruction of the *Bet Hamikdash*) and the *galut*. Even the era of the second *Bet Hamikdash*, which followed the seventy years of the Babylonian exile, was also a state of *galut*: the second *Bet Hamikdash* lacked five things,[3] because it did not constitute a complete redemption.

The period from Zedekiah to Mashiach, therefore, is one of "He couches, he lies down..." The *Tzemach Tzedek* writes[4] that the term *shachav* (he couches) in this interpretation is an idiom of "*vayishkav* (he lay down) and was fast asleep;"[5] "on *mishkavi* (my couch) in the nights;"[6] and "he

---

1. [Numbers 24:9]

2. *Bereishit Rabba* 98:7

3. *Yoma* 21b [the Holy Ark with its cover and the Cherubim; the miraculous fire of the altar; manifestation of the Shechinah; manifestation of the Holy Spirit; and the working of the Urim and Tumim. Other versions have slight variations on the identity of these five things, see—] *Yerushalmi, Makot*, end of 2:6, and *Horayot* 3:2; *Bamidbar Rabba* 15:10. [See also *Tanchuma*, Beha'alotecha:6.]

4. *Ma'amar "Kara Shachav"*—5605. [See *Or Hatorah*, Balak, pp. 1045 and 1048.]

5. [Jonah 1:5]

6. [Song 3:1]

does not die but *nafal lemishkav* (became bed-ridden);"[7]
thus an indication of *galut*.

Galut relates to the body. One might think, though,
that it applies also, Heaven forbid, to the soul, that is, to
the aspects of Torah and *mitzvot* which are bound up with
the soul. Our text thus states that "he couches, he lies
down": this is not the couching of one who has lost his
strength, but the measured restraint of one who ascertains
his own limitations and restrains himself. Thus it is said,
"He couches, he lies down like an *ari*, like a *lavi*": *ari* is a
lion with ordinary strength while *lavi* signifies a lion with
extraordinary strength, as the *Zohar*[8] states that *lavi* signifies greater strength.

In other words: Even a time of "He couches, he lies
down" does not mean, Heaven forbid, that the nations of
the world have mastery over Israel. Jews are always like
an *ari* and a *lavi*, except that "*Mi* (lit., who) shall make him
rise?"[9] The word *Mi*, in this verse, has the same meaning
as in the expression, "*Mi* (who) revealed this secret to My
children,"[10] which, in turn, is bound up with "*Mi*(who)
shall grant that their hearts shall forever remain that way
with them, to fear Me..,"[11] referring to the Almighty.[12] In
our verse, then, "*Mi* shall make him rise" refers to the
Holy One, blessed be He, for He shall redeem us from the
galut, as it is said, "Out of Zion, *Mi* shall grant the salvation of Israel."[13]

---

7. [Exodus 21:18]

8. *Zohar* I:237b

9. [The words following the cited phrase of Numbers 24:9.]

10. *Shabbat* 88a

11. Deuteronomy 5:26

12. [See *Zohar* I:3b and II:105a; *Tikunei Zohar* 49:85b and 63:94b.]
See *Likkutei Torah*, Bamidbar, p. 15a-b.

13. Psalms 14:7 and 53:7. [See *Likkutei Torah*, Bamidbar 15b, citing
Midrash Tehilim 14:6.]

Until the very time when *"Mi* shall make him rise," therefore, the nations do not really master Israel, Heaven forbid. As Israel is like an *ari* and a *lavi*, no one can domineer them.

[This principle is reflected in *Halachah*, as ruled in *Shulchan Aruch*,[14] that lions (*ari* and *lavi*) cannot be mastered, to the point that there is a question whether or not they can be truly tamed.]

From a normative, rational point of view, therefore, the *galut* makes no sense at all,[15] except that the *ari* and *lavi* is compelled to couch and lie down by Divine decree.

Thus it follows that the *galut* does not affect Torah and *mitzvot* of which it is said that "G-d spoke all these words."[16]

II.   By force of habit, however, people get used to the *galut*, and "We do not see our signs."[17]

[There are miracles nowadays as well, except that "we do not see," i.e., the person for whom a miracle is performed does not recognize the miracle.[18]]

The darkness of the *galut* gives rise to the illusion that the world runs on its own, pursuing a natural course. The term *olam* (world) is an idiom of *h'elem vehester* (concealment and hiding).[19] There is an illusory perception that the world has mastery over the *ari* and *lavi*. Thus every so often, including the time of the *galut*, we are shown mani-

---

14. Choshen Mishpat 389:8

15. [See R. Judah Loewe (Maharal), *Netzach Yisrael*, ch. 1, 13, 24, 31, *et passim*, that the *galut* is something altogether irregular, unnatural, and thus irrational.]

16. [Exodus 20:1]

17. Psalms 74:9. [See *Midrash Tehilim* 74:3 on this verse.]

18. *Nidah* 31a

19. [*Sefer Habahir* 8 (10); *Tikunei Zohar* 42:82a. Cf. *Pesachim* 50a.] *Likkutei Torah*, Shlach, p. 37d. *Sefer Hama'amarim 5710*, p. 116.

fest miracles from Above to remind us that even in the *galut* "There is naught but He alone."[20] (One of these manifest and comprehensive wonders of our generation was the miracle of *Yud-Bet - Yud-Gimel Tamuz*.[21])

In this context our sages said that originally G-d intended "to create the world with the attribute of *din* (justice; stern judgment); but He saw that the world could not endure [that way, so] He combined it with the attribute of *rachamim* (mercy; compassion)."[22] In *Sha'ar Hayichud*, the second part of *Tanya*,[23] this statement is explained to refer to the manifestation of G-dliness through the *tzadikim* and the signs and miracles recorded in the Torah.

Miracles breach the fixed measures and restraints of the world, of the natural order, so that even physical eyes will see that "the mansion has an owner and caretaker."[24]

Consciousness of this principle leads to the realization that the Jewish people always are an *ari* and *lavi*. With regards to the soul, in terms of Torah and *mitzvot*, one is not subjected to *galut*.

B

III.   Mystical texts[25] state that there is an inherent connection between Bil'am and Amalek. An allusion to this is seen when one writes these two names one below the other, Bil'am on top and Amalek directly under it:

---

20. [Deuteronomy 4:35]

21. [See below, Yud-Bet Yud-Gimel Tamuz.]

22. Cited by Rashi on Genesis 1:1. [See *Bereishit Rabba* 12:15; and *Torah Shelemah*, Bereishit, ch. 1:par. 209, and ch. 2:par. 82.]

23. Chapter 5.

24. [See *Bereishit Rabba* 39:1; *Lekach Tov* on Genesis 12:1.]

25. See R. Shimshon of Ostropole, *Likutei Shoshanim*. [*Cf. Zohar* III:194a and 281b; also *ibid.*, I:25a.]

when combining the first two letters of Bil'am (*bet-lamed*) with the first two letters of Amalek (*ayin-mem*) directly below them, it spells Bil'am; and when combining the remaining two letters of Bil'am (*ayin-mem*) with the remaining two letters of Amalek (*lamed-kof*) directly below them, it spells Amalek.

We can rid ourselves of the *kelipah* of Bil'am and Amalek by means of *ahavah* (love [of G-d]) and *yirah* (fear, reverence [of G-d]). *Ahavah* and *yirah* have an analogous relationship, as seen when writing these two words one below the other, *yirah* on top and *ahavah* directly under it: combining the first two letters of *yirah* (*yod-resh*) with the first two letters of *ahavah* (*aleph-he*) directly below them, spells *yirah*; and combining the remaining two letters of *yirah* (*aleph-he*) with the remaining two letters of *ahavah* (*bet-he*) directly below them, it spells *ahavah*.

What does that mean?

Amalek was able to wage war against Israel because that nation descended from Esau. Amalek argued that he, too, is a great-grandson of Isaac, and a great-great-grand-son of Abraham; thus he, too, is entitled to speak out on matters relating to Torah and holiness.

Allowing Amalek a slight opening made it possible to having one that "knows his Master, yet purposely sets out to rebel against Him."[26] This led to the consequences of Amalek's attack.[27]

It is likewise with Bil'am. The *Gemara* states that Bil'am was descended of Laban.[28] Laban argued, "The daughters are my daughters, and the sons are my sons ..

---

26. See *Sifra*, Bechukotai, ch. 3: parsha 2.
27. See *Zohar* II:65a ["one should not allow any place for evil things, lest man's action have unwarranted effects." The sequel notes how Israel's inappropriate behavior resulted in the attack by Amalek.]
28. *Sanhedrin* 105a

and all that you see is mine!"[29] In other words, he, too, is related to the Jews, because the whole House of Israel developed from his daughters.

All this has a moral for every generation:

Someone may come and say things that stand in contradiction to Torah and *mitzvot*. He may even assert his authority by showing a certificate proving that he is a great-grandson of Isaac and a great-great-grandson of Abraham. Moreover, he may prove that he is the ancestor of those from whom the whole House of Israel developed.

That person must be told clearly: "We have but our Father in Heaven! Our sole criterion for anything is the Torah! Neither pedigree nor anything else of that sort is decisive for us. The Torah is the exclusive touchstone and standard: whatever accords with the Torah is fine; but if something conflicts with Torah, even if it comes from Bil'am or Amalek, the very fact that it is counter to Torah proves that it has no bearing upon us whatsoever."

In deciding the validity of a proposal, to see whether it accords with Torah, it is essential to keep in mind the following: when possessed of a sense of self-esteem or arrogance one cannot determine whether he rejects another's proposal or decision because it is counter to Torah or counter to his own pride.

Avodah, therefore, must be based on *ahavah* (love of G-d) and *yirah* (fear, reverence of G-d). These themselves must be in the order of first *yirah* and then *ahavah*, just as in the order of the reading of these two terms when they are combined as stated above. Thus it is said in *Tanya*, that *yirah* is "the very beginning of *avodah*, its core and root."[30]

In *Chinuch Katan* of *Tanya*[31] it is said that *ahavah* is the

---

29. Genesis 31:43
30. *Tanya*, ch. 41.
31. [*Tanya*, Introduction to *Sha'ar Hayichud Veha'emunah*.]

root for all positive precepts, and *yirah* is the root for all negative precepts.[32] Moreover, these are subject to *chinuch*, to being taught and instilled. This means that even one who is not yet rational and understanding (and everyone knows his own status) is subject to having *ahavah* and *yirah* taught and instilled.

An approach based on the consciousness of *ahavah* and *yirah* precludes any affectation by Amalek—notwithstanding the fact that Amalek is descended of Abraham and Isaac, and by Bil'am—notwithstanding the fact that "'[No other prophet like Moses] has arisen in Israel;'[33] in Israel there did not rise, but well among the nations, namely Bil'am."[34] [To be sure, *Sifre* compares Bil'am to the King's cook;[35] nonetheless, there does remain an analogy.]

This applies even to the most simple among Jews: when following the order of first *yirah* and then *ahavah*, Bil'am and Amalek cannot affect him.

C

IV. In Bil'am's prophecy it is said: "I see [this people] from the top of rocks, I view it from hills."[36] The term "rocks" refers to the patriarchs, and "hills" refers to the matriarchs.[37] This is analogous to the verse, "The voice of

---

32. [See Rambam's Mishnah-commentary on *Avot* 1:3; Ramban on Exodus 20:8; *Tanya*, ch. 4.]

33. [Deuteronomy 31:10]

34. *Sifre*, Berachah, end of par. 357; *Bamidbar Rabba* 14:20; *Zohar* II:21b; and various other sources.

35. [Bil'am is compared to a king's cook who is familiar with the private expenses of the king's kitchen. Moses is like a prominent minister of the king who is not familiar with those details. Cf. *Lekach Tov* on this verse.]

36. [Numbers 23:9]

37. *Bamidbar Rabba* 20:19

my Beloved .. leaping over mountains, skipping over hills."[38]

Bil'am descended from Laban.[39] [The Torah refers to him as "Bil'am the son of Beor."[40] Beor is identified with Laban,[41] thus Bil'am was Laban's son; or Beor is Laban's son,[42] thus Bil'am was Laban's grandson.] Laban had said: "The daughters are my daughters, and the sons are my sons.. !"[43] Thus it was necessary to nullify this claim by having one of Laban's descendants admit, "I see it from the top of rocks, I view it from hills"—"'Rocks' refers to the patriarchs, and 'Hills' refers to the matriarchs."

It follows, then, that Laban's claim, "The daughters are my daughters, and the sons are my sons," has some validity. If it had been altogether baseless, it would not have been mentioned in the Torah, nor would it have been necessary that Bil'am, a descendant of Laban, should nullify that claim.

V.   What is the significance of Laban's claim that "The daughters are my daughters, and the sons are my sons?"

A *neshamah* descends into a body and becomes involved with material things. To be sure, it does so in order to refine and sublimate matter. Nonetheless, "he who wrestles with a filthy person is bound to become soiled himself."[44] Indeed, the struggle is but for a very short time—"For a brief moment I forsook you"[45]—and then one is released from it. Even so, for the duration,

---

38. Song 2:8. [See *Rosh Hashanah* 11a.]
39. *Sanhedrin* 105a
40. [Numbers 22:5]
41. *Sanhedrin* 105a
42. [*Zohar* I:166b; *Tanchuma*, Balak:12.]
43. [Genesis 31:43]
44. *Tanya*, ch. 28. See there also ch. 8.
45. Isaiah 54:7

albeit a short while or moment, one is involved with physical and material things, thus separated from G-dliness.

[Any separation from G-dliness, Heaven forbid, however brief, is caused by a "spirit of folly."[46] Without that
"spirit of folly" there cannot be a separation from G-dliness, however brief, because of the intellect bound up
with holiness, or, for that matter, because of man's common sense, i.e., sound reasoning. For even a momentary
lapse is an irretrievable loss, especially, as explained in
Tanya[47] in detail, because that moment has an aspect
which transcends time.]

Moreover, the present separation will affect him later
on as well. For, as stated there in *Tanya*, to allow a separation now on the assumption of being restored later on, is
tantamount to the case of "If one says, 'I will sin and
repent afterwards,' he is not given an opportunity to
repent."[48] Eventual restoration, therefore, will necessitate
extraordinary effort.[49]

Laban thus argues, "The daughters are my daughters,
and the sons are my sons": "As you are in need of physical substance you will have to become involved with
physical reality. Thus you will be separated from G-dliness in any case, at the very least during that momentary
involvement; and even that short moment will have a last-
ing effect (as stated above)." This is Laban's argument.

In truth, however, this argument is incorrect. The ultimate intent is for G-d to have an abode in this lowly
world.[50] Man's temporary involvement with matter and

---

46. ["No person commits a sin unless a spirit of folly has entered
into him;" *Sotah* 3a. See *Tanya*, ch. 19 and 24.]
47. *Tanya*, ch. 25.
48. *Yoma* 85b
49. [*Tanya*, ch. 25]
50. *Tanchuma*, Nasso:16. [See above, Shlach, note 36.]

lowly things for the purpose of realizing this Divine intent, therefore, is not a decline but an ascent. It is an advancement to the point that even Bil'am (a descendant of Laban), "the man with an open eye,"[51] perceived that "I see [this nation] from the tops of rocks, I view it from the hills."

VI.   All this is relevant to our service of G-d.

It may be argued that one must be involved with physical matters, even according to the Torah, in view of the fact that the *neshamah* descended into a body. To provide for the needs of the members of one's household is no less than a *mitzvah* and a duty.[52] Thus it follows that everyone should prepare himself for an occupation and take all appropriate measures to that end.

Moreover, Chassidism itself explains that "G-d, your G-d, will bless you in all *you do*,"[53] that is, in and through the physical means of human initiative. The 'garments' (channels) of the supernal constellations are not enough; there must be 'garments' (channels) of this physical world.

Any involvement, therefore, is for the sake of serving G-d: his mundane preoccupations allow for an increase in Torah-study and the observance of *mitzvot*. Nonetheless, at least for the duration one is involved with mundane matters the same as, Heaven forbid, a non-Jew.

One must realize that this kind of approach is in essence Laban's argument of "The daughters are my daughters, and the sons are my sons," the argument that the material substance of a Jew belongs to Laban.

---

51. [Numbers 24:3; see Rashi there.]
52. See *Ketuvot* 49bf. [*Shulchan Aruch*, Even Ha'ezer 69-73.]
53. Deuteronomy 15:18. [Note *Sifre*, Re'ey, par. 123, and *Lekach Tov* on this verse: "I might think that the blessing will come even when man is idle, Scripture thus says, 'with all you *do!*'"] See *Kuntres Uma'ayan*, ch. 19ff. [*Cf. L.S.-Shemot*, Vayakhel, sect. III.]

In truth, however, "I see [this nation] from the top of rocks, I view it from hills." The *sichah* of 12-13 Tamuz[54] elaborated on the point that when stepping out from the domain of Torah and prayer into a new situation, to deal with mundane matters, one must set up a guard-rail. With this guard-rail for the "new house,"[55] one will sense the Divine intent underlying mundane matters even when preoccupied with them. Thus "I see it from the top of the rocks, I view it from hills": for the patriarchs and the matriarchs were like a 'chariot' in all their involvements.[56] It is likewise with anyone fulfilling a *mitzvah*, and also (as explained there) when doing anything else with the consciousness of "Acknowledge Him in all your ways."[57]

The same principle applies to Torah as it is studied with the faculty of human reason: it, too, needs a guard-rail. (As discussed at length in the aforementioned *sichah*,) there is a need for the "Fiftieth Gate,"[58] joining the "dot with the palace"[59]: the 'dot', the core-point of Jewishness,

---

54. [Published in *L.S.-Devarim*, Ki Tetze-B.]

55. ["When you build a house, you are to make a fence (guard-rail) for your roof.." (Deuteronomy 22:8)—the proof-text for that *sichah*.]

56. [See *Bereishit Rabba* 47:6. This expression signifies total submission to the Divine Will, with all their limbs detached from mundane matters, "serving as a vehicle solely for the Divine Will alone;" *Tanya*, ch. 23, and *ibid.*, beg. of ch. 34. See above, Shlach, sect. XV, and notes 93-95 there.]

57. Proverbs 3:6 [referring to all of man's involvements, including all mundane preoccupations such as eating, sleeping, conducting business, and so forth; see Rambam, *Hilchot De'ot* 3:2-3].

58. ["Fifty gates of *binah* (understanding) were created in the world"—*Rosh Hashanah* 21b. The fiftieth gate is the most sublime, the ultimate essence of *binah*.]

59. [A Zoharic expression (*Zohar* I:6a and 15aff.; etc.) referring to the relationship between *chochmah* (wisdom; the 'dot' that signifies the very source and core of wisdom) and *binah* (understanding; the

must be sensed when involved with the apprehensions and understanding of human reasoning.

Generally speaking, this means that the Divine intent must be sensed in anything we do, whether it be mundane involvements in the literal sense or Torah-study with our human mind. This will preclude any decline, even at the time of actual involvement. In fact, there will be an advancement, an ascent, because the Divine intent is realized in and through that act itself.

D*

VII. "Behold, the people shall rise like a *lavi* (fierce lion), and lift itself like an *ari* (lion)."[60] This verse refers to the time of the redemption to come.

Prior to this verse it is said, "At that time Jacob and Israel shall be told what G-d has done."[61] This means that prior to the future redemption there will a restoration of prophecy in Israel.[62]

Yerushalmi[63] comments that Bil'am said this prophecy at the midpoint of the world's age.

Rambam writes in *Igeret Teyman* (Epistle to Yemen)[64] that Bil'am said this in the year 2488, and the word *ka'et* ('at that time;' or '*like* that time') implies that when the same amount of years will have passed—thus in the year 4976—prophecy shall be restored to Israel.[65]

'palace,' i.e., the wide expanse of *chochmah* fully developed and explicated). See *Mystical Concepts in Chassidism*, ch. III, sect. 4.]

60. [Numbers 23:24]
61. [Numbers 23:23]
62. Rambam, *Igeret Teyman*, end of ch. 3.
63. *Yerushalmi, Shabbat*, end of 6:9.
64. [See note 62.]
65. This is the calculation in *Shalshelet Hakabalah* and *Igeret Teyman*. The author of *Seder Hadorot* emends this date to 4972 [see *Seder*

At and around that time—i.e., the year 4976—lived R. Shmuel Hanavi,[66] the father of R. Yehudah Hachassid; R. Eleazar, author of *Roke'ach*;[67] R. Mosheh ben Nachman (Ramban), who authored several Kabbalistic texts and of whom it is said in the writings of R. Isaac Luria that he is one of the few reliable Kabbalists;[68] R. Abraham ibn Daud (Rabad), whose academy was illumined by the Holy Spirit;[69] R. Ezra Hanavi;[70] and R. Yehudah Hachassid, of

---

Hadorot, p. 162b, section beginning 4962], and this date appears also in R. Judah of Barcelona's commentary on *Sefer Yetzirah*, and in *Korban Ha'eidah* on the *Yerushalmi* cited. Some claim that a manuscript of *Igeret Teyman* has the date of 4970. The suggested emendation, and all those who question the proper version of Rambam, are rather strange in view of the fact that it follows from Scripture itself that Bil'am's prophecy occurred in the 40th (and not the 38th) year after the exodus, thus in the year 2488. The interpretation of *ka'et*, therefore, renders the year 4976. Clearly, then, any variant version must be attributed to a scribal error.

66. [Usually referred to as R. Shmuel Hachassid (the Pious); see, e.g., *Tossafot* on *Yevamot* 61b and *Sotah* 12a. R. Eleazar, author of *Roke'ach* (and disciple of R. Yehudah Hachassid), refers to him as *navi*, a prophet (see his *Darkei Teshuvah*, appended to Responsa of R. Meir of Rothenburg (the relevant passage is cited by Chida, *Shem Hagedolim*, s.v. R. Eleazar), and so does R. Shelomoh Luria (Maharshal) in his responsa, no. 29.]

67. "It is known of [the author of] *Roke'ach* and of R. Yehudah Hachassid and their associates that they had great miraculous powers;" R. Menachem Mendel of Lubavitch, *Sefer Hachakirah*, p. 65a. [Note also R. Ya'akov Yehoshu'a Falk's comment on R. Eleazar, in *Pnei Yehoshu'a* on *Megilah* 16a.]

68. [R. Chaim Vital, Introduction to *Eitz Chayim*.]

69. [See Rabad's gloss on Rambam, *Hilchot Lulav* 8:5. See also his glosses on *Hilchot Bet Habechirah* 6:14, and *Hilchot Mishkav Umoshav* 7:7; and his *Tamim De'im*, no. 50. Note R. Menachem Rekanati's commentary on Numbers 6:22ff., cited in R. Chaim Vital's introduction to *Eitz Chayim*.]

70. [R. Ezra of Montcontour, teacher of Ramban. He is referred to as a *navi* in various texts, including *Tossafot* on *Gitin* 88a and *Shevu'ot* 25a.]

whom it is said[71] that if he had lived in the period of the *amoraim* he would have been an *amora*, if in the period of the *tannaim* he would have been a *tanna*, and if in the period of the prophets he would have been a prophet.

About that time, then, there was a restoration of prophecy in Israel. Thus there was also the potential for the sequel of "At that time..," i.e., "Behold, the people shall rise like a *lavi*, and lift itself like an *ari*"—which refers to the future redemption. As "that generation was not fit," however, we are still in distress.

VIII.   Many generations later, bringing us still closer to the coming of Mashiach, there was another case of prophecy restored to Israel. This was with the revelation of our master the *Baal Shem Tov* and his disciples up to the time of the *Alter Rebbe*[72]—of whom was said the same as of R. Yehudah Hachassid, and with greater emphasis yet.[73]

This continued through the generations of the *Rebbes* who succeeded him, up to our own generation and our

---

71. [R. Shneor of Speyer, a contemporary of R. Yehudah Hachassid, quoted in *Sefer Ma'asiyot* (cited in the biographical sketch prefacing R. Margolius' edition of *Sefer Chassidim*, p. 2).]

72. "The Baal Shem Tov—there has not been one like him since the days of the *rishonim*. Through him came about wondrous wonders and miracles beyond nature. Thus I heard from my master and grandfather [the *Alter Rebbe*] that [the Baal Shem Tov] and his disciple, the Maggid, could literally see with their eye from one end of the world to the other, and would relate what they saw, as was clearly evident to their disciples. They were able to do so because to them was manifest the light created on the first day [of creation] which G-d hid in the Torah [see *Chagigah* 12a and *Zohar* I:264a. See *Keter Shem Tov*, sect. 84, 355, and 360; and note *Degel Machaneh Ephrayim*, Bereishit, on Genesis 1:4.] All these true wonders reveal the manifestation of the unrestricted *En Sof*, blessed be He. From my grandfather, too, we heard completely accurate predictions of the future." *Sefer Hachakirah*, p. 65a.

73. [See *Likkutei Sichot*, vol. IV, p. 1120, note 36.]

own *nassi*, the *Rebbe*, my father-in-law. The *Zohar* notes[74] that the phrase "When the morning was light"[75] refers to the "dawn of Joseph."[76] The *Zohar* relates this "morning— the dawn of Joseph" to the verse, "At dawn I will prepare myself for you,"[77] and concludes: "What is the meaning of 'I will prepare myself for you'?.. as it is said,[78] 'I prepare a lamp for *Meshichi* (My anointed),'"[79] which refers to the complete redemption that will occur speedily, in our very own days, through our righteous Mashiach.

---

74. *Zohar* III:204a; and see the commentary in *Bi'urei Hazohar*, ed. R. Dov Ber of Lubavitch, p. 109a (which also reconciles this passage with that in *Zohar* I:203b).

75. [Genesis 44:3]

76. [In context of the preceding, it is suggested that this may also be read as an allusion to the Rebbe's father-in-law: he was not only the *nassi* of his generation (thus, in effect, succeeding Joseph), but also had the same name, which originated with the Biblical Joseph and thus also reflects his very nature. See above, Shlach, note 17, on the significance of names.]

77. [Psalms 5:4]

78. [Psalms 132:17]

79. [*Zohar* III:204b]

YUD-BET YUD-GIMEL TAMUZ

י"ב-י"ג
תמוז

A*

I. A *nassi*, generally speaking, has a *neshamah kelalit*,

---

* [Yud-Bet Yud-Gimel Tamuz (the 12th and 13th of Tamuz) marks the liberation of the sixth Lubavitcher *Rebbe*, R. Yosef Yitzchak (12 Tamuz 5640 (1880)—10 Shvat 5710 (1950)). After becoming head of the Chabad-Chassidic movement (1920), the *Rebbe* was the leading force in the battle against the Soviet communist attempts to strangle Judaism and Jewish observance in Soviet Russia. In spite of vicious threats and persecutions by the secret police (Tcheka) and the Yev-Sektzia (Jewish Section of the Communist Party, notorious for its anti-religious oppression), the *Rebbe* organized his followers to establish Torah-schools, *mikva'ot*, and other religious institutions, throughout the country; founded committees to help Jewish artisans and workers observe the Shabbat; and sent out teachers, preachers and other representatives even to the most remote Jewish communities to encourage and strengthen their religious life. The *Rebbe's* relentless struggle came to a head when he was arrested on the 15th of Sivan 5687 (1927) and placed in solitary confinement in the infamous Spalerno Prison in Leningrad, where he was subjected to psychological and physical torture. The authorities issued a death-sentence against him, but this was miraculously commuted to banishment into exile for 10 years. This sentence was again commuted to 3 years of exile in Kostrama, in the Urals. After barely a week in Kostroma, the *Rebbe* was informed on his 47th birthday (12th of Tamuz 5687) that he is free altogether; but as that day was a local holiday (with all government agencies closed) he was not given his release-papers until the next day, the 13th of Tamuz. These two days of Yud-Bet (12) and Yud-Gimel (13) Tamuz have thus become days of celebrating the *Rebbe's* liberation and as a festival for the triumph of efforts on behalf of Torah over those that would oppose it.]

a comprehensive soul.[1] Most of his aspects, therefore, relate not only to himself but also to all those bound up with him.

The *Rebbe*, my father-in-law, is the *ba'al simchah* (celebrant of this joyous occasion). When he commissioned the writing of a Torah-scroll with which to welcome Mashiach,[2] the *Rebbe* said that he himself could very well provide all the expenses for the parchment, ink and writing, but he wished for all Jews to have an opportunity to participate.[3]

This means that he did not want to take that *zechut* (merit) all for himself. He also did not want to take it upon himself on behalf of everybody else, by virtue of a *neshamah kelalit* and a *nassi* being able to act on behalf of everybody else.

[It is said[4] that every Jew must fulfill all 613 *mitzvot* of the Torah. When failing in this goal, the soul must return to this world by way of reincarnation until it will complete the fulfillment of all 613 precepts. The precepts incumbent upon a king, however, are excluded from this obligation, because the king observes these on behalf of all Jews.[5] From this we learn two things: a) The precepts incumbent upon a king relate to all Jews, i.e., *all* are obligated by them. This is reflected in the following statement of the *Gemara*: "[A Torah-scholar takes precedence over a king of Israel, for] when a scholar dies there is none to replace

---

1. [*Tanchuma*, Chukat:23; *Bamidbar Rabba* 19:28; *Zohar* II:47a and 198a. See *Chassidic Dimensions*, p. 101f.]

2. [In 5702 (1942). For details see *Sefer Hasichot 5702*, pp. 14 and 118; and *Sefer Hama'amarim-Melukat*, vol. I, p. 98-100.]

3. [*Sefer Hama'amarim-Melukat*, vol. I, p. 98.]

4. [R. Chaim Vital, *Sefer Hagilgulim*, ch. 4; *idem, Sha'ar Hagilgulim*, ch. 11, and *Sha'ar Hamitzvot*, Introduction. *Tanya*, Igeret Hakodesh, sect. VII, XIX, and XXIX.]

5. *Tanya*, Igeret Hakodesh, sect. XXIX.

him; but when a king dies, all Israel is eligible for kingship."[6] b) All Jews fulfill the precepts incumbent upon a king through the king himself: when the king fulfills these *mitzvot*, he discharges all Jews from their obligation. It follows, then, that there are things which are done by a *neshamah kelalit* on behalf of all others as well.]

The *Rebbe* insisted that all others participate through their own effort.[7] There are things of which it is said that "it is more meritorious when done personally than through an agent."[8] An act can be fulfilled through an agent as well, but it would be lacking *hidur*[9] and special merit. The *Rebbe* thus wanted that every Jew have the *hidur* as well, to "Choose life"[10] by participating and having a letter in the Torah-scroll with which to welcome Mashiach.

II.   The *Rebbe* also showed generosity with the redemption of *Yud-Bet Yud-Gimel Tamuz*, which followed after his arrest. Obviously, there cannot be a redemption and liberation unless there had been an imprisonment.

The *Rebbe's* imprisonment was not for something private or personal. It was for disseminating Torah and strengthening *mitzvot*, something incumbent upon all Jews that lived in those days and in that place. The *Rebbe* was the leader who directed these activities. If, therefore, the Yev-Sektzia (Jewish section of the communist party in Russia) deemed such activities to warrant imprisonment, they should have arrested all those who were obligated to

---

6. *Horiyot* 13a; *Yerushalmi, Horiyot* 3:5 (8).

7. [See *Likkutei Sichot*, vol. II, p. 501, sect. XIII (cited in *Chassidic Dimensions*, p. 212*f.*)]

8. *Kidushin* 41a. *Shulchan Aruch*, Orach Chayim 250:1 [see there *Ba'er Heitev*, note 2].

9. [See above, Shlach, note 7.]

10. [Deuteronomy 30:19; and see Rashi there.]

engage in them, and especially all those actually involved under the guidance and direction of the *Rebbe*. The *Rebbe*, however, took the imprisonment completely upon himself on behalf of everybody else. Thus he discharged all others from being arrested and from all the sufferings that preceded and followed the imprisonment,[11] except for a select few individuals who also merited to be subjected to these.

It was different, though, with regards to the redemption and the ensuing festival. When Jews establish and fix a festival below, the Celestial Court confirms that which is undertaken on earth.[12] Thus it was decreed Above that this day (of the redemption) be a *yom tov* (festival), an auspicious day for drawing forth all and any illuminations and emanations that are bound up with Torah and *mitzvot*.[13]

This festival, then, the *Rebbe* did not take just for himself, to be celebrated by him as a representative for all others. He did it in such a way that every Jew share and partake in it; that everyone inspire his household and environment with the significance of this festival by explaining the events of the fasts and the outcry of prayers that occurred and the redemption that followed; that everyone be able to participate in the celebration, with his possessions, body and soul.

III.   There is a principle that "He who gives a gift does so in a liberal spirit," generously offering the gift along with all its appurtenances.[14] In a legal context there are some qualifications to this principle; a sincere donor, however, gives generously, throwing in "the cistern and

---

11. [See the *Rebbe's* memoirs of his imprisonment in *Likkutei Diburim*, vol. IV, p. 1219*ff*.]

12. [*Cf. Megilah* 7a; *Yerushalmi, Berachot* 9:5.]

13. [See below, beginning of sect. VI, and notes 24-26.]

14. *Baba Batra* 53a, and parallel passages cited there.

the upper story, the things below along with the things above."[15] The recipient, too, should show a spirit no less liberal than that of the donor, and properly utilize all that is given to him.

The *Rebbe* notes in his letter [for the first anniversary of the 12th of Tamuz][16] that this festival is to be utilized by organizing a *farbrengen*. He elaborates in that letter that one should not confine oneself to his own domain for private meditation on all that occurred in those days, but to organize a *farbrengen* and to inspire oneself along with the whole environment.

This day is an auspicious occasion for extraordinary success in the realization of all resolutions undertaken for the strengthening of Torah and *mitzvot*. The effects will extend throughout the whole year, in deed, speech, and even in thought.

B*

IV.   "And it came to pass in the thirtieth year.."[17]

Every month has its unique aspects. Some of these are central to the whole month, and in some months these aspects are central to the whole year.

A month is a concept of time, and every aspect in a month has its own time when it becomes manifest.

As regards the month of Tamuz, up to thirty years ago there were only the manifestations of negative things that happened in this month.[17*] Thirty years ago (in 5687), however, there was a manifestation of this month's posi-

---

15. [*Baba Batra* 71a. *Shulchan Aruch*, Choshen Mishpat 215:6.]

16. Published in *Sefer Hama'amarim 5688*, p. 146*ff.* [and see there also p. 209*f.*], and in *Sefer Hama'amarim 5708*, p. 263*ff.*

17. Ezekiel 1:1

17*. [See *Ta'anit* 4:6. Cf. *Zohar* II:78b; *ibid.* 12a; and *Zohar Chadash*, Eichah: 92d.]

tive content: the days of redemption of 12-13 Tamuz, with the strengthening of Torah and *mitzvot* associated with these.

The redemption of 12-13 Tamuz is no doubt a central aspect. As noted by the *Rebbe* (in his letter for the celebration of the first anniversary[18]), it was not a liberation for an individual person but for all those who care about our holy Torah, who observe *mitzvot*, and even for anyone who simply "assumes the name of Israel."[19]

Torah and *mitzvot* represent the very purpose of the whole creation.[20] The redemption of 12-13 Tamuz, therefore, signifies a redemption for all aspects in the creative process, including the most sublime manifestations up to the ultimate Essence. As Torah and *mitzvot* are the purpose of everything, it follows that the days of 12-13 Tamuz brought about a redemption for all these aspects, up to the ultimate Essence.

V.   All aspects of a month begin to come about on the *Shabbat mevarchim*, the preceding Shabbat when that month is blessed. Moreover, our sages said[21] that "All the days are blessed by the [preceding] Shabbat."[22] That

---

18. [See above, note 16.]

19. See *Sefer Hama'amarim 5711*, p. 287, that this compounds all groups and types of Jewish men and women; see there at length. [The phrase "assume the name of Israel" is from Isaiah 44:5.]

20. [See *Bereishit Rabba* 1:4; *Oti'ot deR. Akiva, s.v.* bet; cited by Rashi on Genesis 1:1.]

21. See *Zohar* II:63b and 88a.

22. This includes also various aspects of the following Shabbat, especially those which need to be prepared on the preceding Friday (as follows also from the example cited in the *Zohar*, i.e., the manna). In Kabbalistic terminology: From the Shabbat (corresponding to [the *Sefirah* of] *binah*) are blessed all the days—i.e., the six *midot* [the six *Sefirot* of *chessed* to *yessod*, which are rooted in *binah*], and the sixth day is pre-eminent in it for its own part and the part of the Shabbat (following [in this context corresponding to the *Sefirah* of] *malchut*).

includes also the day of *rosh chodesh*, the beginning of the month, which compounds all the days of that month. This Shabbat, *Shabbat mevarchim* [of Tamuz], therefore, marks the beginning of the redemption of 12-13 Tamuz.

In fact, the actual beginning is still earlier, albeit potentially: our sages state the principle that the Holy One, blessed be He, prepares the cure before the affliction.[23] As the imprisonment happened in the middle of Sivan, the redemption, therefore, must have been prepared before then.

VI.   All that has been stated applies each and every year. Every year things are renewed. Thus it is said in the writings of R. Isaac Luria,[24] in comment on the verse "These days are remembered and enacted":[25] with the "remembered," i.e., as these days are recalled properly, there is also the "enacted," that all the [original] effects and emanations of these days recur and are re-enacted [on their anniversary].[26]

Even so, this is merely like the renewal of something of old. It is not an original, new event, as it was the very first time.

To be sure, it is said in *Igeret Hakodesh*[27] that every year there is the emergence of an altogether new illumination which had never been before. Every year, therefore,

---

23. See *Megilah* 13b.

24. R. Mosheh Zaccuto, *Sefer Tikun Shovevim*; cited in Chida's *Lev David*, ch. 29. [See also R. Joseph Ergas, *Shomer Emunim*, Responsa, no. 5; *Likkutim Yekarim*, Yosher Divrei Emet, ch. 48 and 53 (partly cited in *Keter Shem Tov*, sect. 401). See also *Tossafot, Sotah* 14b, s.v. mipnei (though there this principle is stated in a negative context).]

25. [Esther 9:28]

26. This applies not only to spiritual aspects but is reflected on the natural and physical level as well, as evident from the Mishnah, *Gitin* 3:8. [See *Sefer Hama'amarim 5704*, p. 13.]

27. *Tanya*, Igeret Hakodesh, sect. XIV.

there are novel aspects. Nonetheless, this is relative to the earlier ones: the earlier aspects are infused with a new illumination, which means, in effect, that there is no more than a renewal of the old.

VII.   A "renewal of the old" is itself subject to a number of variations. The passing of specific periods of time from the event, such as one or more decades etc., marks a greater emanation and change, which differs altogether from the annual effect and renewal.

This concept is analogous to the distinctions found in the *Mishnah*[28] of "at twenty years .. at thirty years .. at forty years ..": every decade there is something novel.[29] This may be explained in context of the principle stated in *Pardes Rimonim*[30] that everything is arranged in an order of ten, corresponding to the ten *Sefirot*. The same applies to the present [30th anniversary of the redemption of 12-13 Tamuz].

In the scale of tens itself, special significance is attached to the number thirty. The *Tzemach Tzedek* interprets[31] the verse "And it came to pass in the thirtieth year" to correspond to the compound of the ten *kelim*, ten *orot pnimiyim* and ten *orot makifim*, which compound everything.[32]

---

28. [*Avot* 5:22]

29. [The *Rebbe* adds here the following comment:] Thus I heard once from my father-in-law, the *Rebbe*, in explanation of the stipulation of waiting ten years for the birth of children (*Yevamot* 64a): one can say that this is analogous to the division of eras in the Mishnah of *Avot* in terms of decades.

30. *Pardes Rimonim*, Sha'ar II.

31. See *Kitzurim Vehe'arot leTanya*, p. 76. *Cf. Zohar* III:246b; and R. Meir ibn Gabbai, *Avodat Hakodesh* IV:ch. 19.

32. [There are ten *Sefirot*, each of which divides into the aspects of *orot* ('lights'; Divine emanations) and *kelim* ('vessels' containing the *orot*). The Divine emanations themselves divide into *orot pnimiyim*

It follows, then, that the completion of thirty years since the redemption marks a new aspect in that redemption, more sublime and more comprehensive than before.

VIII.   Many things have been achieved until now in matters of Torah and *mitzvot* by virtue of that redemption. As of now and further, however, this is no longer enough. New and greater aspects of the redemption have now become manifest, and this implies that there must also be ever greater achievements and manifestations in matters of Torah and *mitzvot*.

Torah and *mitzvot* express themselves in the three modes of "Torah, *avodah* (service of G-d) and *gemilut chassadim* (performance of kindness)."[33] This means, therefore, that there must be increases in the aspect of Torah, the aspect of *avodah*, and the aspect of *gemilut chassadim*.

Ability and energy to do so is given from *Shabbat mevarchim* onwards. For on *Shabbat mevarchim* all the days of the coming month are blessed to be "for life and for peace..," i.e., all the expressions and facets enumerated in the prayer for the blessing of the month. This includes also the blessing and infusion of ability to enhance Torah and *mitzvot*.

Avodah with Torah and *mitzvot* will bring about, very speedily indeed, the revelation of the ultimate redemption through our righteous Mashiach.

C*

IX.*   We are now in the days of *Yud-Bet Yud-Gimel*

(immanent *orot*, 'within' the *kelim*) and *orot makifim* (transcendent *orot*, the source-lights emanating from 'without' and transcending the lower ones). For a detailed explanation see *Mystical Concepts in Chassidism*, ch. V, section 2.)]

33. [See *Avot* 1:2]

* [This *sichah* was delivered to the children of Camp "Gan Yisrael," at the dedication of the camp.]

Tamuz.[34] These are the days of the *Rebbe's* liberation from prison after his arrest for disseminating Torah and *mitzvot.*

The *Rebbe* disregarded all difficulties and obstacles and carried on his work. In the end he triumphed and was freed. This offers every one of us the lesson to remain strong in the study of Torah and the observance of *mitzvot.* We must not desist therefrom even when confronted by all kinds of obstacles, and in the end we shall triumph.

X.   Among the themes the *Rebbe* discussed at various occasions there are a good many related to children, and I shall recall a few of these now.

This camp bears the name *Gan Yisrael* (Garden of Israel). *Yisrael* is the name of all Jews. All Jews are referred to by the name *Yisrael.*[35] This was also the personal name of the first one to reveal Chassidut in the world. He was called *Yisrael,* and later on became known by the title *Baal Shem Tov.*

The *Rebbe* related[36] the following. When the Baal Shem Tov was a child of five years, his father told him: "My dear child, do not be afraid of anyone but G-d. Love every single Jew with the full ardor of your soul, regardless of who he is or whatever he may be."

The Baal Shem Tov then pursued his holy work throughout his lifetime with these two principles of *yirat Hashem* (fear of G-d) and *ahavat Yisrael* (love of Israel).

---

34. [Though the *sichah* was delivered on the 15th of Tamuz, this day is within three days of the festival of redemption and thus related to it: Jewish law stipulates that the three days prior to, and the three days following, a distinct date, are related to it. See *Pesachim* 106a.] See *Shulchan Aruch,* Orach Chayim 299:6. See also *Avodah Zara* 2a; and other sources. [See at length *L.S.-Vayikra,* Bechukotay, sect. IX, and the notes there.]

35. [*Sanhedrin* 44a. See *L.S.-Vayikra,* Pesach, sect. X-XII, and especially note 59. See also *Sefer Hama'amarim 5711,* p. 287, note 4.]

36. *Likkutei Diburim,* vol. III, p. 770. [*Sefer Hasichot 5701,* p. 153*f.*]

As the *Rebbe* told us of this incident, it follows that it provides a lesson for all of us, and obviously also for children: the two principles mentioned must be the light to guide us throughout our life.

XI. Some, including children, ask: how is it possible for so young a child not to be afraid of anything but G-d? One answer can be found in a teaching of the Baal Shem Tov's disciple, the Maggid of Mezhirech:[37]

A father is much more educated and wiser than his child. Nonetheless, he will express the love for his child by restraining his superior level and bringing himself down to little things of the child, so that even the child on its inferior level can understand the father's love.

It is the same with the Jewish people, G-d's children:[38] the Almighty "lowers Himself" to them and provides them with all they need, including material and 'little things,' and He protects them against everything. Thus there is no reason whatsoever to be afraid of anything in the world.

XII. On the other hand, the fact that the Jewish people are G-d's children may possibly lead to arrogance. One might argue: "As I am the child of this great G-d, I can do anything I want to do, and surely the Almighty will forgive me!"

In this context the *Rebbe* related[39] an incident with the *Alter Rebbe*, the first to reveal *Chabad*-Chassidut to the world at large:

When a child starts learning *Chumash*, the custom is to start with *parshat Vayikra*.[40] Thus when one of the *Alter*

---

37. See his *Or Torah*, Bereishit, sect. 1.

38. [Deuteronomy 14:1. See *Kidushin* 36a, and Responsa of Rashba, I:nos. 194 and 242.]

39. See *Sefer Hasichot 5700*, p. 68.

40. [*Tanchuma*, Tzav:14; *Vayikra Rabba* 7:3. See also *Midrash Sechel Tov*, ed. Buber, p. 342.]

Rebbe's grandchildren turned three[41] and learned *parshat Vayikra*, he asked his grandfather: "Why is the word *Vayikra* written with a small *aleph*?"[42]

The *Alter Rebbe* answered that every Jew is born with unique talents, and for sure also *Mosheh Rabeinu*, our master Moses. Nonetheless, Moses was very humble[43] and regarded himself as 'small' and insignificant — a 'small *aleph*'[44] (unlike the big *aleph* that is written with Adam[45]). For that very reason Moses merited the highest levels of achievement: he received the Torah; he freed the Jewish people from Egypt; and he will also free them from the last *galut*, the present one,[46] with the true and final redemption.

This, too, is a lesson for all Jews: one must be humble and do all that G-d commands, regardless of whether one enjoys doing so or not. The very fact that it is a command from the Almighty proves that it must be good.

XIII.   Even so, there is a *yetzer hara*, an evil inclination which disturbs man. In this context the *Rebbe* related[47]

---

41. [The normative age that a child is to be taught to read; *Tanchuma*, Kedoshim:14; Rashi on *Avot* 5:21; *Shulchan Aruch*, Yoreh De'ah 245:8 (gloss of Rema).]

42. [Some letters in the Torah-scroll are to be written larger than the normative size, and others smaller. See *Midrash R. Akiva al Oti'ot Ketanot .. Oti'ot Gedolot*, in *Batei Midrashot*, ed. Wertheimer, vol. II, pp. 478-488. See also *Zohar* I:3b, and the parallel passages cited there in *Derech Emet*, note 1. The *aleph* in the first word of *Vayikra* is to be written smaller than the normative size.]

43. [Numbers 12:3]

44. [See commentaries of *Rosh*, *Tur*, and *Tzror Hamor*, on Leviticus 1:1.]

45. [I Chronicles 1:1. *Cf. Midrash R. Akiva al Oti'ot Gedolot*, *s.v.* aleph; and *Zohar* I:239a.]

46. [*Shemot Rabba* 2:4; *Devarim Rabba* 9:9; *Zohar* I:253a. See *L.S.-Shemot*, Introduction, note 54.]

47. See *Hayom Yom*, *s.v.*, Tevet 20.

the advice of the *Alter Rebbe's* son, the *Mitteler Rebbe*, how to make it easier to overcome the *yetzer hara*:

Discuss the problem of fighting the *yetzer hara* with a fellow-Jew—with a friend, a counselor, or your teacher of Torah. Thus there will be two *yetzer tovs*—two Divine souls—against one *yetzer hara* (one natural soul); and you know very well that in a fight of two against one, the two will prevail.

XIV.   (The *Rebbe shalita* asked the children to sing *Ani Ma'amin*, and then continued:)

In order to merit all that was mentioned above, we were given the *mitzvah* of *tefilah*, prayer.

In prayer we ask G-d to give us all our needs. Thus it is important to know the meanings of the words in prayer, or—in the case of very small children—to know at least what prayer is all about.

The *Rebbe* thus related[48] that his great-grandfather (the *Tzemach Tzedek*) instructed the teachers of his small grandchildren to teach them also the meanings of the words of prayer. Regardless of the *Tzemach Tzedek's* busy schedule, he would test his grandchildren once a month to see whether they know and understand what they say in their prayers.

XV.   In the *Shemoneh Esrei*, which is the major prayer, our first request[49] is, "Bestow upon us .. wisdom, understanding and knowledge." We ask the Almighty to give us intelligence. A wise person knows the most important thing, namely the purpose of life.

XVI.   The *Rebbe* thus related[50] how his grandfather (the *Rebbe Maharash*) explained to his children (when they

---

48. See *Hayom Yom*, s.v. Tevet 8.

49. [*Cf. Yerushalmi, Berachot* 4:4; *Shulchan Aruch*, Orach Chayim, sect. 115.]

50. See *Likkutei Diburim*, vol. III, p. 841*ff*. [*Sefer Hasichot 5703*, p. 72*f*.]

were still quite young) that every Jew must set for himself a goal in life, a goal that goes beyond eating, drinking, sleeping and playing games: a goal of conducting oneself according to the will of G-d.

XVII.   Related to all this is a rule which one must always keep in mind. This rule was expressed by the *Rebbe's* father (the *Rebbe Reshab*) when he said to the *Rebbe* (who at that time was a child of four years):[51] G-d gave man two eyes, so that he will look at his toys and candies with the *"left* eye," and at a fellow-Jew with the *"right* eye"—that is, to see his good qualities.

Acceptance of these principles confers an ability for good conduct, that you should forever improve, so that everybody will be happy with you, first and foremost your parents and teachers.

XVIII.   The Torah states that the human being is compared to a tree.[52]

With a tree we can see that any good change or adjustment in the seed, however small, will be reflected in the tree growing from it: the tree will grow much better to become a large, good tree producing many good fruits.

It is the same with a human being. Any improvement—however small—in a child will express itself as a much greater improvement when that child grows older. How much more so when there is a great improvement while one is still young.

May the Almighty grant you success to follow all that was mentioned. You should forever grow higher and better until we shall go with you towards Mashiach, very speedily, and say: "See these children that we have raised; they are worthy to be the soldiers of Mashiach!"

---

51. *Likkutei Diburim*, vol. IV, p. 1412.
52. Deuteronomy 20:19. [*Zohar* III:24a. See *Ta'anit* 7a, and *Likkutei Sichot*, vol. IV, p. 1114*ff.*]

Mashiach will come very speedily, in our days, and redeem us from the *galut* through the true redemption. Amen.

D*

XIX.   *Yud-Bet Tamuz*, the Chassidic festival of the present month of Tamuz, is the day of the *Rebbe*'s liberation from imprisonment for disseminating Judaism.

Bar-mitzvah is the time a Jew reaches maturity. When the *Rebbe* became *bar-mitzvah*, his father, who was also his mentor, told him to ask some question. (This was a custom with all the *Rebbes*, since the days of the *Alter Rebbe*.)[53]

The *Rebbe* then asked why it is said in the *Sidur* of the *Alter Rebbe* that before prayer one is to say, "I hereby take upon myself the positive precept of 'Love your fellow-being like yourself'":[54] what is the connection between this *mitzvah* and prayer? If it is to teach us that the first thing every day must be a bonding with fellow-Jews, then surely one should say it earlier, with the morning-blessings, and not wait until the beginning of the order of prayers!

His father explained that in prayer one asks for all needs. G-d is the Father in Heaven of all Jews, young or old, male or female.

When submitting a request to a father, one should first do something to please him. There is no greater pleasure for a father but to see his children relate one to another harmoniously, with brotherly love:[55] though there are many children, each of which differs from the other, every

---

53. *Sefer Hasichot 5700*, p. 156*f*.

54. [See above, Bamidbar, note 53.]

55. See the comment of the *Alter Rebbe* on this principle, cited in *Kovetz Michtavim-Tehilim* (appended to *Tehilim Ohel Yosef Yitzchak*), p. 199; and in *Likkutei Diburim*, vol. III, p. 1129.

one loves the other like himself—"love your fellow like yourself."

That is why one is to affirm this *mitzvah* right before the order of prayers.

This incident marked the very beginning of the *Rebbe's* life as a mature Jew, and it served as a preparation for his future leadership.

The fact that the *Rebbe* told us about this incident, no doubt shows that it provides a lesson for every one of us as well. Every one of us has some influence and authority over some circle, whether it be just his family or at the very least himself. Thus at the very beginning of every-one's working on himself, and as an introduction to his particular form of 'leadership', one must know that when asking for the Divine blessing of success in these, the initial step and preparation is a loving bond with every Jew.

This will be the preparation and instrument for the Almighty to fulfill one's requests. For peace is the instrument that contains both material and spiritual blessing.[56]

XX.   This principle relates in a special way to the present days.

We are now in the midst of the "Three Weeks" during which we are to remember the *churban* and the events that occurred *beyn hametzarim*.[57]

Our duty to remember these is obviously not for the mere sake of having a good memory, but in order to derive a moral for our present conduct and actions.

---

56. [See *Uktzin* 3:12.]

57. [On the 17th of Tamuz the walls of Jerusalem were breached, the city was invaded, and three weeks later, on the 9th of Av, the *Bet Hamikdash* was destroyed. This three-weeks period, therefore, is a time of mourning the *churban*. It is referred to as the period of *beyn hamet-zarim*, based on Lamentations 1:3 "all her pursuers overtook her *beyn hametzarim* (between the straits, or boundaries)": "within the days of distress from the 17th of Tamuz to the 9th of Av.." (*Eichah Rabba* 1:29).]

What are we to learn from remembering and mourning the *churban*?

First and foremost we must nullify the very cause of the *churban*.

Our sages tell us that the *churban* was caused by *sinat chinam*, gratuitous hatred.[58] Thus we must nullify that cause: *sinat chinam* (gratuitous hatred) is nullified by *ahavat chinam* (gratuitous love).[59]

There must be love for every Jew — *chinam*, unqualified. This applies even to one who has never done you any favor, and you will never need him for any favor. It applies even to a Jew one has never met or seen,[60] and even to one who is *chinam*,[61] for whom one cannot find any reason, any positive quality, that would warrant feelings of love; even a person like that must be loved.

This love, this peace and unity, is the instrument of blessing, including the greatest blessing of G-d speedily sending us our righteous Mashiach to redeem us with the complete and ultimate redemption.

XXI.   May the Almighty grant that each and every one of us make an effort in that direction. This will then bring "Pinchas who is Elijah,"[62] i.e., the prophet Elijah, the harbinger of the redemption.[63] For in the current *parshah* it

---

58. *Yoma* 9b. [See *Tossefta, Menachot* 13:22.]

59. [See *Tanya*, Igeret Hakodesh, sect. XXXI; "The Dynamics of Ahavat Yisrael," *Chassidic Dimensions*, p. 78f. Cf. *Tanchuma*, Nitzavim:1; *Bereishit Rabba* 98:2; *Agadat Bereishit*, ch. 82(83).]

60. [See *Keter Shem Tov*, Hossafot, par. 140. *L.S.-Shemot*, Pekudei, sect. X. Cf. *L.S.-Devarim*, Shemini Atzeret-Simchat Torah, sect. IV; and *Likkutei Sichot*, vol. XXI, p. 51.]

61. See *Sifre*, Beha'alotecha, sect. 87: "*Chinam* (for naught)—i.e., devoid of *mitzvot*."

62. *Targum Yehonathan* on Exodus 6:18; Ralbag on I Kings 17:1. [See below, Pinchas, sect. II, and note 12 there.]

63. [*Pesikta Rabaty* 36:4, in comment on Isaiah 52:7 (and *cf.*

is said of Pinchas, "Behold I give him My covenant of peace,"[64] which is also part of the principle that "Pinchas is Elijah":[65]

Pinchas signifies "My covenant of peace," i.e., peace and unity between one Jew and another, and is identified with Elijah;[66] that is, this peace will bring very speedily the prophet Elijah to announce that verily tomorrow[67] Mashiach will come to redeem us with the ultimate redemption.

E*

XXII.   "A star steps out of Jacob and a rod rises out of Israel."[68] The *Targum* and Midrashim[69] state that this refers to Mashiach. *Yerushalmi*,[70] however, interprets this verse to refer to every Jew. There is no contradiction here: *Me'or Einayim*[71] cites the Baal Shem Tov to the effect that every Jew contains within himself a part of the soul of Mashiach; thus both interpretations converge, for ultimately they state one and the same.

This does not mean that the spark of Mashiach in

Malachi 3:23). See also *Targum Yehonathan* on Exodus 6:18; and *Eruvin* 43b.]

64. [Numbers 25:12]

65. [See *Pirkei deR. Eliezer*, ch. 47, and *Bi'ur Haradal* there, note 40.]

66. [The prophet Elijah will come to establish peace in the world; Malachi 3:24; *Eduyot* 8:7.]

67. *Eruvin* 43b

68. [Numbers 24:17]

69. [*Tanchuma*, ed. Buber, Devarim, Hossafot:6. See also *Devarim Rabba* 1:20; and *Eichah Rabba* 2:4.]

70. *Ma'aser Sheni* 4:6

71. R. Nachum of Czernobyl, *Me'or Einayim*, end of Pinchas [on Numbers 25:12].

every Jew is only a latent aspect. As stated, the *Yerushalmi* reads this into the verse of "A star steps out of Jacob and a rod rises out of Israel." The words "steps out" and "rises out" imply that it comes out into the open. This means, therefore, that every Jew is able to bring out into the open the spark of Mashiach within himself.

To put this into simple terms: every Jew is able to speed up and bring about the actual manifestation of Mashiach. One is able to do so by means of Torah and *mitzvot*. For Torah and *mitzvot* effect a purification of the world. One reduces the spirit of impurity, "bit by bit I will drive it away,"[72] to the point of "I shall remove the spirit of impurity (altogether) from the earth."[73] This will be with the coming of Mashiach who shall reveal goodness and holiness in the world, culminating in "the earth shall be filled with the knowledge of G-d as the waters cover the sea"[74] (i.e., totally filled with it).

In context of the first *mitzvah* in the Torah—"Be fruitful and multiply"[75]—the *Gemara* states that "the scion of David will not come until all the souls in the *guf* will be disposed of."[76] This means that all the souls in the Supernal Treasure, which is referred to as *guf*, will be disposed to become vested in bodies on earth. Now just as the *Gemara* says this of the first *mitzvah*, it applies equally to all the *mitzvot* in the Torah. For all *mitvot* imply the concept of "Be fruitful and multiply."

The *mitzvah* "Be fruitful and multiply" signifies drawing forth a soul and manifesting this on the mundane level. The soul was in existence already, but it was in the

---

72. [Exodus 23:30]
73. Zechariah 13:2
74. Isaiah 11:9
75. [Genesis 1:28]
76. *Yevamot* 62a. [See *Zohar* II:253a.]

'Treasure of Souls.' By the *mitzvah* of "Be fruitful and multiply" it is drawn downwards and revealed. It is the same
with all the *mitzvot*: one reveals the spark of Divinity in
the physical object used to perform the *mitzvah*.
Observance of *mitzvot*, therefore, brings that spark out into
the open, just like the birth of a child.[77]

In this sense every Jew has the ability to speed up the
redemption by performing any *mitzvah*. One must be careful, though [as discussed on the preceding Shabbat], to
assure that the *mitzvot* be *ma'asim tovim ume'irim*, deeds
that are good and radiating.[78] There is always a possibility
that one will not only fail to effect purification in the
world by means of the *mitzvot*, but also enhance momentarily the vitality of the *kelipot*, as explained in *Hilchot
Talmud Torah* of the *Alter Rebbe*.[79] This, in turn, would
increase 'darkness.' In plain terms:

When the study of Torah and the observance of
mitzvot enhance a person's ego and arrogance, he
enhances the "alien god within you,"[80] the vitality of the
kelipot. Of a person like this it is said, "I and he cannot

---

77. See *Likkutei Torah*, Va'etchanan, p. 9d, interpreting the statement that Israel was dispersed among the nations in order that proselytes might join them (*Pesachim* 87b) [to refer to the sublimation of the
sparks of Divinity inherent in physical objects by means of using them
in the observance of Torah and *mitzvot*. Cf. *Keter Shem Tov*, Hossafot,
par. 137.]

78. [*Ma'asim tovim* does not mean simply that the actions themselves are good but that they leave an impact on the one performing
them, that they have a "radiating effect." This is achieved by a proper
attitude and preparation prior to the act. See *Likkutei Torah*, Shemini
Atzeret, p. 85a, and Shir, p. 17c.]

79. Chapter 4:3.

80. ["'There shall be no alien god within you.. ' (Psalms 81:10)
Which is the alien god that resides within man? It is the *yetzer hara*.'
Shabbat 105b.]

dwell together."[81] All this is avoided when the initial step
is an *avodah* of prayer. This will preclude the study of
Torah and subsequent observance of *mitzvot* from enhanc-
ing the ego and debasing oneself. Moreover, it will effect a
self-purification and a negation of ego: the Torah and
mitzvot will refine him [as explained at length last
Shabbat].

An initial *avodah* of prayer effects deeds that are good
and radiating. Every *mitzvah* disperses the darkness bit by
bit, and adds light in the world. This will lead to "I shall
remove the spirit of impurity from the earth" along with
"The earth shall be filled with the knowledge of G-d as the
waters cover the sea."

XXIII.   A question remains: how can a Jew refine the
world by means of Torah and *mitzvot*? After all, the world
per se was created before man, thus has a claim to priority.
Even on the sixth day of creation itself, the world existed
for several hours before man was created!

For this very reason we find that the verse "A star
steps out of Jacob and a rod rises out of Israel" is preceded
by the verse of "I see [the people] from the top of rocks, I
view it from hills."[82] The soul of every Jew, even of people
like ourselves, is rooted in the "Top of the Rocks,"[83] bound
up with "G-d, my Rock (of strength) and my Redeemer."[84]
Chassidut explains[85] that every soul is rooted in *pnimiyut
hamach'shavah*, the very essence of the 'Divine Thought'.
Every Jew, therefore, is able to control the world, because
the world was created by way of 'Divine Speech': "The

---

81. [*Sotah* 5a]
82. [Numbers 23:9]
83. [*Cf. Yalkut Shimoni* on this verse, par. 766.]
84. [Numbers 23:9]
85. [See *Tanya*, Igeret Hateshuvah, ch. 4. Cf. also *Likkutei Torah*,
Massey, p. 92a and 93d.]

heavens were made by the word of G-d.."[86] To be sure, this 'Speech' is said to derive from 'Thought'; nonetheless, it is but from *chitzoniyut hamach'shavah,* the external aspect of the 'Divine Thought.' The souls of Israel, however, are rooted in *pnimiyut hamach'shavah,* and that is why one is able to change the world.[87]

This concept conforms also with the Midrashic interpretation[88] that the term "rocks" refers to the patriarchs and "hills" refers to the matriarchs. The reality of every Jew's soul being bound up with "G-d, my Rock and my Redeemer" derives from the patriarchs and matriarchs: we inherited this from them. "How good is our portion, how pleasant our lot, and how beautiful our heritage" that they bequeathed unto us the aspect of "my Rock and my Redeemer," the aspect of *pnimiyut hamach'shavah,* which gives every Jew control over the world.

All this relates to the soul which is of *pnimiyut hamach'shavah,* thus even to the soul's status prior to its descent to earth. Nonetheless, the goal of "A star *stepping out* of Jacob" and "the rod *rising out of* Israel," i.e., the revelation of the future redemption, is not effected by the soul as it is above, but only after it descends to earth. For the ultimate intent of creation is to establish a *"dirah betachtonim*—an abode [for Divinity] in the lower worlds."[89] To be sure, the soul in its original state above, too, has the quality of being of the "Rock;" but there it is

---

86. Psalms 33:6. [*Avot* 5:1]

87. [Thought precedes speech: speech is rooted in thought, and therefore controlled by it. By analogy, the soul, rooted in the very essence of the Divine 'Thought,' transcends the world which is rooted only in the Divine 'Speech.' Cf. *Tanya,* Igeret Hateshuvah, ch. 4.]

88. [*Bamidbar Rabba* 20:19. *Tanchuma,* Balak:12.]

89. [*Tanchuma,* Nasso:16. See *Tanya,* ch. 36; and cf. *L.S.-Vayikra,* Vayikra, note 54.]

not bound up with the lower worlds. When the soul descends and carries out its task, however, it will actualize the goal of *dirah betachtonim* intended by the "Rock." Thus it will bring about the future redemption.

This accords with the principle that "the scion of David will not come until all souls in the *guf* will be disposed of": it is not enough to have souls in the "Treasure of Souls" which is called *guf*, or "beneath the Throne of Glory,"[90] and so forth. The soul must come down to earth. This alone will bring about the coming of the scion of David.

XXIV. We can now understand the great joy related to the birth of a child. There is surely great joy for the people of Israel when another Jew is added in this world. As for the baby born, however, it would seem to be otherwise. After all, birth marks a tremendous descent for the newborn, as stated in the *Gemara*[91] that when the fetus is in its mother's womb "a light burns above its head .. and it is taught the whole Torah." The Kabbalah and Chassidut elaborate on the extraordinary status of the soul on its supernal level. Generally speaking this includes also the period of pregnancy. For the newborn, therefore, birth signifies a decline in terms of "Turn away from evil" as well as in terms of "Do good."[92] There is a decline in terms of "turn away from evil" because the fetus does not have a *yetzer hara*; if it had been otherwise, it would rebel in the mother's womb and emerge, as stated in the *Gemara*.[93] There is also a decline in terms of "do good" because the fetus enjoys most sublime revelations by virtue of being

---

90. ["All souls are cut from beneath the Throne of Glory;" *Zohar* III:29b.]

91. *Nidah* 30b. [See here also the sequel, "there is no time in which man enjoys greater goodness than in those days."]

92. [Psalms 34:15. See *Tanya*, ch. 30.]

93. *Sanhedrin* 91b

taught the whole Torah. Why, then, is there any joy for the newborn? Nonetheless, the Torah regards birth as a joyous occasion. Thus we must say that there is joy not only for the people of Israel as a whole, and for the parents in particular, but also for every individual, including the newborn.

We can understand this in context of two statements in the *Gemara* distinguishing between a fetus and a newborn child. One source[94] says that a Noachide commits a capital offense when killing a fetus, because a fetus, too, is referred to as *adam* (man). In a second source[95] Rashi explains that an Israelite is not executed for killing the fetus because it is not referred to as *nefesh* (lit. soul). It follows, then, that a fetus differs from one that is born in that it has the status of *adam* but not that of *nefesh*.

Scripture has four designations for man: *adam, ish, gever* and *enosh*. The *Zohar*[96] states (and this is explained in Chassidut[97]) that the term *adam* denotes the highest quality. This quality is possessed by a fetus as well. The *Zohar*,[98] and Chassidut,[99] based on the prooftext "He created them male and female .. and He called their name *adam*,"[100] state that the special quality of *adam* is in the fact that *adam* signifies joining two opposites (male and female; soul and body). This aspect applies to a fetus as well. For a fetus, too, has a body, especially in the later stage of pregnancy of which the *Gemara*[101] says, "its head lies between its

---

94. *Sanhedrin* 57b

95. *Ibid.* 72b

96. *Zohar* III:48a

97. [*Likkutei Torah, Shir,* p. 25a; *Torat Hachassidut,* ch. 7 (*Hayom Yom, s.v.* Elul 4); *Likkutei Sichot,* vol. IV, p. 1116.]

98. *Zohar* I:55b

99. [See *Or Hatorah,* Tazri'a, p. 516f.]

100. [Genesis 5:2]

101. [*Nidah* 30b]

knees..," indicating that there is a head, knees, and the form of all 248 organs. The fetus also has a soul which is bound up with the body.[102] The fetus, therefore, is an *adam*, a compound of the two opposites of soul and body.

Now, the fetus is indeed referred to as *adam*, but not as *nefesh*. Offhand this is rather difficult. *Nefesh* signifies vitality. A fetus, too, has vitality, as it is said that "it eats what its mother eats and drinks what its mother drinks!"[103] Moreover, there is also spiritual life, as follows from the premise that it is taught the whole Torah! Why, then, is it not referred to as *nefesh*?

The difference between a fetus and one that is actually born, however, is in the very fact that the fetus "eats what its mother eats and drinks what its mother drinks." It eats and drinks, but it does not achieve anything independently. It deals only with things already prepared for it.[104] Birth, on the other hand, marks the beginning of *avodah*, of *birur* (refinement), of effort on the personal level. This is an extraordinary quality, because the whole purpose for the descent of the soul is to be active on one's own.

G-d is the quintessence of goodness, and it is "the very nature of the good to do good."[105] Thus we would think that the Almighty should provide all and any manifestations without any effort on our part. In reality, however, G-d provides everything by way of our *avodah*, and He does so precisely because He is the very essence of

---

102. [*Sanhedrin* 91b]

103. *Nidah* 30b

104. See *Torah Or*, Esther, p. 124bf.

105. [*Emek Hamelech* I:ch. 1; *Tanya*, Sha'ar Hayichud Veha'emunah, ch. 4. See *Eitz Chayim*, Sha'ar Hakelalim:ch. 1; and *Shomer Emunim* II:12ff.]

goodness, and ultimate good means that it should not be "bread of shame."[106]

This, then, is the advantage of having been born over the previous status of being a fetus: the former has vitality and life *of his own*, for which he toiled, and by virtue of which he is himself a *nefesh*. The whole concept of *avodah* does not apply to a fetus. That comes only after birth.

This explains the great joy associated with a birth. It is a joy not only for the parents but also for the infant. Indeed, while in the state of a fetus one enjoys the most sublime manifestations, but lacks the aspect of *avodah*. The fetus consumes that which its mother eats and drinks, but these are not its own. Coming out into the world, however, means the beginning of *avodah*. To be sure, any obligations of *mitzvot* begin much later (at least not earlier than the age of being subject to *chinuch*, training and education), and not from the moment of birth. Nonetheless, from the moment of its coming into the world, the child eats, drinks and refines on its own. It is likewise on the spiritual level: there is already the potential of *avodah* and personal effort, as well as the preparation for actualizing this potential (i.e., observance of the commandment to study Torah when growing up, because a father must start teaching Torah to a child from the time it is able to speak,[107] and so forth; moreover, even prior to that stage, the infant consumes food and refines it, thus developing the body with which it will later observe Torah and *mitzvot*).

---

106. [See *Yerushalmi, Orlah* 1:3. *Cf.* R. Joseph Caro, *Maggid Meisharim*, Bereishit, *s.v.* Tevet 14; and above, *Shavu'ot*, sect. XXXIV, and the notes there. For a wider discussion of this basic principle see *Likkutei Sichot*, vol. III, p. 1009f.; *ibid.* vol. XV, p. 94f.; and especially the Pesach-letter of the 11th Nissan 5732. *Cf.* also *L.S.-Shemot*, p. 174.]

107. [*Sifre*, Ekev, par. 46; *Sukah* 42a.]

XXV.   [*At this point follows an explanation for the distinction between the two laws stated above, notes 94-95. As it is too complex, we took the liberty of omitting it in this translation.*]

XXVI.   This, then, is the special nature of the great joy associated with the event of a birth. Birth signifies the beginning of an individual's personal *avodah*, which in turn leads to a refinement of the world and hastens the future redemption. To be sure, the ability to refine the world derives from the *neshamah* (soul), the aspect of "I see it from the top of rocks" which is already in the *neshamah* even as it is still above. Nonetheless, the soul actually starts carrying out its mission of *dirah betachtonim*, to establish an "abode in the lower worlds," only from the time of birth, the time of its becoming manifest in the world. It does not do so earlier, regardless of its status, however sublime the soul may be. Throughout the period of pregnancy the world remains as it is. All and any manifestations and changes begin only with the moment of birth.

Thus it is said of Moses that "at the time *of his birth* the whole house was filled with light."[108] He had been in the house prior to his birth as well, as a fetus in his mother's womb. Nonetheless, the house remained dark. The house was filled with light only at the time of his birth, because the event of birth signals the beginning of the *avodah* which the soul must carry out.

Thus it is said in the *Zohar (parshat Balak)*,[109] that the verse "I shall proclaim that which is inscribed.. I have begotten you this day"[110] refers to the birth of Mashiach, i.e., Mashiach the scion of David (and not the Mashiach

---

108. *Sotah* 12a
109. *Zohar* III:203b
110. [Psalms 2:7]

descended of Joseph). Offhand one may ask how this
interpretation relates to the plain sense of the words "I
have begotten you this day." It is readily understood,
however, in context of what was said above: the actual
event of the soul's birth, when the "I see it from the top of
rocks" becomes manifest below—not in a state of pregnancy, but with the event of actual birth—marks the
beginning of "a star steps out of Jacob and a staff rises out
of Israel" to the point of "Israel shall be valiant,"[111] which
refers to the ultimate redemption, as explained in various
sources.[112]

XXVII.   This explains the meaning of the verse, "A
[good] name is better than good oil, and the day of death
[is better] than the day of birth."[113] What is the relationship
between these concepts?

The term "oil" refers to the performance of *mitzvot*, as
stated in the *Zohar*[114] (cited in *Tanya*[115]), in comment on
"Let there not be a lack of oil above your head."[116] As for
the term "name," our sages state that "the Holy One,
blessed be He, went on a five hundred years' journey to
acquire a name for Himself."[117] "A name is better than
good oil" thus means that man's *avodah* is not for his own
sake but to establish and effect the acquisition of G-d's
Name. How is the superiority of "name" achieved? By
means of "good oil," the observance of *mitzvot*, good
deeds.

111. [Numbers 24:18]
112. [See Rambam, *Hilchot Melachim* 11:1; R. Yitzchak Abarbanel,
Mashmi'a Yeshu'ah, s.v. hamevaser tov harishon.]
113. Ecclesiastes 7:1
114. [*Zohar* III:187a]
115. [*Tanya*, ch. 35]
116. [Ecclesiastes 9:8]
117. *Kohelet Rabba* 7:1(2). See *Or Hatorah*, Shemot, p. 29f.

The same applies to the second half of the verse, "and the day of death [is better] than the day of birth." On the day of his birth, man's future is unknown. On the day of his death, however, one can see the realization of "You shall be blessed in your coming, and you shall be blessed in your going,"[118] that his departure from this world is as his coming into this world[119] and, moreover, it marks the completion of his mission. Even so, this itself was achieved by virtue of his "day of birth"! On the day of birth there is already the full potential of the totality of man's *avodah*, of everything that he will accomplish throughout his life on earth. As stated earlier, the "day on which I have begotten you" compounds everything, including the revelation of Mashiach.

When Moses was born, the whole house was filled with light. It is likewise with "the extension of Moses in every generation," referred to in *Tikunei Zohar*,[120] to the point of this being "like the sun radiating to the sixty myriad stars from below the earth":[121]

Yud-Bet Tamuz, the twelfth of Tamuz, is the birthday of the *Rebbe* (R. Yosef Yitzchak). Considering the status of his soul and the parents to whom he was born,[122] no doubt but that throughout the period of pregnancy he was surely taught the whole Torah on a most sublime level. Nonetheless, this did not measure up to the reality of the physical house and the world. The day of actual birth

---

118. [Deuteronomy 28:6]

119. *Baba Metzi'a* 107a

120. *Tikunei Zohar* 69:112a and 114a. ["There is an 'extension' of Moses in every generation, in every *tzadik* and sage occupied with Torah."]

121. [*Zohar* III:216b and 273a.] See *Tanya*, Igeret Hakodesh, end of sect. XXVII-B.

122. [See *Zohar Chadash*, Bereishit:11a, cited in *Tanya*, ch. 2.]

alone marks the beginning of—and compounds—his *avo-dah* to radiate to the "sixty myriad stars," the totality of Israel:[123] to infuse special ability to all, even to all those that simply "assume the name of İsrael"[124] (cited in his letter of *Yud-Bet Tamuz*[125]), and surely to Chassidim and all those bound up with him, to enable them to acquire Torah and good deeds and to transform the whole world into an abode for Divinity, that the 'whole house' (G-d's abode) be filled with light.

This is the great joy with the birthday of the *Rebbe*,[126] and "these days are remembered and enacted" every year.[127] It is a joyous occasion not only for those who merited to benefit from his teaching but also for those who but "assume the name of Israel." For with his birth he began to illuminate the whole world.

The joy resulting from an individual's *avodah* is in many respects greater than the joy associated with the creation of the world and the joy of *matan Torah* (the Giving of the Torah). For with the latter there was only potentiality; everything was latent. *Avodah*, on the other hand, actualizes the potential. There is a birth, a coming out into the open, "this day I have begotten you"—which, as stated, relates to the manifestation of Mashiach, very speedily indeed.

XXVIII.   We discussed the birthday of the *Rebbe*, a concept related to time. Time, however, is bound up with

---

123. [Israel consists of 600,000 root-souls; see above, Chukat, note 23.]

124. [See above, note 19.]

125. [See above, note 16.]

126. [See *Bereishit Rabba* 63:1; and *Tossafot* on *Eruvin* 13b (*s.v.* no'ach) and *Avodah Zara* 5a (*s.v.* she'ilmale); that the birth of a *tzadik* is an occasion of great joy for himself and for his generation.]

127. [See above, notes 24-26.]

space. The 'space' of the *Rebbe's* birth was in our former
country (Russia). The redemption of *Yud-Bet Yud-Gimel
Tamuz,* too, occurred in that same place.

I already related once[128] that there is a register of the
Rebbe, the celebrant of this festival of redemption, in
which he recorded a vision he had on a birthday of his
father, the *Rebbe Reshab.*[129] He notes there that his father
then said a *ma'amar* on Psalms 84. This happened twenty-
four years after his father's passing.[130] It follows then that
the spiritual ascents which occur with every birthday continue even after a person has departed from this world:
every year there is an ascent to a higher level.[131]

The *Rebbe's* new chapter of Psalms as of this *Yud-Bet
Tamuz* is Psalms 83.[132] There it is said: "G-d, do not hold
Your silence; be not silent and be not still.. They scheme
deceitfully against Your people, and they conspire against

---

128. [*Sefer Hama'amarim Bati Legani,* vol. I, p. 293f.; *Likkutei Sichot,*
vol. II, p. 496.]

129. [Born on the 20th of Marcheshvan 5621.]

130. [He passed away on the 2nd of Nissan 5680. The vision
occurred on the 20th of Marcheshvan 5705, the 84th birthday of the
Rebbe Reshab. The significance of the discourse on Psalms 84 is in terms
of a tradition, passed on by the Baal Shem Tov, that every day one is to
recite the chapter of Psalms that corresponds in number to one's current year; for example, with the ninetieth birthday one begins the nine-
ty-first year, thus is to begin reciting chapter 91; and so forth. (*Kovetz
Michtavim-Tehilim,* p. 214. See *Ma'amarei Admor Hazaken-Haketzarim,* p.
341, for an explanation by the *Alter Rebbe* for this custom; and *cf.* also
Likkutei Sichot, vol. X, p. 75.) The 20th of Marcheshvan 5705 thus
marked the conclusion of the *Reshab's* 84th year.]

131. [For a discussion of this principle, with references to both
Halachic and Kabbalistic texts. see the sources cited above, note 128,
and *Likkutei Sichot,* vol. V, p. 103.]

132. [The *Rebbe Reyatz* (R. Yosef Yitzchak) was born on the 12th
of Tamuz 5640. This *sichah* was delivered on his 82nd birthday, thus
the beginning of his 83rd year.]

those You shelter." The chapter concludes: "Then they will know that there is just You, whose Name is *Havayah*, the Supreme Being over all the earth."

Midrash Tehilim[133] relates the verse "Do not hold Your silence" to the principle of "The *tzadik* decrees, and the Holy One, blessed be He, confirms and fulfills it."[134]

"Your people are all *tzadikim*"[135] applies to all Jews. Thus as they decree, the Almighty confirms and fulfills it. What does Israel decree? "Do not hold Your silence; be not silent and be not still." There may be a number of reasons for being silent and still, but as Jews decree "Do not hold Your silence.. and be not still," it is a case of "the *tzadik* decrees, and the Holy One, blessed be He, confirms and fulfills it."

The verses following explain the context: "*Ya'arimu sod*—they scheme deceitfully against Your people, and they conspire against *tzefunecha*, those You shelter." The *Midrash*[136] comments that the deceitful schemes against Jews are related to *sod*, i.e., the fact that Jews study the Torah—"*Sod Hashem* (the secret of G-d) is for those who fear Him."[137] "They conspire against *tzefunecha*;" this, the commentators say,[138] refers to the people of Israel who are sheltered by G-d.

This raises a difficulty. The deceitful schemes against Israel are not based solely on Israel's preoccupation with the *sod* (esoteric dimension) of the Torah, but on the very

---

133. [*Midrash Tehilim* 83:1]

134. [*Tanchuma*, ed. Buber, Va'eira:22. *Bamidbar Rabba* 14:4; *Zohar* I:45b. See also *Mo'ed Katan* 16b; and *cf. Shabbat* 59b and 63a.]

135. Isaiah 60:21

136. [*Midrash Tehilim* 83:2]

137. [Psalms 25:14]

138. Ibn Ezra, Redak, and Metzudot, on this verse; and R. Bachaya on Deuteronomy 32:41.

fact that they study Torah altogether, even *nigleh*, the exoteric meaning of the Torah. The nations thus plot even
against those who merely assume the name *Yisrael* (which
is an acronym for *Yesh Shishim Ribuy Oti'ot Latorah*[139]), as
we have seen in reality. Why, then, does our text use the
term *sod?* Also, why does our text use the term *tzefunecha*
to refer to the uniqueness of Israel?

The concluding verse, "Then they will know that
there is just You, whose Name is *Havayah*, the Supreme
Being over all the earth," too, presents a difficulty. The
phrase "just You, whose Name is *Havayah*" signifies the
ultimate transcendence of G-d[140] which is altogether
beyond the creative process [as will be explained later on
at length[141]]. The phrase "the Supreme Being over all the
earth," however, is related to the world [the immanence of
G-d], albeit the aspect of the "Supreme Being" over all the
earth. How can these two concepts be paired together?

The Jewish people have *mesirat nefesh* for Torah and
mitzvot, including *galya deTorah*, the revealed (exoteric)
part of the Torah. This *mesirat nefesh* derives from *satim
denishmata*,[142] the concealed (inner) aspect of the soul
which is bound up with *satim deKudsha Berich Hu*, the concealed reality of G-d, through *satim de'orayta*, the concealed dimension of the Torah.[143] This fact disturbs
"Esau"[144] tremendously. "Esau" is prepared to endure and

---

139. [See above, Chukat, note 23.]
140. [The ineffable Name, *Havayah* (the Tetragrammaton), signifies Divine transcendence. *Zohar* III:257b reads this Name as a compound of *Hayah-Hoveh-Yihyeh* (He was-He is-He will be)—"He was
before all beings, He is in all beings, He will be after all beings," indicating the timelessness or infinity of G-d which transcends creation.]
141. In the *Ma'amar "Ki Merosh Tzurim"*, delivered that Shabbat.
142. This is explained in *Tanya*, ch. 18.
143. [See *Zohar* III:73a.]
144. ["Esau" (or Edom), the archenemy of Israel, is the symbol

deal with the revealed and manifest aspects. For "Esau,"
too, has a share in the revealed part of Torah (i.e., the laws
of the seven precepts of the Noachide Code[145]). The fact
that "Esau hates Jacob,"[146] therefore, does not derive from
the exoteric. It stems from *satim de'orayta* and *satim denishmata*, the concealed aspect of the Torah and the concealed
aspect of the soul which illuminate and penetrate the exoteric aspects as well. Esau does not share in these, and that
is why he cannot bear them. Thus it is said, *"ya'arimu sod"*:
the principal reason for which "they scheme deceitfully
against Your people" is because of the aspect of *sod*.

This is seen also in the arrest and liberation of *Yud-Bet
Yud- Gimel Tamuz*. The *Rebbe* sacrificed himself for everything, even for the simple learning of *aleph-bet*; but everything was permeated by *pnimiyut*, the aspect of *satim* and
sod.

The Almighty deals with man "measure for mea-
sure":[147] as the Jewish people arouse *satim denishmata* (the
concealed aspect of the soul) by means of *satim de'orayta*
(the concealed aspect of the Torah), they are bound up
with *satim deKudsha Berich Hu*, the concealed reality of
G-d. That is why they are referred to as *tzefunecha*, those
hidden (sheltered) by G-d.

"Esau" cannot bear this. Thus "they scheme deceitfully against Your people and they conspire" because of the
aspects of *sod* and *tzefunecha*. In this context Israel decrees
"Do not hold Your silence, be not silent and be not still."
As they decree this, G-d confirms and fulfills it. Thus

---

for all that scheme against Israel. In the later verses—Psalms 83:7-9—
ten nations are mentioned, but Edom ("Esau") is the principal enemy.
Cf. *Midrash Tehilim* 83:3.]

145. [*Sanhedrin* 56aff.]

146. [*Sifre*, Beha'alotecha, par. 69; cited by Rashi on Genesis
33:4.]

147. [See above, Shevu'ot, note 244.]

"*veyede'u*—they will know that just You.." *Veyede'u* is an idiom of *yedi'ah*_(knowledge), as well as an expression of breaking asunder — as in "*vayoda*, he broke with them the men of Sukot."[148] The implication is that the *kelipot* are broken asunder and there is a manifestation of Divinity in the world.

This manifestation will be in a manner of "Then they will know that just You, whose Name is *Havayah*, are the Supreme Being over all the earth." For the Almighty deals "measure for measure." Thus even as the Jewish people effect through their *avodah* a joining of the concealed (*satim*) with the revealed (*galya*), that the *galya* will be permeated by the *pnimiyut*, the Almighty will cause the aspect of "just You, whose Name is *Havayah*" will radiate on earth, to become manifest within the world itself.

This aspect was evident with the redemption of *Yud-Bet Yud-Gimel Tamuz*, an event of G-d doing great and wondrous things *on earth*. Thus it is a preparation for the ultimate redemption when "your Master shall not hide Himself any more [but your eyes shall see your Master],"[149] and "all flesh shall see..:"[150] even the material reality will perceive Divinity in a way of it no longer being hidden.[151]

As stated, the redemption of *Yud-Bet Tamuz* occurred in our former country. The anticipated manifestations, too, will begin in that selfsame land presently suffering the greatest oppression.[152] From that lowest level starts the

---

148. Judges 8:16

149. Isaiah 30:20

150. ["The glory of G-d shall be revealed, and together all flesh shall see that the mouth of G-d has spoken;" Isaiah 40:5.]

151. [See *Tanya*, ch. 36; and the *Mitteler Rebbe's Sha'ar Ha'emunah*, ch. 25.]

152. [By now, the time that this translation is published, we have already been privileged to witness the fulfillment of these prophetic

"*ufaratzta*—you shall spread abroad to the west and to the east, to the north and to the south..,"[153] and from there this shall extend to the rest of the whole world. "Then they shall know that just You, whose Name is *Havayah*, are the Supreme Being over all the earth": even on the lowest level there will be a manifestation of Divinity with the ultimate redemption through our righteous Mashiach, very speedily indeed.

---

words, with the miracle of the radical changes in Russia and Eastern Europe over the past few years which affected the formerly oppressed Jews in particular.]

153. [Genesis 28:14]

PINCHAS   פינחס

A

I. We are told that the confrontation with Zimri happened in the presence of Moses, the sons of Aaron, and the elders,[1] yet none knew how to react. Pinchas was of junior rank in that assembly.[2] (This follows from the *Gemara's* description of the order how Moses taught the Torah to Israel: first he taught Aaron, then Eleazar and Ithamar, then the seventy elders, and finally all the people.[3] Pinchas thus learned along with the people.) Even so, he stepped forward and stated that the case of Zimri is subject to the law of "zealous people may attack him." He was then told, "Let him who reads the letter be the agent [for executing its contents]."[4]

There is a moral in this incident:

Sometimes things happen about which the leaders of the generation remain silent. This does not mean that nothing is to be done. Nor does it mean that this silence could be used as an argument to dissociate oneself from the event. On the contrary: when aware that you are able to do something about it, you are obligated to do so. The fact that others, greater than yourself, say nothing, may

---

1. [See Rashi on Numbers 25:6. *Sanhedrin* 82a; *Pirkei deR. Eliezer*, ch. 47 (and *Be'ur Haradal* there, note 24).]
2. [See *Bamidbar Rabba* 20:25, and *Perush Maharzav* there, s.v. vayakam. See also *Korban Ha'eidah* on *Yerushalmi, Sanhedrin* 10:2, s.v. mitoch Sanhedrin shelo.]
3. *Eruvin* 54b
4. *Sanhedrin* 82a [cited by Rashi on Numbers 25:7].

very well be for the sake that "Pinchas acquire the priest-hood."[5] In other words, the event may have special bear-ing upon *you*: it is part of those things that *you* are to refine and rectify in order to achieve your own perfection.

On the physical level everyone has his own portion, and "no one can infringe upon the sustenance of another."[6] It is likewise, and self-evidently even more so, on the spiritual level: everyone has his personal share and portion in Torah and in the observance of *mitzvot* that he is to accomplish, and "no one can infringe upon the suste-nance of another."

[That is why we say, "Grant us *our share* in Your Torah."[7] This relates not only to an understanding of Torah, but also to discovering novel insights in it.[8] The *Gemara*[9] thus relates that Rabbi Akiva once recited a legal ruling of which Moses was unaware.]

As for the principle "If he merits he will take his own share as well as the share of another,"[10] this relates to *Gan Eden*, the afterlife, to the *reward* for *mitzvot*. As for the *mitz-vah* itself, however, which itself transcends the reward for its fulfillment,[11] everyone has his own share.

It follows, then, that the reason of no one else doing

---

5. *Bamidbar Rabba* 20:24. [*Tanchuma*, Balak:20.]

6. As it is said, "No one can touch that which is prepared for his fellow..;" *Yoma* 38b.

7. *Avot* 5:20. [See sources cited in next note.]

8. [R. Chaim Vital, *Sha'ar Ru'ach Hakodesh*, ed. Tel Aviv 1963, p. 108b; *idem*, *Sha'ar Hagilgulim*, ch. 17, and *Eitz Hada'at Tov*, Yitro, on Exodus 20:1 (p. 12d); *Tanya*, Igeret Hakodesh, sect. XXVI (p. 145a). See also R. Judah Hachassid, *Sefer Chassidim*, sect. 530, and *Berit Olam* there.]

9. *Menachot* 29b

10. *Chagigah* 15a

11. [See *Tanya*, beg. of ch. 37, and *ibid*. ch. 39 (p. 53a), in context of *Likkutei Torah*, Re'ey, p. 28df.]

anything about certain matters may be because it is something relating to yourself, that it is up to you to accomplish the effect.

II.   Of Pinchas it is said, "Pinchas is Elijah."[12] This statement is questioned in view of the fact that Pinchas preceded the prophet Elijah; thus it would be more appropriate to say "Elijah is Pinchas!"[13] The paradox is resolved in context of a passage in *Zohar*[14] which states that Elijah did in fact precede Pinchas, except that at the time he was not a human being but an angel. That is why it is said that "Pinchas is Elijah."[15]

The implication for man's *avodah* is as follows:

It was stated above that no one should pay attention to what others do or fail to do. If an opportunity arises to accomplish something, one must go ahead and do it. If it should be asked, "where will one find the strength to do so?," we are told, "Pinchas is Elijah!" When the Almighty places a person into a situation that requires *mesirat nefesh*, that person is also given the necessary abilities,[16] and may

---

12. *Targum Yehonathan* on Exodus 6:18; *Yalkut Shimoni*, Pinchas, par. 771; *Zohar* II:190a. [See also *Zohar* III:215a (and *cf. ibid.* 124a); *Yelamdenu* cited in *Aruch*, *s.v.* zero'a; Rashi on *Baba Metzi'a* 114b, *s.v.* kohen; Redak on I Kings 17:1 and 19:4; and Ralbag on I Kings 17:1. Some texts note that the *gimatriya* (numerical equivalent) of Pinchas is the same as that of Eliyahu multiplied four times (*cf. Berachot* 4b and *Sha'arei Zohar* there).]

13. [*Zohar* III:215a does state "Elijah is Pinchas." Generally, though, the expression is always "Pinchas is Elijah," which raises the question stated; see R. Joseph Karo, *Maggid Meisharim*, Pinchas; and Chida, *Chomat Anoch* on I Kings 17:1, and *Midbar Kedemot*, *s.v.* aleph:par. 27.]

14. *Zohar* I:46b. See there *Derech Emet*, note 8.

15. [*Chomat Anoch* and *Midbar Kedemot* cited in note 13. *Maggid Meisharim* offers a different answer.]

16. [*Cf.* above, Shevu'ot, note 251.]

even be infused with a spark of someone who is not human.

III.   This offers a lesson for all young people in our time. One is not to think in terms of "this one or that one can do the job." One must be aware that anything coming your way belongs to your own share. You have the abilities to deal with it, and must do so with *mesirat nefesh*.

The *Rebbe* said that *mesirat nefesh* does not mean ascending to a roof and, Heaven forbid, throwing yourself down. *Mesirat nefesh* must be without noise and bustle, for "G-d is not in the commotion."[17] *Mesirat nefesh* must permeate all the activities of our daily life — "stopping his ears.. and shutting his eyes.."[18] For Torah, too, there must be *mesirat nefesh*: not to take the Torah to oneself, but to take oneself to the Torah. With a truly sincere will, one shall succeed.

Following the example of the *mesirat nefesh* of Pinchas will also effect that "Pinchas is Elijah" — i.e., the one who proclaims the redemption.[19] In other words, all of the present *avodah* is a preparation toward Mashiach, to transform this world into a sanctuary for G-dliness.

B

IV.   The Torah relates the story of Pinchas who zealously took up the cause of the Almighty.

"A study session cannot pass without some novel insight."[20] This is said of *Torah shebe'al peh*, the oral Torah. How much more so, then, that this applies to *Torah shebike-*

---

17. I Kings 19:11.
18. Isaiah 33:15. See *Kuntres Ha'avodah*, ch. 2.
19. *Targum Yehonathan* on Exodus 6:18. [*Pesikta Rabaty* 36:4, in comment on Isaiah 52:7 (and *cf.* Malachi 3:23); *Eruvin* 43b.]
20. *Chagigah* 3a

tav, the written Torah, where we derive complete laws from single letters.[21] No doubt, then, that there must be some novel teachings from a whole story,[22] like the story of Pinchas.

The novel teachings in this narrative are the rulings of "Zealots shall punish him,"[23] and "Such is the law, but it is not promulgated."[24] This means that there are cases where one inquires of the *bet din* (court) what to do about certain situations, and they will not offer any instructions because such is the ruling of the *Shulchan Aruch* (Code of Jewish Law).[25] That same code, however, also states that "zealots shall punish him!" In other words, if one would not come to inquire of the *bet din* but acts on his own, prompted by the dictates of his innermost soul, he will have acted correctly (for "*such is the law,* except that it is not promulgated"). His reaction thus happens to coincide with the Divine Will.

As a rule one must always consult the *bet din* for all matters. Even so, situations that require a zealous taking up the cause of the Almighty, are analogous to a case of *pikuach nefesh* (saving endangered life): to ask for directions when confronting a situation of *pikuach nefesh* is tantamount to bloodshed.[26] One ought to care enough to act immediately, on your own, without asking for instructions from the *bet din.* Likewise, when truly concerned about a condition that requires taking up the cause of G-d, one does not seek guidance from the *bet din.* In a situation like

---

21. [*Cf. Chagigah* 1:8; and *Menachot* 29b.]

22. [*Cf. Zohar* 149a-b and 152a (cited and translated in *The Mystical Tradition,* p. 31*ff.*).]

23. [*Sanhedrin* 81bf.; *Shulchan Aruch,* Choshen Mishpat 425:4.]

24. [*Sanhedrin* 82a; *Shulchan Aruch,* Choshen Mishpat 425:4.]

25. [See *Encyclopedia Talmudit, s.v.* halachah ve'ein morin kein.]

26. *Yerushalmi, Yoma* 8:5. [*Shulchan Aruch,* Orach Chayim 328:2.]

this one should not seek the assurance of a "solid bridge,"
not to do anything without prior consultation of a *bet din*,
because every moment counts. Moreover, even when
knowing beforehand that the *bet din* would rule not to do
anything, there remains the principle that "zealots shall
punish him"! This is the very will of G-d, for the principle
of "zealots shall punish him" is an explicit law in *Shulchan
Aruch*.

We can understand this by the following:

"A person will not sin unless a spirit of folly enters
into him."[27] As stated by the *Alter Rebbe*, it is intrinsic to
every Jew that he does not want to be—nor can he be—
separated from G-dliness.[28] The fact that he may act like
an animal derives from the 'spirit of folly,' from the 'animal' within him (the 'animal' soul). When therefore moved
by pure zealousness—"I have been very zealous for the
sake of G-d.."[29]—as opposed to that of "his own glory or
the glory of his family,"[30] and being so concerned about it
that he does not even think whether or not he may be
committing a sin, he negates altogether his ego and any
personal considerations. By disregarding the body and
animal soul one leaves but the Divine soul which is "forever faithful with G-d."[31] That is why he is overcome by a
spirit of zealousness. No doubt but that for as long as the
animal soul will not interfere, the *neshamah* by itself will
surely direct him to the Divine intent.

Thus when Pinchas executed Zimri, "the plague was
arrested."[32] He saved thousands of Israelites from the

---

27. *Sotah* 3a

28. [See *Tanya*, ch. 24. *Sefer Hama'amarim 5710*, p. 115; discussed
in *Sefer Hama'amarim Bati Legani*, vol. I, pp. 46 and 48*ff.*]

29. [The words of Elijah in I Kings 19:10 and 14.]

30. [*Cf. Ta'anit* 20a; *Megilah* 3a; and parallel passages.]

31. *Tanya*, ch. 24.

32. [Numbers 25:8]

most serious sin of the idolatry of Ba'al Pe'or. The *Midrash*[33] relates that the transgression of Ba'al Pe'or is one that forever incites anger, except that Moses nullifies that incitement. We do not find that with any other transgression! Yet Pinchas saved the Jewish people from this sin. Thus he merited that "I am giving him My covenant of peace,"[34] that "Pinchas is Elijah" who attends every *berit milah* (the covenant of circumcision)[35] and will announce the redemption.[36]

V.   Our day and age, too, is experiencing a plague, may the Merciful One save us. My father in-law, the *Rebbe*, said that the Almighty has put the walls of the *galut* on fire.[37] This is so clearly evident that it is not in need of any proof or explanations. We can actually see how so many Jews, both in the diaspora and in the Holy Land (may it be rebuilt and re-established speedily), are being lost to *Yiddishkeit*. They walk a crooked road leading them to opposing, Heaven forbid, G-d and His Torah. In a time like this, therefore, a time of raging fires, a time when Jewish boys and girls could—Heaven forbid—be lost to *Yiddishkeit*, one need not consult a *bet din* or check sources whether or not one may suspend learning for an hour, or similar questions. There is imminent danger when delaying even one moment. This is a time for action.

In a time like this it is incumbent upon every Jew to kindle zealousness in his soul. This can be done by means

---

33. Cited in *Tossafot, Sotah* 14a, *s.v.* mipnei. See also *Pirkei deR. Eliezer*, ch. 45.

34. [Numbers 25:12]

35. *Pirkei deR. Eliezer*, end of ch. 29, cited in *Abudraham*, Sha'ar IX. [Elijah is called *"malach haberit* — the messenger of the covenant;" Malachi 3:1, and see Redak there. See also below, note 63.]

36. [See above, note 19.]

37. [*Igrot Kodesh-Maharyatz*, vol. VI, p. 372 (and see there also p. 307), cited in —] Preface to *Hayom Yom*.

of *pnimiyut Hatorah* and by leaving one's privacy to go out to fellow-Jews to speak to them with pleasant, sincere and warm words. There is no point in engaging them in philosophical debates or discussions, for that is altogether inappropriate in the face of a raging fire.[38] Moreover, in a situation of *pikuach nefesh* one does not win with logic. One must speak with feeling, with soul-words, and thus one will kindle the fire within them—"its flashes—flashes of fire, a flame of G-d"[39]—and the plague shall be arrested.

This will lead to "Pinchas who is Elijah," who will come "before the great and awesome day .. and he shall turn the heart of the fathers to the children.."[40] and proclaim the redemption by our righteous Mashiach, speedily in our own days.

C

VI.   The laws dealing with the order of inheritance are one of the original themes in *parshat Pinchas*.

The topic of sacrifices, as well as the topic of enumerating the Jewish people, can be found also in other *parshiyot*, even with details. The order of inheritance in general, and especially the division of the Land of Israel as an inheritance, is explained in *parshat Pinchas*.

The division of the Land of Israel was by means of a lottery: "The land shall be divided by lot."[41] The *Gemara*[42] and *Midrash*[43] explain that the division took place by lot as well as by means of the Urim and Tumim.

---

38. [See *Igrot Kodesh-Maharyatz*, vol. VI, p. 306.]
39. Song 8:6. [*Cf. Tanya*, ch. 9 and 43f.]
40. Malachi 3:23-24.
41. [Numbers 26:55]
42. *Baba Batra* 122a
43. *Bamidbar Rabba* 21:9. [*Tanchuma*, Pinchas:6; Rashi on Numbers 26:54.]

The physical division of the Land of Israel reflects its spiritual division, i.e., the division of the *avodah*-symbolism of the Land of Israel.[44] That spiritual division, therefore, is by lot. This raises an obvious problem: *avodah* must be based on mind and reason; a lottery, however, is something beyond reason![45]

To be sure, the very foundation of *avodah* is *kabalat ol*, a submissive acceptance of the "yoke of Heaven;" but this refers only to the *foundation* of *avodah*. The beginning of *avodah* itself, however, the determination how to act, to know what is permitted and what is forbidden, that depends altogether on the Torah. Knowledge of Torah depends on mind and understanding. How, then, could it be said that the "division," i.e., the determination and categorization of man's *avodah* and his conduct, is "by lot"?

Moreover, Scripture states, "The land shall be divided *ach* (but; only) by lot." The word *ach* is exclusive,[46] in effect stating that the division is to be by lot only. How could this be when it should be exclusively by reason and intellect?

VII.   In a *maamar* of the *Tzemach Tzedek*,[47] as well as in discourses of later *Rebbes*,[48] there is an explanation how our text—"The land shall be divided only by lot"—relates to the soul and *avodah*. That explanation answers our question:

A lot is beyond reason. The division of the land must be specifically by means of a lot, because that division is rooted in something beyond reason.

---

44. *Torah Or*, Vayeshev, p. 26c*ff.*; and *Torat Chayim*, Vayeshev, p. 57a*ff.*

45. [See *Tanya*, Igeret Hakodesh, end of sect. VII.]

46. [*Yerushalmi, Berachot* 9:7; cited by Rashi on Leviticus 23:27.]

47. *Or Hatorah*, Pinchas, p. 1059*ff.*

48. *Torat Shemuel-5626*, p. 171 [and see there p. XIV, for references to discourses of the *Rebbes* thereafter].

This means:

Every Jew must follow all the *mitzvot*. Nonetheless, every Jew has some specific aspects that relate uniquely to him. Thus it is explained in *Tanya-Igeret Hakodesh*,[49] that we find various Tannaim and Amoraim who showed extraordinary zealousness for certain *mitzvot*.[50] They were careful with *all mitzvot*, but for certain things they demonstrated additional care because those things had a unique bearing upon them personally. The extra heed shown for those aspects effected inspiration and elevation for all their other *mitzvot*.[51]

The fact of there being such a unique relationship between an individual and his specific aspects cannot be explained in terms of reason or intellect. It is not a relationship based on some rational insight, but transcends reason altogether. This is the very concept of a lot or lottery.

VIII.   To experience unusual obstacles and difficulties with the observance of a certain *mitzvah* is evidence that one has a special relationship to that *mitzvah*.[52] The very fact of strong opposition shows that this *mitzvah* affects him ever so much more.

One may fail altogether to detect any logical reason why that *mitzvah* should be so significant to him. In fact, he notes that it presents for him more difficulties than anything else, or that he is unable to find any delight or

---

49. Sect. VII. See also R. Chaim Vital's Introduction to *Sha'ar Hahakdamot* (reprinted in *Kuntres Eitz Hachayim*, see there end of p. 73). *Sefer Hasichot 5700*, p. 22. [See also *Eitz Chayim* 49:5; and *Sefer Hagilgulim*, ch. 4.]

50. [*Shabbat* 118b. See *Sefer Chassidim*, sect. 529; and *Sha'arei Zohar* on *Avodah Zara* 5a.]

51. [See *Keter Shem Tov*, Hossafot, par. 74, and note 75 there. Cf. *L.S.-Shemot*, p. 46f., and note i there.]

52. See *Kuntres Ha'avodah*, ch. 6 [especially pp. 41f. and 43ff.].

success in that whole area of Torah. Nonetheless, this particular aspect is uniquely his, relating to him in a very specific and personal way, and it will elevate his over-all involvement with Torah and *mitzvot*. The *yetzer hara* fights him in this matter for precisely the reason that it is so crucial to him.

One must not, therefore, drop it and move on to other things. On the contrary: there must be extra effort to pursue it because it is so crucial to him. The very fact of neither understanding the personal relationship nor recognizing its significance, is one of the obstacles and impediments for its achievement.

IX. We can now understand why it says, "The land shall be divided only by lot," referring to the concept of "lot" which signifies something that is supra-rational.

In the land of Israel there are different kinds of areas: mountains, lowlands and valleys, fields of corn and fields of orchards, and so forth.[53] When one received his share in mountainous territory and another in a valley, or one received cornfields and another orchards, this division of the physical land of Israel reflected each one's individual relationship to the spiritual land of Israel.

That is why it says, "The land shall be divided only by lot": the relationship of each one to his individual part is not subject to reason and intellect; it is supra-rational. On our human level this is reflected in the concept of a lottery-system.

X. The very fact that the above is an integral part of the Torah indicates that it relates to each and everyone of us; for the Torah is eternal, relevant to all times and all places.[54]

---

53. See *Baba Batra* 122a, explained in *Torat Shemuel 5626*, p. 205.

54. [See *Keter Shem Tov*, par. 393, and my notes there; and the Maggid's *Likkutei Amarim*, sect. 4, and *Or Torah*, sect. 38 and 406. *Cf.* *L.S.-Bereishit*, p. XIV.]

Everyone has something unique that relates specifically to him or her. One must disregard any obstacles and
impediments in its pursuit. Indeed, as stated, the very
experience of vehement opposition against this from the
yetzer hara, the world about him, must evoke ever greater
efforts to pursue it. For it is most significant and crucial to
that individual, and will inspire and elevate everything
else relating to himself.

D*

XI.   There are varying views on the spelling of
Pinchas, whether it is to be *malei* ("full"; *with* a *yod*) or
chasar ("defective"; *without* a *yod*).[55] The concept of *malei* is
related to Mashiach and the Messianic age, as it is said of
the verse, "These are *toldot* (the generations; written *malei*)
of Peretz;"[56] for then there will be a restoration of conditions just as when the world was created in its fullness.[57]

Pinchas is related to the Messianic redemption:

Of Pinchas it is said that he took up the cause of G-d

---

55. [See the sources cited in *Likkutei Sichot*, vol. VIII, p. 355, note
32. See also *Torah Or*, Miketz, p.40a.]

56. Ruth 4:18. [The word *toldot* is always written *chassar* (with
one *vav* instead of two), except for two instances: Genesis 2:4—which
speaks of the creation of heaven and earth in their "fullness" (i.e., perfection), and this verse in Ruth which traces the genealogy of King
David, the ancestor of Mashiach in whose days the "fullness" of the
world will be restored as it was at the time of creation. See references
in next note.]

57. *Bereishit Rabba* 12:6. [*Tanchuma*, Bereishit:6; and parallel passages. See especially *Midrash Hagadol* on Genesis 2:4. The restoration to
"its fullness" refers specifically to the six things (enumerated in these
sources) which the world lost because of man's sin. These six things
are alluded by the letter *vav* (which also represents the number six)
missing in the word *toldot* throughout Scripture (see preceding note).]

with zeal in the incident with Zimri.[58] The same is said later of the prophet Elijah, with whom Pinchas is identified:[59] "I have zealously taken up the cause of G-d, the G-d of Hosts."[60] The Almighty thus said, "Behold, I give unto him My *covenant* of peace":[61] Elijah ["Pinchas is Elijah"] is to attend every *berit* (covenant of circumcision)[62] to see and attest to the fact that the Jewish people are not at all as he had thought[63] (and "women have the status of those that are circumcised"[64]).

The implication is that Elijah's zealousness brought about an effect of *ahavat Yisrael*: he observes the virtues of

---

58. [See Numbers 25:11 and 13.]
59. See above, note 12.
60. I Kings 19:10 and 14.
61. [Numbers 25:12. See *Zohar* I:66b.]
62. [See above, note 35.]
63. [The prophet Elijah, in his zealousness for G-d, spoke evil of Israel: "I have been very zealous for G-d, the G-d of Hosts, for the children of Israel have forsaken Your covenant." (I Kings 19:10 and 14) The Almighty disapproved of Elijah's criticism of Israel, and he was censured for it, because "he defended the honor of the Father but did not insist upon the honor of the child (Israel)." *Mechilta*, Bo: Petichta; *Shir Rabba* 1:6 (1); *Eliyahu Zutta*, ch. 8; *Pirkei deR. Eliezer*, end of ch. 29 (and see there *Be'ur Haradal*, note 61, and the sources cited there). To rectify this criticism of Israel (which emphasized specifically the neglect of circumcision—see I Kings 19:10, and Redak there; *Pirkei deR. Eliezer*, ch. 29; and *Zohar* I:66b and 93a), Elijah is to attend every circumcision to see and attest that Israel is not at all as bad as he had thought. See *Zohar* I:93a; *ibid.* 209b (and *Or Hachamah* there), and II:190a; *Zohar Chadash*, Noach:23b (stating that Elijah attests not only the observance of circumcision but all and any good deeds performed by Israel; *cf. Ruth Rabba* 5:6).]
64. *Avodah Zara* 27a. [The ritual of circumcision relates only to the males; the addition of this phrase, therefore, shows the inclusion of the females, for they are of themselves already part of the covenant as even in their natural state they are classified as "circumcised."]
65. [See above, note 19.]

220   **LIKKUTEI SICHOT**

Israel, and thus he will also be the one to proclaim the redemption.[65]

Elijah was a disciple of Achiyah the Shilonite,[66] the master of the Baal Shem Tov.[67] The Baal Shem Tov was guided by the principle of *ahavat Yisrael*;[68] and thereafter likewise the *Alter Rebbe* and the *Rebbes* that followed after him.[69] They conducted themselves according to the principle of *ahavat Yisrael* and demanded the same from their followers. By virtue thereof we shall merit the coming of Elijah, the harbinger of the redemption.[70]

XII. We must know fully well that the *Rebbe*, my father-in-law, demands *ahavat Yisrael* of everyone: to befriend all Jews, including the simplest of them all. Aside of the fact that the simple ones, too, are beloved unto G-d even as a father loves his child, they also have the intrinsic quality of simplicity.[71]

Yeshivah-students who spend their free time as emissaries of *Merkas Le'inyanei Chinuch*[72] must keep in mind

---

66. [*Yerushalmi, Eruvin* 5:1, cited by—] Rambam, Introduction to *Mishneh Torah*.

67. [See *Keter Shem Tov*, par. 143; *ibid.*, Hossafot, par. 203 (and note 207 there).]

68. [See above, Yud-Bet Yud-Gimel Tamuz, sect. X. See also *Keter Shem Tov*, Hossafot, par. 101, and *ibid.*, par. 139*ff*.]

69. [See above, Yud-Bet Yud-Gimel Tamuz, sect. XIX*ff.Cf.* above, Bamidbar C-D.]

70. [See *Tanchuma*, Nitzavim:1; *Bereishit Rabba* 98:2; *Agadat Bereishit*, ch. 82(83); and above, Yud-Bet Yud-Gimel Tamuz, sect. XX.]

71. [See above, Bamidbar, sect. XXIV, and note 102 there.]

72. Students of Lubavitch Yeshivot undertake (especially during their vacations) missions on behalf of *Merkas Le'inyanei Chinuch* (Central Organization for Jewish Education of Lubavitch) to all places where Jews are to be found. They are to acquaint themselves with local conditions of *yiddishkeit* in general and of Jewish education in particular; to encourage the members of those communities, old and young, and to disseminate all kinds of literature to strengthen Jewish life.

that zealousness must be applied to themselves. With regards to another, however, there must be *ahavat Yisrael*. This will bring about the realization of "Behold, I shall send unto you Elijah the prophet.."[73] to proclaim the ultimate redemption very speedily in our own days.

E*

XIII.   Pinchas is identified with the prophet Elijah, the harbinger of the ultimate redemption that will come about very speedily. One aspect of the connection between Elijah and the redemption follows from the difference between Moses and Elijah:[74] When Moses was born, the whole house was filled with light.[75] Even so, his exalted state did not pervade physical matter, and that is why his body required burial. Elijah, on the other hand, signifies the aspect of *Ban*[76] (the numerical equivalent of his name is also the same as that of *Ban*). He achieved so thorough a purification of his physical body that it ascended by a whirlwind into Heaven.[77] This relates to the future

---

Oftentimes they carry out more specific missions to enhance Jewish identity, education and observance. [This practice was instituted by the *Rebbe Reyatz*, shortly after his arrival in the U.S.A. in 1940.]

73. Malachi 3:23

74. Explained at length in the discourse *Ki Merosh Tzurim 5722* [delivered just before this *sichah*].

75. [*Sotah* 12a]

76. [*Ban* is a short form signifying one aspect of the Divine Name *Havayah*; see Glossary at end of this volume, and *cf. L.S.-Vayikra*, p. 53, note 34.]

77. [II Kings 2:11. For a detailed discussion of this aspect of Elijah, and the distinction between Moses and Elijah, see *Sefer Halikkutim-Tzemach Tzedek, s.v.* Eliyahu, p. 1212*ff.*; and *ibid. s.v.* Mosheh, p. 1619*ff.* See also R. Mosheh Cordovero, *Pardes Rimonim* 24:13; and *Likkutei Sichot*, vol. II, pp. 458 and 516.]

redemption when "all flesh shall see..,"[78] that is, when the physical flesh shall be so purified that it will perceive Divinity.[79]

All this started when it was said, "Behold, I give unto him My covenant of peace."[80] As explained elsewhere, if not for various incidents, the Jewish people would have entered the Holy Land shortly after *matan Torah*[81] (led by Moses, and this would have been with permanence[82]). So, too, when the Almighty conferred the covenant of eternal priesthood upon Pinchas—"I give unto him My covenant of peace," there was the potential to enter the Land of Israel under the leadership of Joshua and that this be with permanence. There could have been a complete redemption, as indicated by the identification of Pinchas with Elijah, the harbinger of the redemption. Unfortunately, though, this was not merited, and instead thereof came all that happened to the point that "all the (indicated) times (for the redemption) have already passed."[83] Now, however, very speedily, the prophet Elijah will come with the

---

78. [Isaiah 40:5]

79. [See *Tanya*, ch. 36; and above, Yud-Bet Yud-Gimel Tamuz, end of sect. XXVIII, and note 151 there.]

80. [Numbers 25:12]

81. [See *Sifre*, Beha'alotecha, sect. 82; and *ibid.*, Devarim, sect. 2; and parallel passages. *Midrash Hagadol*, and Rashi, on Deuteronomy 1:2.]

82. [If Moses had entered the Holy Land and built the *Bet Hamikdash*, this would have been with permanence: the *Bet Hamikdash* would never have been destroyed. See *Or Hachayim* on Deuteronomy 1:37 and 3:25, referring to *Sotah* 9a (and *cf. Pesikta Rabaty* 2:6 and *Midrash Tehilim* 62:4, that this would have been also if David had built the *Bet Hamikdash*); *Yalkut Re'uveni*, Va'etchanan (p. 26), citing *Megaleh Amukot*, ofan 187. This principle is explained at length in Chassidut; see R. Dov Ber of Lubavitch, *Sha'arei Teshuvah* II:p. 26a; and *Or Hatorah*, Va'etchanan, especially pp. 65*ff.* and 93*ff.*]

83. [*Sanhedrin* 97b; *Zohar* III:122a.]

glad tiding of the coming of our righteous Mashiach who will redeem us with the true and complete redemption.

F*

XIV. *Zohar, parshat Pinchas*,[84] states that Pinchas saw an "open *mem*"[85] floating in the air. He feared lest it combine with the letters *vav* and *tav*,[86] [the first two letters in the words] *vatikach* (and she took), *vatochal* (and she ate), *vatiten* (and she gave),[87] and *vatipakachnah* (and they were opened)[88]—which brought about the opposite of life in every sense.[89] Pinchas therefore quickly attached the *mem* to himself, thereby bringing about "*romach* (a spear);" as it is said there that the numerical equivalent of the name Pinchas is the same as that of *Yitzchak* (Isaac), namely *reish-chet* (the Hebrew number for 208), and when adding the *mem* [to *reish-chet*] it spells *romach*. Thus it is said, "[Pinchas saw..] and took a *romach* (spear) in his hand."[90] With this *romach* he arrested the plague from striking the Israelites.[91] The 24,000 who died[92] were all of the children of the *erev rav*.[93]

---

84. *Zohar* III:237a [and see *Or Hachamah* there].
85. [The 'open *mem*' is the regular letter as opposed to the 'closed *mem*' or 'final *mem*' (closed off in all four sides, in the shape of a square) which appears only as the final letter of a word.]
86. [Thus spelling *mavet*—death.]
87. [Genesis 3:6, the three actions in the first sin of eating of the fruit of the Tree of Knowledge.]
88. ["The eyes of both were opened" (Genesis 3:7), resulting from that first sin.]
89. [Genesis 2:17. *Bereishit Rabba* 16:6; and *Pirkei deR. Eliezer*, ch. 14.]
90. [Numbers 25:7]
91. [Numbers 25:8]
92. [Numbers 25:9]
93. [The *erev rav* were "a mingling of various nations who

XV. The *Gemara*[94] states that "an 'open *mem*' denotes an open teaching, and a 'closed *mem*' denotes a closed teaching." The commentators explain that an "open teaching" refers to the revealed (exoteric) Torah, while a "closed teaching" refers to the hidden (esoteric) Torah.[95] That is why the verse *"Lemarbeh* (for the one that increases) the authority.."*[96] has a 'closed *mem*' where there should be an 'open *mem*';[97] for that verse speaks of the future to come[98] when one will perceive the "inner (esoteric) dimension" of that which is "manifest (exoteric)."[99] In the very place of the 'open *mem*' there is thus a 'closed *mem*', because one will see and understand the inner meaning of even the manifest aspect of the Torah.

The 'open *mem*' denotes the manifest Torah which expresses the very wisdom and will of the Almighty. "Torah is not subject to impurity, as it is written, 'Is not My word like unto fire..'[100]: just as fire does not incur

---

became proselytes" and ascended with Israel from Egypt (Exodus 12:38 and Rashi there; see also *Zohar* II:45b), and were forever a source of aggravation and trouble to Israel (see *Shemot Rabba* 42:6, cited by Rashi on Exodus 32:7; *Zohar* I:28b; *ibid*. II:45b and 120b). After they converted to Judaism they married women from the tribe of Shimon. The 24,000 who died in the plague were their children. (This passage in the *Zohar* thus supports the view of Rashi in his commentary on Numbers 26:13.)]

94. *Shabbat* 104a
95. [See Rashi there, *s.v.* ma'amar.]
96. Isaiah 9:6
97. [The *mem* in *lemarbeh* is in the middle of the word, thus should be an 'open *mem*,' but in fact is a 'closed *mem*.' See *Sanhedrin* 94a.]
98. [*Sanhedrin* 94a]
99. [*Eliyahu Zutta*, ch. 20; *Oti'ot deR. Akiva*, *s.v.* zayin. See Rashi on Song 1:2. Cf. *Vayikra Rabba* 13:3; *Kohelet Rabba* 11:8; and *Zohar* III:23a. *Likkutei Torah*, Tzav, p. 17a.]
100. [Jeremiah 23:29]

impurity, so words of Torah (including the exoteric Torah) do not incur impurity."[101] Nonetheless, the one who studies Torah improperly can come to harm. The Torah itself will not be affected, for the words of Torah cannot contract impurity; but this cannot be said of the one who studies it in a non-meritorious way, the one who fails to study it *lishmah* (for its own sake) and in order to observe it, as stated by our sages.[102]

This is the meaning of the fear "lest the 'open *mem*' floating in the atmosphere be joined to the *vav* and the *tav*." When the *mem* floats about in the atmosphere it is not bound up with any *hamshachah* (drawing forth) of supernal influence. As far as the Torah itself is concerned this does not matter, for the words of Torah do not contract impurity. The letter *vav* signifies 'drawing forth,' from above downwards. Texts of the Kabbalah[103] and Chassidut[104] explain that the very shape of the *vav*, a line going downwards, indicates *hamshachah*, drawing from above downwards. If the floating *mem*, therefore, were to join with a *vav*, and this unit is drawn downwards unto the letter *tav*, the consequences would be detrimental. For the *Gemara*[105] states that the letter *tav* denotes the two aspects of life and its opposite. Thus when the Torah is bound up with the *tav*, it becomes a "Tree of Good and

---

101. *Berachot* 22a
102. *Yoma* 72b [If one is meritorious, and uses the Torah the right way, it becomes for him an elixir of life; if one is not meritorious, then it becomes for him a deadly poison. See also *Yerushalmi, Berachot* 1:2 and *Vayikra Rabba* 35:8, with regards to "He who studies with the intention not to practice."]
103. [Cf. *Zohar* II:181a; *Zohar Chadash*, Bereishit:5c; and *Tikunei Zohar* 19:39a. *Pardes Rimonim* 27:9.]
104. [*Tanya*, Igeret Hateshuvah, ch. 4.]
105. *Shabbat* 55a

Evil," as stated in the *Zohar, parshat Nasso*[106] and explained in *Tanya*, Igeret Hakodesh, sect. XXVI.

To put all this more explicit: The *neshamah* descends into a physical body and an animal soul. (Rashbatz[107] would say of this: "*Chochmah ila'a* (Supreme *Chochmah* from Above) put into a pot of seething flesh and bones.") Man finds himself in a material condition, with an animal soul and a *yetzer hara* "who comes earlier to plead his cause;"[108] furthermore, there is also the "*derech eretz* of the world which precedes Torah."[109] When one sets out to study Torah in these conditions without doing anything about self-improvement, thus *lo zachah*, he did not *refine* himself[110] for the study of Torah, the Torah becomes for him the opposite of a life-giving substance, as stated by our sages.[111]

XVI.   This negative process begins, first and fore-

---

106. [*Zohar* III:124b]

107. [Acronym for R. Shemuel Betzalel Sheftel, a famed *chassid* of the *Tzemach Tzedek* and his successors, and teacher of the *Rebbe Rayatz* (R. Yosef Yitzchak). See *Hatamim* I:p. 67ff. for a short biography.]

108. [*Zohar* I:179b. The *yetzer hara* (evil inclination) precedes the *yetzer tov* (good inclination): the *yetzer hara* is born with man (see Genesis 8:21: "the *yetzer* of man's heart is evil from his youth;" Rashi: from the moment the fetus bestirs itself to leave the mother's womb, the *yetzer hara* is given to it), while the *yetzer hatov* enters only at the point of maturity (bat-mitzvah or bar-mitzvah). *Avot deR. Nathan* 16:2; *Kohelet Rabba* 4:13 and 9:15. See also *Sefer Halikkutim-Tzemach Tzedek*, s.v., yetzer tov-yetzer hara, p. 1271ff.; *Kuntres Uma'ayon* XIII:2; and below, Matot, notes 18-20.]

109. [*Vayikra Rabba* 9:3. *Derech eretz* (lit. the way of the land) may mean proper social conduct, or the necessary practice of working for a livelihood (as in *Avot* 2:2; see *Bartenura* there).]

110. [*Zachah*, to be worthy or meritorious, in the *pi'el*-form of *zikah* means to purify or refine. This word, therefore, referred to in the above quotation of *Yoma* 72b (note 102), has both meanings.]

111. [Above, note 102.]

most, from *vateireh* (she saw),[112] i.e., looking at things which one should not view. One may protest loudly, "I am only *looking*, thus not doing anything," and feel confident that this is altogether harmless. Yet this *vateireh* is followed immediately by *"vatikach* (and she took.. *vatochal* (and she ate)"—i.e., corrupting oneself.[113] In turn, this leads to *"vatiten* (and she gave)"—corrupting others as well.[114] The end was that *"vatipakachnah*—the eyes of both of them were opened and they realized that they were naked":[115] there is a realization that they lost even the one and only *mitzvah* they had, and thus they remained 'naked,' without any *mitzvot*.[116]

A great number of the 613 *mitzvot* relate to the *Bet Hamikdash* (Holy Temple). The *mitzvot* that we are still able to fulfill nowadays, therefore, are a small minority of the 613.[117] At the very least, then, we should be extra careful with those few *mitzvot* so as not to lose them, Heaven forbid.

If one does not want to become "'naked'—i.e., without *mitzvot*," it will just not do to guard oneself only against the *vatiten*, nor even against the *vatochal*. One must not allow even any *vateireh*. The *vateireh*, the mere look, is

---

the first step to descend and fall ever lower, Heaven forbid.[118]

One may argue: "I am a scholar! I have studied a lot of Torah! I have achieved my status by virtue of great personal effort and energy. Thus I can safely view whatever I want and it will not harm me." A person like that is answered: "Adam was created by the very hands of G-d, as it were, and Eve was formed from the ribs of Adam; nonetheless, even they were led ever further astray by the *vateireh.*"

There is a way to guard oneself against the "evil one who lurks for the righteous in order to slay him,"[119] a way to protect oneself against the *yetzer hara* who seeks out every device to achieve the nakedness from *mitzvot*: one must, as stated in the *Zohar* cited, encompass the 'open *mem*'—*nigleh* (the exoteric Torah)—with Isaac, for he represents the 'closed *mem*'[120] which signifies the "closed (i.e., concealed) teaching," i.e., *pnimiyut Hatorah.*

---

118. [See Numbers 15:39, "You shall not stray after your heart and after your eyes": for the heart and the eyes are the "spies of the body," the "agents for sin": the eye sees, the heart covets, and the body commits the sin. *Tanchuma*, Shlach:15; *Bamidbar Rabba* 17:6; cited by Rashi on this verse. See also *Sifre*, Shlach, sect. 115; and *Yerushalmi, Berachot* 1:5. Cf. *Tzava'at Harivash*, sect. 121, and my notes there. See above, note 113.]

119. [Psalms 37:32. *Sukah* 52b reads this as a reference to the *yetzer hara.*]

120. *Likkutei Torah Arizal*, Toldot [on Genesis 25:20], in context of *Eitz Chayim* 15:4ff.

MATOT   מטות

I. *Parshat Matot* discusses vows and the annulment of vows.[1] There are three forms of annulment: (a) release by an expert sage,[2] which has the effect of altogether dissolving the vow retroactively;[3] and (b) annulment by the father,[4] or (c) the husband,[5] both of which negate the vow as of the moment of nullification.[6]

In the case of a husband there are two possible situations: a) between the time of betrothal (*erusin*) and marriage (*nisu'in*); and b) *after* marriage. In both cases there is the prerogative to nullify the vow, but the laws relevant to the betrothed (*arus*) and the husband (*ba'al*) differ.

Offhand it would seem that the authority of the *ba'al* (husband) should be greater than that of the *arus* (betrothed). Nonetheless, in the context of nullifying vows we find that the law grants an advantage to the *arus* beyond that of the *ba'al*:

A husband (*ba'al*) cannot nullify any vows his wife made prior to the marriage.[7] The *arus*, however, can annul even vows made by his fiancee before the betrothal.[8]

---

1. [Numbers 30:3-17]
2. [Numbers 30:3, as interpreted in *Chagigah* 10a. See *Shulchan Aruch*, Yoreh De'ah 228:7; and *cf. ibid.* par. 26, and *Siftei Kohen* there.]
3. [*Ketuvot* 74b]
4. [Numbers 30:4-6. *Ketuvot* 46bf.]
5. [Numbers 30:7ff. *Ketuvot* 46b; *Nazir* 62b.]
6. [*Shulchan Aruch*, Yoreh De'ah 234:51]
7. *Nedarim* 67a. *Shulchan Aruch*, Yoreh De'ah 234:35 [and see there also par. 10].
8. *Nedarim* 67b. *Shulchan Aruch*, Yoreh De'ah 234:5.

This raises an obvious question: how can an *arus* have greater authority than the *ba'al*?

One of the answers explains this in context of the fact that the *arus* cannot annul the betrothed's vows on his own but only in conjunction with her father: "In the case of a betrothed maiden, her father and her betrothed (*arus*) annul her vows."[9] For the father, of course, there are no temporal restrictions about earlier vows. As he is now conjoined with the *arus*, the father's prerogative extends to the *arus* as well so that the latter, too, can annul the earlier vows.

A husband (*ba'al*), however, annuls on his own. The act of marriage negates the authority of the wife's father, and the husband becomes an authority on his own. The husband, therefore, is subject to the legal restrictions.[10]

II.   All this is relevant to man's spiritual reality.

The service of G-d entails two forms of *avodah*: the *avodah* of *erusin* (betrothal), and the *avodah* of *nisu'in* (marriage). The era of the *galut* is generally compared to *erusin* (the stage of betrothal), while the aspect of *nisu'in* (marriage) will be only in the future to come [in the Messianic age].[11] In a more specific way, however, even the period of the *galut* itself, too, comprises both stages of *erusin* and *nisu'in*.

Erusin signifies "forbidden to all the world,"[12] thus severed from the world. This level of *avodah* has not yet affected him to the point of "He shall cleave .. and they

------

9. *Nedarim* 66b

10. [See *Ran* and *Perush Harosh* on *Nedarim* 67b (raising this question and offering this answer).]

11. [*Shemot Rabba* 15:31]

12. [*Kidushin* 2b, and see there *Tossafot, s.v.* de'assar lah. When a man betrothes a woman she becomes forbidden to any other man ("all the world") for the duration of the betrothal and the subsequent marriage.]

shall become one,"[13] i.e., unification with G-dliness. Nonetheless, there is already a severance from worldliness.

The *avodah* of *nisu'in* signifies "they shall become one": to become unified with G-dliness. This unity is to achieve the purpose of *nisu'in*, i.e., to beget offspring of the same kind. To cite our sages: "What are the offspring of the righteous? Good deeds!"[14] In other words, man and all his actions become an instrument for G-dliness, an instrument that negates itself to, and unifies itself with, its essence and purpose.

III. The *avodah* of *nisu'in* transcends that of *erusin*. Even so, there is an advantage to the *avodah* of *erusin* beyond that of *nisu'in*.

One might think that having attained the *avodah* of *nisu'in* is an indication of having become a *tzadik gamur* (perfect saint), thus no longer in need of Divine assistance: he is now the "husband who can annul on his own, independent of the father."

In fact, however, this is not the case. Once upon a time there was an individual who made such a claim, and then they knew immediately that he was not "*Bar-kochba* —the son of the star, i.e., of 'a star steps out from Jacob'[15]," but "*Bar-koziba*—the son of falsehood."[16] In his case it was in context of physical warfare; how much more so in context of spiritual warfare!

---

13. Genesis 2:24

14. *Bereishit Rabba* 30:6 [and *Tanchuma*, No'ach:2], as cited by Rashi on Genesis 6:9.

15. [Numbers 24:17]

16. [Bar Kochba, who led a revolt against the Roman Empire after the destruction of the second *Bet Hamikdash*, was blessed with extra-ordinary strength. His strength and early successes led him to arrogant self-reliance to the point that when leading his soldiers to battle he would say: "Master of all worlds: do not help us, and also do not harm us!" (*Yerushalmi, Ta'anit* 4:5; *Eichah Rabba* 2:4—see ed. Buber

Here, then, is the advantage of an *arus*, of the *avodah* of *erusin* which goes beyond that of *nisu'in*. The *arus* on his own is inferior, but he has the advantage of being associated with the 'Father': he acts with the power of the Almighty. In this condition all restrictions are removed and one is able to reach goals which one could never attain on his own.

Tohu precedes *tikun*.[17] In *tohu* are rooted all physical entities[18] and the *yetzer hara*[19] who "comes first to plead his case."[20] Man's personal power is insufficient to annul "pre-nuptial vows." On one's own one cannot reach to the level of *tohu*, thus cannot refine those aspects which derive from *tohu*. On the other hand, when associated with the

---

there, note 55.) He proclaimed himself to be Mashiach (*Sanhedrin* 93b); and because of his unnatural strength many were inclined to accept him as such, taking this verse of Numbers 24:17 (which refers to Mashiach; see above, Yud-Bet Yud-Gimel Tamuz, beginning of sect. XXII, and note 69 there) as an allusion to Bar Kochba. Rabbi (R. Judah the Prince) therefore expounded that verse: "Do not read *kochav* (a star) but *kozav* (a lie; falsehood)." (*Yerushalmi* and *Eichah Rabba* there; and see *Eichah Rabba*, ed. Buber, there note 57*.]

17. [In the creative process we speak of two schemes. There is the original scheme of *tohu* (lit. unordered; 'chaotic'; Genesis 1:2) in which the *Sefirot* emanated "unordered" in the sense of not being inter-related, thus not interacting. The realm of *tohu* is that of the "primordial worlds" of which the Creator said "These do not please Me." The subsequent scheme of *tikun* (lit. correction; restitution) has the *Sefirot* inter-related, thus interacting: "new worlds" of which it is said, "G-d saw everything that he had made, and behold it was very good." (Genesis 1:31) *Bereishit Rabba* 3:7 and 9:12. *Tohu*, therefore, is "chaotic," while *tikun* is well-ordered and formed. For a detailed explanation of these terms and their implications, see *Mystical Concepts in Chassidism*, ch. IX.]

18. [See *Likkutei Torah*, Emor, p. 37cff.; and next note.]

19. [See *Sefer Halikkutim-Tzemach Tzedek*, s.v. yetzer tov—yetzer hara, p. 1268ff.; *Kitzurim Vehe'arot Letanya*, p. 48ff.]

20. [*Zohar* I:179b. See *Kuntres Uma'ayon* 13:2. See above, Pinchas, note 108.]

'Father' — the Almighty who is not restricted in terms of "before and after," of "*tohu* preceding *tikun*" — He enables even the *arus* to reach back into *tohu*. One is able to conquer the *yetzer hara* who had pre-declared his case by virtue of "the Holy One, blessed is He, helps him."[21] Thus he is able to sift and extract the sparks of *tohu* within physical entities.[22] This is the very concept of "annulling a vow": permission, and infusion of ability, to deal with the refinement and sublimation of material reality.[23]

IV.   The point of all this is as follows:

Man may attain very sublime levels. Indeed, he may have achieved even an *avodah* of *nisu'in*. Nonetheless, he must realize that one cannot proceed with no more than one's own strength. One must always be bound up with something higher, beyond oneself, because there remain ever higher goals which have not yet been attained and relative to which one is but at the very beginning of his *avodah*.

---

21. ["Were it not that the Holy One, blessed be He, helps him, one would not be able to withstand [the *yetzer hara*];" *Sukah* 52b.]

22. [All objects are sustained by "sparks" from the Divine emanations of *tohu*. When these objects are used in their Divinely intended context, these "sparks" are sifted out, extricated or freed, and material reality is sublimated to become absorbed in holiness—the ultimate purpose for their creation. See *Mystical Concepts in Chassidism*, ch. XI (especially p. 156*ff.*); and *L.S.-Vayikra*, p. 53, note 34.]

23. [In the Halachic context of vows, the husband (*arus* and *ba'al*) can annul in a permanently effective way only vows which involve self-denial of physical benefits ("every vow and every binding oath to *afflict the person*;" Numbers 30:14, and see Rashi there). *Nedarim* 79a-b; *Shulchan Aruch*, Yoreh De'ah 234:55*ff.* The annulment thus permits the woman to benefit again from the relevant materials or activities. In the spiritual dimension, therefore, the concept of "annulment of vows" implies permission—and ability—to refine and sublimate material substances. *Cf.* also *Sefer Halikkutim-Tzemach Tzedek, s.v.* nedarim, p. 44*ff.*]

When bound to that which is higher, when aware that one has not yet completed his task in terms of the ever more sublime goals, the Father will draw to Himself even the *arus*, to the point that the *arus*, too, is no longer restricted and thus able to annul "pre-nuptial vows."

MASSEY   מסעי

A

I.   *Parshat Massey* starts with the verse, "These are *massey* (the journeys) of the children of Israel *asher* left from the land of Egypt.. "[1]

The word *massey* is in plural form, indicating that there were numerous journeys by means of which the Israelites left Egypt. This raises an obvious question: there was but one journey to go out of the land of Egypt itself, namely from Rameses to Sukot.[2] All the other journeys were after the Israelites had already left Egypt. Why, then, the plural form of *massey*?

Moreover, what is the significance of there being 42 journeys between leaving Egypt and arriving in the Land of Israel, the "good and spacious land"[3]? *Mitzrayim* (Egypt) is an idiom of (and signifies) *meytzarim ugevulim*, restrictions and boundaries.[4] With the very first journey

---

1.   [Numbers 33:1. The word *asher* may refer to the Israelites, thus "*who* left;" or it may refer to the journeys, thus "*which* they left from the land of Egypt." The *sichah* takes the second meaning, thus raising the questions following.]

2.   [Numbers 33:5. Exodus 12:37, and see there Rashi (citing *Mechilta*, Bo, Pis'cha: ch. 14) that Sukot is 120 miles beyond Rameses (other versions, cited in the notes on *Mechilta*, ed. Horovitz, p. 47, suggest a still greater distance).]

3.   [Exodus 3:8. See *Lekach Tov*, and *Midrash Hagadol*, on this verse for the significance of the adjectives "good" and "spacious." Cf. *Torah Or*, Tetzaveh, p. 84c.]

4.   [See *Torah Or*, Va'eira, p. 57c; *Likkutei Torah*, Shlach, p. 48c. Cf. *Likkutei Torah-Arizal*, Vayeishev (p. 101a); and *Sha'ar Hapessukim*, Vayeishev (p. 89b).]

taking them out of *Mitzrayim* (Egypt), therefore, there is already a condition of *merchav* (spaciousness; expansiveness): to leave *meytzar* (restriction) implies of itself to come into a state of expansiveness. What, then, did the 42 journeys add to the principle of 'expansiveness'?

The concepts of *meytzarim* and *merchav*, however, are both subject to numerous levels and gradations. A certain situation may be *merchav* (expansiveness) relative to a particular kind of restriction, yet remain *meytzarim* (confining restraints) relative to higher levels. True *merchav* is attained only after the last journey, when arriving at *Yarden Yericho* (the Jordan near Jericho)[5]—which refers to Mashiach of whom it is said that *mari'ach veda'in* ("he smells and then judges").[6] Until that time, however, all attainments are conditions of *merchav* only relative to lower levels, but they remain states of *meytzarim* relative to higher levels.

This, then, is the meaning of the 42 journeys from *Mitzrayim* (Egypt) until the "good and expansive land." The first journey removed them from *Mitzrayim*, thus of itself into *merchav*; but this was merely a relative *merchav*. In terms of higher levels it remained a state of *Mitzrayim*. Thus there was need for a further journey to leave that state of *Mitzrayim* as well; and so forth. This explains why

---

5. [Numbers 33:48]

6. [The name *Yericho* is derived from *rei'ach* (smell), because of the pleasant smell from the balsam-trees growing in that city (Rashi on II Kings 20:13 and Ezekiel 27:17). The sense of smell is specifically associated with Mashiach, of whom it is said, *'veharicho* in the fear of G-d" (Isaiah 11:3): Raba said, that Mashiach 'smells' a person and judges him, as it is written (Isaiah 11:3-4), "*Vaharicho* in the fear of G-d, and he will not judge with the sight of his eyes, nor reprove after the hearing of his ears, yet shall judge the poor with righteousness." *Sanhedrin* 93b. See *Likkutei Torah, Massey,* p. 89b. *Cf.* also *Zohar* II:8b on the role of Jericho in the Messianic redemption.]

it is said, "These are *massey* (the journeys; in plural form) with which they left from the land of *Mitzrayim*." For every one of the journeys was a going forth from *meytzarim* until reaching *Yarden Yericho*, the ultimate ascent.[7]

II.   The Torah is timeless, relating to every single generation.[8] This applies especially to the concept of *yetzi'at Mitzrayim*, the exodus from Egypt, of which it is said that everyone must forever see himself as if he had personally left Egypt that very day.[9] Our text, therefore, provides a lesson for man's *avodah*. One may have achieved an *avodah* beyond his faculty of reason and intellect, beyond normative capacity and limitation, thus in effect "left the *Mitzrayim* of *kedushah* (the limitations of the realm of holiness)."[10] Nonetheless, this is not yet sufficient. Relative to higher levels it is still a state of *Mitzrayim*. Thus one must labor still more and continue to proceed ever further.

This concept is understood also from the *avodah* of prayer. *Tefilah* (prayer) signifies the *avodah* of man. Thus we distinguish between Torah and *tefilah*: Torah is "from above downward," while prayer is the *avodah* of man "from below upward"[11]—a "ladder standing in the earth and its top reaching into Heaven."[12] In prayer, therefore, one moves from a low level upward, leaving straits for expansion.

---

7.   *Likkutei Torah*, Massey, p. 89bff.

8.   [See above, Pinchas, note 54.]

9.   *Pesachim* 116b; *Tanya*, ch. 47.

10.   [See *Torah Or*, Shemot, p. 49d; and the sources cited above, note 4.]

11.   *Tanya*, Igeret Hateshuvah, ch. 10. See *Torah Or*, Bereishit, p. 1c; *Sefer Hama'amarim 5708*, p. 80.

12.   *Zohar* I:266b; *ibid.* III:306b; *Tikunei Zohar* 45:83a. [See "The Dynamics of Prayer," *Deep Calling Unto Deep*, ch. VI and XVf.]

In prayer itself there are a number of ascents. With each ascent one leaves the previous status. However, this is not sufficient. One must continue to ever greater heights.

The first step is the *preparation* for prayer. Man is finite. He is very much restricted, vested in a body and animal soul, and especially so when yet tarnished by sin. How, then, can man set out to pray, to approach the Almighty—the Infinite, who is beyond all and any restrictions? To do so, therefore, one must first free oneself from all personal matters, from self-consciousness, and only then set out to pray.[13]

The very act of "setting out" to pray (which precedes actual prayer, thus before starting to say *Hodu*, or even *Mah Tovu*), as by putting on a *gartel*[14] and readying himself, already implies stepping out of personal matters and becoming more refined. In other words, he is leaving his *meytzarim*, his restrictions and limitations.

(This explains the Halachic ruling that before prayer one is to discharge bodily wastes and wash the hands.[15]

---

13. [*Cf. Berachot* 30b; *ibid.* 31a and 32b. *Shulchan Aruch*, Orach Chayim 93. Note the interpretation of *Berachot* 8a in *Netivot Olam*, Avodah, ch. 5, cited in "The Dynamics of Prayer," note 61.]

14. [Before prayer one ought to girdle oneself with a *gartel*, a sash wound around the waist; *Shulchan Aruch*, Orach Chayim 91:2. Aside of the Halachic aspect of separating between the upper and lower halves of the body (see there, and in the commentaries, especially *Kaf Hachayim*, par. 4ff.), this is also an act of preparing for prayer in context of Amos 4:12, "Prepare towards (meeting) your G-d, O Israel" (*Shulchan Aruch*, there): girding the loins is an expression of quickening with strength (Rashi on II Kings 9:1 and Jeremiah 1:17). Thus girdling oneself with a *gartel* for prayer is an indication of special alertness for prayer (*Levush*, cited in *Kaf Hachayim*, there, par. 6).]

15. *Berachot* 15a [and 23a. *Shulchan Aruch*, Orach Chayim 92:1 and 4f.; in *Shulchan Aruch Harav*, 92:3-5.]

First one is to remove all external and inner wastes, and then wash the hands to remove impurity. Indeed, that impurity is merely external and transcendent to man's true being, without any concrete reality of its own;[16] nonetheless, it, too, must be removed prior to prayer.)

To attain this new status is not yet sufficient, and one must yet start to recite the actual prayers. This will take man beyond the state he reached by his preparation for prayer, for even that state is a form of restrictive limitation relative to the higher level following. Thus he must move even from that restriction to the status of a greater expanse.

Moreover, in the actual prayer itself there are numerous ascents, generally divided into four rungs.[17] (These ascents are by means of the Divine Name of *Mem-Bet*.[18])

---

16. *Cf.* Rambam, *Hilchot Mikva'ot* 1:12 [that the laws of purity and impurity are of the *mitzvot* classified as *chukim*, i.e., supra-rational principles: they are Divine decrees about which the human mind cannot form any judgments. Impurity is not some mud or filth which water can remove but a matter of Scriptural decree, subject to the intention of the heart]. See *Bamidbar Rabba* 19:1 [stating the same principle, and concluding that this matter is one of "I have legislated a statute (*chukah*), I have issued a decree! You are not permitted to transgress My decree!"] See also *Likkutei Torah*, Acharei, p. 29a [and see there also Tavo, p. 43c and Shir, p. 9c]. Impurity, therefore, is not something tangible: there is no waste which is empirically evident, and all that can be said about it is that "I have legislated a statute.."

17. *Sefer Hama'amarim 5708*, p. 80. [The "ladder of prayer" has four rungs (*cf. Moreh Nevuchim* II:10), corresponding to the ascending order of the four "Worlds" of *Asiyah, Yetzirah, Beri'ah* and *Atzilut*; see *Peri Eitz Chayim*, Sha'ar Hatefilah, ch. 1 and 4-6. For a detailed discussion of this principle, and how the order of prayer is divided into these four components, see "The Dynamics of Prayer," ch. XIV-XV.]

18. [See *Peri Eitz Chayim*, Sha'ar Hatefilah, ch. 15, and *ibid.*, Sha'ar Hakadeishim, ch. 1. *Cf. Eitz Chayim* 9:2.

The "Name of *Mem-Bet*," i.e., the Divine Name consisting of 42

Each of these rungs, however, is a restrictive limitation relative to the next, superior one.

The progression continues until one reaches the *Shemoneh Esrei*, the ultimate ascent: there is a total departure from one's own reality (whatever it may be, including the one that has been fully refined by his *avodah* on all preceding levels), and one stands in total self-negation like a slave before his master. There is no longer any personal reality, to the point that one says: "G-d, open my lips that my mouth may declare Your praise,"[19] i.e., may G-d open my lips and I will be no more than one who repeats what is said to him.[20]

III. This explains an apparent paradox in the *Shemoneh Esrei*: a) there is ultimate self-negation, and one is but like one who repeats after the reader; yet b) the *Shemoneh Esrei* contains requests for all one's needs, not only spiritual needs but also material needs! The sections preceding the *Shemoneh Esrei*—*Pessukei Dezimra*; the blessings for the reading of the *Shema*; and the *Shema* itself— do not contain any requests for material needs (for in

---

Letters (*Kidushin* 71a) is generally defined as the acronym of the 42 words in *Ana Beko'ach*, the prayer of R. Nechunyah ben Hakanah (*Tikunei Zohar* 4:19a; see also *Zohar* III:108b and *Tikunei Zohar* 21:50b). *Tossafot* on *Chagigah* 11b, *s.v.* ein dorshin, states that *Ma'aseh Bereishit* (The Work of Creation) refers to this Name which emerges from the 28 letters of the first verse of the Torah and the first 14 letters of the second verse (*cf. Tikunei Zohar*, Introduction:13a, and *ibid.* 4:19a. For a detailed explanation see *Pardes Rimonim* 21: ch.12-13). The 42 journeys correspond to this Name of "42 Letters" (*Likkutei Torah-Arizal*, Massey), to subdue the forces of evil and impurity (*Likkutei Torah*, Massey, pp. 88d and 91b; and see *Sefer Halikkutim-Tzemach Tzedek*, *s.v.* Mem-Bet, p. 6-9).]

19. Psalms 51:17

20. See commentary of R. Mosheh Alsheich on this verse; *Likkutei Torah*, Shir, p. 2c; and *Torat Shemuel 5627*, p. 436.

those stages one is not concerned with self, as stated above). The *Shemoneh Esrei* itself, however, does contain such requests!

This paradox can be resolved as follows:

By virtue of the fact that the *Shemoneh Esrei* signifies the ultimate ascent, it is able to absorb two contraries. Thus it was explained in the *ma'amar** that the higher and more sublime levels can compound proportionally greater absorptions.[21] This reflects somewhat the future manifestations, when "All *flesh* shall see..;"[22] that is, even the physical flesh will then sense the manifestation of Divinity,[23] thus in effect compounding two contraries.

IV. The *Shemoneh Esrei* signifies the ultimate ascent, yet the very next day one must again set out to pray. One must again start with the preparation for prayer, then recite *Hodu*, the *Pessukei Dezimra* and so forth. For regardless how lofty the level attained yesterday, it is still restricted in terms of what one is to attain today.

This facet of the *avodah* of prayer applies also to man's general *avodah*. A human being must forever move, progress.[24] One may have departed fully from evil and

---

* [Discourse delivered prior to this *sichah*.]

21. [See *Sefer Halikkutim-Tzemach Tzedek, s.v.* hitkalelut, p. 386*ff*.]

22. [Isaiah 40:5]

23. [See *Tanya*, ch. 36; and above Yud-Bet Yud-Gimel Tamuz, end of sect. XXVIII.]

24. ["I will give you *mehalchim* (lit., goers) among these *omdim* (that stand);" Zechariah 3:7. This verse contrasts man and angels. Angels are called *omdim* (Isaiah 6:2), while man is called a *mehalech*— one that goes, moves onwards, proceeds further. Angels are essentially static: they remain in their qualitative levels. Man, on the other hand, has the ability to improve, to enhance himself dramatically, progressing and ascending ever further. See *Chomat Anoch* on Zechariah 3:7; *Torah Or*, Vayeishev, p. 30*aff.*; *Likkutei Torah*, Bechukotai, p. 45a; and *Sefer Halikkutim-Tzemach Tzedek, s.v.* malachim, p. 468*ff*. See also *Tanya*, Introduction to part II (p. 76a, column 2); and below, sect. VIII.]

attained a most sublime level, yet one must remain aware
that all that is not enough. Relative to higher levels there
remains some connection to evil.

(One can prove this to oneself by the fact of detecting
some evil in another. In this context there is a well-known
teaching of the Baal Shem Tov: to note evil in another is
evidence that this same evil is present within oneself as
well, at the very least in some subtle fashion.[25])

It is imperative that one depart from that evil as well.
One must forever work on purifying one's physical reality.
This does not mean that one is to crush it, by means of
fasts and self-mortification, but to refine it, as known from
the Baal Shem Tov's interpretation of the verse "When you
see the donkey of your enemy.."[26] Immediately upon rising in the morning one is to harness his *chamor* (donkey),
i.e., his *chomer* (matter; material reality).[27] This is the very
way of attaining the manifestation of the future era when
"All flesh shall see..," i.e., that the physical substance will
be refined and purified to the point of itself actually *seeing*
Divinity.[28]

V.   One might argue: "I have already worked so
hard on myself that I rid myself of all blatant and crude
evil. I have already reached a high level. Who says that I
must toil further? I am quite satisfied with the level I
attained."

A person like this is told that the task and purpose of
man is to be a *mehalech*, one that keeps going and progressing, and not to be an *omed*, one that remains stand-

---

25. [*Keter Shem Tov*, sect. 89, 116, and 363; *ibid.*, Hossafot, par.
152, and see there notes 160-163 (explaining the Baal Shem Tov's principle that looking at someone else is like looking into a mirror).]

26. Exodus 23:5. See above, Shavu'ot, note 106.

27. [*Chamor* (donkey) and *chomer* (matter) are etymologically
related.; see reference in preceding note.]

28. [See above, notes 22-23.]

ing, static. Each day that he is granted by G-d, man must carry out his purpose in life, as it is written, "Days were fashioned, and *lo echad* in them."[29]

This, then, is the lesson from the journeys enumerated in this *parshah*. One must never be satisfied with whatever has been achieved.

VI. The theme of the "journeys" teaches another lesson, from a different perspective.

Man may find himself most unworthy, on the very lowest level. Even so he should not despair. It is always

---

29. Psalms 139:16.

["Days were fashioned" refers to the days allotted to man, his lifespan. The word *velo* is written with an *aleph* (thus meaning "and there is not"), but read as if written with a *vav* (thus meaning "and to him"). Both versions relate to the earlier phrase:

Man is allotted a certain amount of days to be used for the realization of his purpose in life — to acknowledge and establish *echad*, the absolute unity of G-d, "G-d is *echad* — one" (Deuteronomy 6:4). The word *echad* has 3 letters which (like all letters) also represent numbers: *aleph* (1) — signifying the One *Aluph* (Master) of the universe, supreme over *chet* (8) — the 7 heavens above and the earth below, and *dalet* (4) — in all 4 directions of east, west, north and south. (*Berachot* 13b; *Shulchan Aruch*, Orach Chayim 61:6).

The days of man's lifespan are regarded as potential "garments" for his soul: properly utilized they garb the soul; neglected or misused they leave the soul naked. (See *Zohar* I:224a — in context of our prooftext; and *ibid.* 129a. See at length the *ma'amar* "*Ve-Avraham Zaken Ba Bayamim 5738*, appended to *Tzava'at Harivash*, and the sources cited there).

The two versions of *lo* are now understood: when man wastes time and does not use every day for Torah and *mitzvot*, then "Days were fashioned but *lo* (with an *aleph*) — there is no *echad* in them" (see *Likkutei Torah*, Shlach, p. 51c). When man utilizes his time as intended, then "Days were fashioned and *lo* (with a *vav*) — he has *echad* in them" (see *Sefer Hama'amarim-Yiddish*, p. 82). See also *Likkutei Sichot*, vol. XXIII, pp. 419 and 457; and —] *Tehilim Yohel Or* on this verses, citing relevant sources.

possible to leave the present state and attain the highest levels.

One must never think that the lowly state detected within oneself renders all efforts futile. The theme of the "journeys" teaches us that a single journey removes from *Mitzrayim* (Egypt) and leads to a "good and expansive land" (i.e., good and expansive relative to one's present status, and even thereafter to progress ever further—to the ultimate elevation).

The Israelites in Egypt had been altogether submerged in the "49 gates of defilement."[30] Moreover, their stay in Egypt was prior to the giving of the Torah, thus in a time when any joining of "Rome" and "Syria" was precluded.[31] Nonetheless, the journeys led them to the "good and expansive land."

------

30. *Zohar Chadash*, Yitro:31a [translated in *Haggadah for Pesach*, ed. Kehot, p. 20].

31. *Shemot Rabba* 12:3.

[When G-d created the universe, He decreed that "The Heavens are the heavens of G-d, but the earth He has given to mankind" (Psalms 115:16); the upper realms were for the upper (spiritual) beings, and the lower realms for the lower beings (*Devarim Rabba* 10:2): "the 'citizens of Rome' must not descend to 'Syria,' and the 'citizens of Syria' must not ascend to 'Rome.'" There was a radical division between Heaven and earth, between spiritual reality and physical reality. This had practical implications for the observance of *mitzvot*. *Mitzvot* could be—and were—performed even then (see *Yoma* 28b; *Kidushin* 82a; and *Vayikra Rabba* 2:10) with physical objects or in physical contexts; but the *matter* involved was unaffected by these *mitzvot* and was not transformed into sacred objects: the *mitzvah* was a purely spiritual affair, and the physical entities remained in their original state of physicality. *Matan Torah* changed this:

"When [G-d] was about to give the Torah, He rescinded the original decree and said, 'Those who are below shall ascend to those on high, while those who are on high shall descend to those that are below." (*Shemot Rabba* 12:3) *Matan Torah* thus removed the original dichotomy and bridged the gulf between spirit and matter. As of then,

How much more so, then, nowadays. Regardless how low one may have fallen, the present *avodah* is altogether much easier. For presently there remain but "small flasks."[32] Moreover, by virtue of the giving of the Torah we are endowed with special abilities. *Matan Torah* nullified the decree which precluded the joining of "Rome" and "Syria", thus allowing a union of those above with those below. Also, there is the factor of a bond between a *Rebbe* and Chassidim, i.e., that the *Rebbe*, my father in-law, joins the individual Jew with the Divine Essence.[33] Every Jew, therefore, is able to leave his status and attain the "good and expansive land," up to the ultimate expanse of *Yarden Yericho*, the revelation of Mashiach who is *mari'ach veda'in*.[34]

VII. In this context we can understand why the *parshiyot* of *Matot* and *Massey* are scheduled to be read invariably in the period of *beyn hametzarim*.[35]

There is a concept of "demolishing in order to rebuild,"[36] i.e., that the act of demolishing is a means

---

the spiritual and the physical can interact: the spiritual can penetrate the physical and sublimate it to holiness and spirituality. See *L.S.-Bereishit*, Chaye Sarah, sect. XVI; *ibid.*, Vayeitze, sect. XII, and Vayishlach, sect. XI; *L.S.-Vayikra*, pp. 141f. and 193f.; and *cf.* above, Shavu'ot, sect. III.]

32. [In a paraphrase of *Chulin* 91a (cited by Rashi on Genesis 32:24) — that Jacob went back to salvage some small flasks, the last stage of the *galut* is seen as a time in which but a few minor things ("small flasks") remain to be rectified and restored to holiness, after which the Messianic redemption will occur. *Cf. L.S.-Bereishit*, Vayigash, sect. VIII and note 13 there.]

33. [This principle is explained in detail in "The Concept of the *Rebbe-Tzadik* in Chassidism," *Chassidic Dimensions*, ch. V-VIII.]

34. See above, note 6.

35. [For this term and its meaning see above, Yud-Bet Yud-Gimel Tamuz, note 57.]

36. [*Shabbat* 31b]

toward the end of establishing a better and greater building. The Baal Shem Tov thus interprets the verse, "It is a
time of *tzarah* (trouble; straits) for Jacob, but he shall be
delivered *mimena* (from it)":[37] delivery and salvation is
attained *mimena*, by way and means of the "time of *tzarah*"
itself.[38] This, too, signifies the absorption of two contraries.

That is why the *parshiyot* of *Matot* and *Massey* are read
in this time of the year. *Matot* signifies *hitkalelut*, a unifying
absorption.[39] *Massey* signifies going out from *beyn hametzarim*, the restrictive straits, never to be overwhelmed in
any sense by whatever the present status may be. In fact,
through the *tzarah* (straits; trouble) itself there is the delivery to reach *Yarden Yericho*.

This is also the reason why the fifth month is called
Menachem-Av, an expression of *nechamah* (consolation).[40]

---

37. Jeremiah 30:7
38. *Keter Shem Tov*, Hossafot, par. 8-9.
39. [See *Likkutei Torah*, Matot, p. 85d*ff.*, the *ma'amar* "*Heichaltzu*,"
and note there especially pp. 86d and 88a-b. The emphasis is on the
word *heichaltzu*—arm yourselves (Numbers 31:1), which implies "*all of
you*," signifying an all-comprehensive absorption and unity. The Torah
speaks there of the battle to be waged against Midian. The term
Midian is an idiom of *madon*—strife and contention (see *Zohar* II:68a).
Midian thus signifies divisiveness, disunity, the very principle of baseless hatred which underlies the whole realm of impurity, as opposed to
kedushah (holiness) which signifies unity (*cf. Zohar* III:16b). The cited
ma'amar discusses this in context of the destruction of the *Bet
Hamikdash* which was caused by baseless hatred (*Yoma* 9b). The *hitkalelut* or *achdut* of *ahavat Yisrael* rectifies the cause of the negative manifestations of the period of *beyn hametzarim*, thus bringing about the
Messianic redemption. See above, Yud-Bet Yud-Gimel Tamuz, sect. XX,
and the notes there.]
40. [The actual name of the month is *Av*, but traditionally it is
mostly referred to as *Menachem Av* (signifying consolation of the
Father) as a prayerful expression in anticipation of being consoled by
our Father in Heaven from the tragic events that occurred in that
month. *Cf. Aruch Hashulchan*, Even Ha'ezer 126:16.]

For ultimately everything is for good,[41] as explained by the example of a father who disciplines his child because of his concern for the welfare of the child.[42] Contemplation on this fact leads to a recognition of the ultimate good. Moreover, one will recognize it not only on the abstract, mental level, but actually come to sense it, to see it with the physical eye. One will actually experience the good in a truly manifest way, as was the case with those who reached the level of saying "This, too, is for good,"[43] and "Whatever the All-Merciful does is for good."[44]

To be sure, there is need for "G-d shall wash the filth off the daughters of Zion..,"[45] as this concept is explained in *Tanya*[46] by means of the simile of a great and awesome king who personally washes the filth from his only child. This itself, however, is done with kindness and compassion (that is, aside of the fact that the cleansing itself is for good, the afflictions effecting this cleansing will also be with kindness and compassion). This is implied by the wording in *Tanya*, "his father who is compassionate, righteous and merciful," signifying that the afflictions will be with kindness and compassion. Most important of all, however, is that ultimately it will be perceived to be visible and manifest goodness, that the *tzarah* (trouble) itself will become *tzohar*, brilliant brightness.[47]

---

41. [See *Bereishit Rabba* 51:3, and the commentary *Yefeh To'ar* there; *Moreh Nevuchim* III:12; *Tzava'at Harivash*, sect. 130, and the notes there; and *L.S.-Vayikra*, Bechukotai, sect. V-VIII. Cf. also *Bereishit Rabba* ch. 9; and see the next two notes.]

42. [Deuteronomy 8:5; Proverbs 3:12.]

43. *Ta'anit* 21a

44. *Berachot* 60b. *Shulchan Aruch*, Orach Chayim 230:5. [On the distinction between these two expressions see *Keter Shem Tov*, sect. 33.]

45. Isaiah 4:4

46. *Tanya*, Igeret Hakodesh, sect. XXII-a.

47. [See note 38; and *Keter Shem Tov*, sect. 33.]

B*

VIII.   The journeys enumerated in this *parshah*, from the time of leaving Egypt until reaching *Yarden Yericho*, signify all the stages that Israelites must pass through until the coming of Mashiach.

Thus it is said in the works of the Kabbalah, and in a teaching of the Baal Shem Tov,[48] that he who understands the meaning of the journeys will know the particular "journey" of his present stage as well as all that still lies before him, i.e., how many and which journeys he still needs to travel until the coming of Mashiach.

Generally speaking,[49] all these journeys are an order of ascents. "These are the journeys of the children of Israel leaving the land of Egypt" refers to journeys in the plural form, notwithstanding the fact that there was but a single journey that took them out of Egypt; but every journey signifies a going out from the *Mitzrayim* (restriction and limitation) of that moment and stage to the expanse relative to that moment and stage.

There are numerous levels and stages. Something may be a "good and expansive land" relative to a lower level, but it would still be *Mitzrayim* relative to higher levels. The "journeys" thus teach us that one must incessantly move on and progress, regardless of past achievements. There must be a continual move from *Mitzrayim* to a "good and expansive land," at the very least in terms of one's current status. This implies a non-gradual progression.

---

48. *Degel Machaneh Ephrayim*, Massey. [See *Keter Shem Tov*, Hossafot, par. 23, and note 21 there; and *Sefer Ba'al Shem Tov*, Massey.]

49. [The remainder of this *sichah* is essentially a brief restatement of the basic theme of the preceding *sichah*. See there for relevant notes and explanations.]

Angels are referred to as *omdim* (standing; static),[50] because their ascents are strictly gradual. Souls that descend to this world, however, are *mehalchim* (going; moving).[51] For souls are able to bypass a gradual order. With a single journey they can instantaneously leave *Mitzrayim* — *meytzarim ugevulim* (restrictions and limitations) — into a "good and expansive land." This would be an ascent from "limited" to "unlimited."

Even so, one is not to suffice with that singular departure from *Mitzrayim*. One must forever progress further in awareness of the fact that whatever stage has been attained remains a form of *Mitzrayim*, restrictive limitation, relative to higher levels. Thus one must continue onwards until reaching *Yarden Yericho*, the coming of Mashiach who is referred to as *mari'ach veda'in*, speedily in our very own days.

---

50. [Isaiah 6:2, and Zechariah 3:7. See next note.]
51. [Zechariah 3:7. See above, note 24.]

GLOSSARY

GLOSSARY

1. The Glossary is restricted to Hebrew and Yiddish words and terms that appear in the *sichot* and have generally not been translated.

2. The reader is advised to also consult the index to find these words and terms in the text, as the various contexts may offer further clarification.*

3. Where the Glossary cannot do proper justice to technical terms, it includes references to accessible sources which offer fuller explanations.

Acharon shel Pessach—Last day of *Pessach*.

Adar—Twelfth month in the Jewish calendar. In a leap-year an extra month is intercalated after *Shvat* (the eleventh month) and is called *Adar Rishon* (the first *Adar*), immediately followed by *Adar Sheni (the Second Adar)*; *Adar Sheni* is then the regular or principal *Adar* for purposes of observing *Purim* and other special occasions related to that month. See s.v. *Purim Katan*.

Agadah—The sections of Rabbinic literature which contain homiletical expositions of the Bible, prayers, stories, maxims, etc., in contradistinction to *Halachah*.

Ahavah—Love.

Ahavat Yisrael—'Love of Israel,' as enjoined by the Biblical precept 'Love your fellow-man like yourself' (Leviticus 19:18).

Akeidah—'Binding (the Sacrifice)'; the story of the attempted sacrifice of Isaac on Mount Moriah (Genesis, ch. 22).

Aleph Bet—the Hebrew alphabet.

Aliyah, *pl.* **Aliyot**—'Ascent'; being

called up to partake in the communal reading of the Torah.

Alter Rebbe—'Elder *Rebbe*': R. Shneur Zalman of Liadi (1745-1813), founder of *Chabad* Chassidism and author of *Tanya* and *Shulchan Aruch*. The term signifies the 'first *Rebbe*' of *Chabad*.

Amalek—Nation descended from Esau; signifies the very essence of evil, and opposition to G-dliness and the people of Israel (see Exodus 17:14-16 and Deuteronomy 25:17-19).

Amora, *pl.* **Amoraim**—'Interpreter(s);' rabbinic authorities of the *Gemara*, in contradistinction to *Tannaim*.

Ari—Acronym for 'Adoneinu (our master) R. Isaac,' i.e., R. Isaac Luria (1534-1572), founder of the Kabbalistic school in Safed which became the dominant system in Jewish mysticism and constitutes the theoretical basis of Chassidic thought.

Asarah Maamarot—The Ten Utterances, Fiats, or Sayings. Term designating the ten Divine utterances in the first chapter of Genesis ('Let there be..'), by means of which everything was created.

Aseret Hadibrot—The Ten Sayings or Statements. Term designating the Ten Commandments publicly proclaimed by G-d at Mount Sinai.

Asiyah—'[World of] Action'; lowest of the Four Worlds, the final level in the creative process which includes the physical universe. See *Worlds*.

Av—Fifth month in the Jewish calendar, also referred to as *Menachem Av*.

Avodah—Service or Worship of G-d in general, and often relating particularly to prayer.

Avot—'Fathers.' Title of tractate in *Mishnah (s.v.)* See below, *Pirkei Avot*.

Ba'al Hahilula—Master, or Subject of the Feast; generally referring to one whose *yahrzeit (s.v.)* or special festive event is observed. See below s.v. *Hilulah*.

Baal Shem Tov—Master of the Good Name: R. Israel Baal Shem Tov (1698-1760), founder of the Chassidic movement.

Baal Teshuvah, *pl.* **Baalei Teshuvah** —One who returns to G-d; a penitent who returns to the Torah way of life after having been astray. See *Teshuvah*.

Ban—'52'; a short form signifying one form of the Ineffable Name *Havayah*, when each of its letters is spelled phonetically like this: יו"ד ה"ה ו"ו ה"ה—as the numerical equivalent of all these letters is

52. This name relates to the pristine immanence of G-d which has its source in the Name *Mah*.

Bar Mitzvah—'Son of the Commandment'; term relating to boy's attainment of religious maturity at thirteenth birthday.

Becheyn—Therefore; term relating to practical implication of subject under discussion. (See *L.S.*, vol. I: pp. XIV and 195).

Beka—Half a *Shekel*.

Beriah—[World of] Creation; second of the Four Worlds, essentially spiritual though much less so than *Atzilut*. See *Worlds*.

Berit—Covenant

Berit Milah—Covenant of Circumcision

Bet Din—Court of Justice; Rabbinic Tribunal for legal decisions.

Bet Haknesset—Synagogue; generally used exclusively for purposes of worship.

Bet Hamidrash—House of Learning; assembly-hall essentially for Torah-study.

Bet Hamikdash — House of the Sanctuary, or Holy Temple, on the Temple Mount in Jerusalem.

Beyn Hametzarim—'Between the Straits;' term for the three-weeks-period between the fasts of the 17th of Tamuz and the 9th of Av, commemorating and mourning the destruction and loss of Jerusalem and the *Bet Hamikdash*.

Binah—Understanding; in Kabbalistic-Chassidic terminology generally referring to one of the Ten *Sefirot*, or the corresponding soul-power in man. See *Chabad*.

Birur, pl. **Birurim**—Refinement; in Kabbalistic-Chassidic terminology referring to the refinement of the material world in general, and of all its individual parts and aspects in particular, by using them or relating to them in their divinely intended context. See *Mystical Concepts in Chassidism*, ch. XI.

Bitul; Bitul Hayesh—Self-negation; concept of man's self-negation to the point of recognizing that G-d is the sole true reality.

Bnei Noach—'Children of Noah.' Term generally referring to mankind at large (as all are descended of Noah); specifically distinguishing between mankind at large and *bnei Yisrael* (the children of Israel), especially in the context of their differing legal and moral codes. (See L.S., vol. II: p. 53, note *xvi*.)

Chabad—Acronym for *Chochmah, Binah, Da'at*.

(a) The three 'intellectual' *Sefirot*, and correspondingly the three intellectual soul-powers or faculties in man: *Chochmah*—conceptual knowledge; *Binah*—the comprehensive understanding or externalization of the subject matter perceived on the conceptual level of *Chochmah*; and *Da'at*—fully sensing or absorbing the knowledge understood, to the point of being affected by it. See *Mystical Concepts in Chasidism*, ch. 111, section 4.

(b) Name of the Chassidic movement or school founded by R. Shneur Zalman of Liadi [*Chabad* Chassidism], because of its predominant emphasis on the need to develop these intellectual faculties .

Chametz—Leavened bread or substances, altogether prohibited to be enjoyed or even possessed on *Pessach* .

Chanukah—Festival of Dedication, commemorating the re-dedication of *the* Sanctuary by the Hasmoneans; celebrated for eight days starting the 25th of *Kislev.*

Chassid—Pious or Saintly Person, designating a person who goes beyond the minimum requirements of the law. Colloquially a follower of the Chassidic movement.

Chassidut—The teachings or philosophy of the Chassidic movement.

Chayah—Second highest of the five levels of the soul. See *Nefesh-Ruach-Neshamah.*

Chazakah—Supposition; legal term denoting an accepted supposition in a legal disputation, or a presumptive title of possession.

Cheder—Room. Colloquialism for Jewish elementary school.

Chessed— Kindness; Benevolence. One of the *Sefirot,* designating the Divine attribute of Kindness and Benevolence.

Chet—Eighth letter in the Hebrew alphabet .

Chinuch—Consecration; mostly referring to education. *Chinuch hakasher* thus means proper education as dictated by Torah-law and tradition.

Chitat—Acronym for *Chumash-Tehillim-Tanya*, referring specifically to the daily study and recitation of these three texts as instituted by the leaders of *Chabad.*

Chochmah—Wisdom; Conceptual Knowledge. In Kabblistic-Chassidic terminology generally referring to one of the ten *Sefirot*, or to the correspondin soulpower in man. See *Chabad*.

Choshen Mishpat—Fourth part of *Shulchan Aruch*, dealing specifically with the laws relating to religious judges, courts, courtproceedings, and Jewish civil law.

Chumash—Pentateuch. The Five Books of Moses.

Churban—Destruction. Term generally referring to the destruction of the *Bet Hamikdash (s.v.)*.

Da'at—Knowledge; in Kabbalistic-Chassidic terminology generally referring to one of the ten *Sefirot*, or to the corresponding soul power in man. See *Chabad*.

Daven(ing)—Yiddish colloquialism for pray(ing).

De'orayta—'Of the Torah;' Biblical ordinance, as opposed to *derabanan* (Rabbinic ordinance).

Derabanan—'Rabbinic;' ordained or instituted by rabbinic decree, as opposed to *de'orayta* (Biblical decree).

Derush—Homiletics; the homiletical interpretation or dimension of the Torah. See *Pardes*.

Devekut—Principle of cleaving, or attaching oneself to Divinity.

Dirah Betachtonim—'An Abode in the lower worlds;' oft-cited Midrashic principle that G-d created the world for the purpose of having 'an Abode in this lowly world.' This is achieved by the sanctification and sublimation of the mundane by means of Torah and *mitzvot*.

Dov Ber of Lubavitch, R.—See *Mitteler Rebbe*.

Dov Ber of Mezhirech, R.—See *Maggid*.

Elokim—One of G-d's sacred Names, specifically relating to the Divine attribute of Justice and the Divine manifestation in nature. (See L.S., vol. I: p. 54; II: p. 83; III: p. 5, notes 15 and 17.)

Emunah—Faith.

En Sof—Without Limit; term denoting G-d the Infinite, unknowable and undefineable. See *Mystical Concepts in Chassidism*, ch. II.

Farbrengen—Chassidic gathering at which the *Rebbe* delivers *Maamarim* and *Sichot;* also gatherings at which Chassidim discuss *Chassidut*, recount Chassidic tales and exchange moral exhortations.

Galut—Exile; Diaspora. Generally the Jewish people's state of exile.

Gan Eden—Garden of Eden.

Gemara—The Talmudic traditions, discussions and rulings of the *Amoraim*, based mainly on the *Mishnah*, and forming the bulk of the Babylonian Talmud and Jerusalem Talmud.

Gemilut Chassadim—Performance of Kindness; extending charity and kindness by word and deed.

Ge'ulah—Redemption. Generally designating the Messianic redemption, but appears also qualified as, e.g., the *'ge'ulah* from Egypt,' etc.

Gevurah—Might. One of the *Sefirot*, designating the Divine attribute of Law and Justice, in contradistinction to *Chessed (s.v.)*

Hafatzah—'Spreading; dispersing;'

concept of spreading and promulgating the teachings of the
Torah among all Jews, especially
among those presently alienated
from their roots. See *Hafatzat
hamayanot chutzah.*

Hafatzat Hamayanot Chutzah—
'Dispersing the spring-wells
abroad;' concept of spreading,
promulgating and popularizing
the teachings and practices of
Chassidism throughout, even—
and especially—to *chutzah* (lit.
'outside'), those presently fur-
thest removed from knowing,
following or appreciating these
values. See "Let Your Wellsprings Be Dispersed Abroad,"
in *The Mystical Tradition.*

Haftorah—Supplementary selection from the Prophets read on
the Sabbath, Festivals and Fast-
days after the reading of the
Torah.

Haggadah; Haggadah for Pesach—
Title of text recited at the *seder*
(*s.v.*) celebrated the first night [in
the Diaspora the first two nights]
of Pesach detailing the events
and significance of the exodus
from Egypt, as well as the procedures for this celebration.

Hakafot—Circuits. (See *L.S.*, vol. I:
p. 76).

Hala'ah—Elevation; Sublimation.
Act of raising or sublimating
something from a lower to a
higher level.

Halachah, *pl.* **Halachot**—(a) A final
decision or ruling relating to
Torah-law. (b) The Jewish legal
system; the sections in Rabbinic
literature which deal with legal
issues, in contradistinction to
Agadah.

Hallel—Praise; Psalms 113-118
recited on Rosh Chodesh and
Festivals.

Hamshachah—A drawing forth;
elicitation; as, e.g., a drawing
forth or elicitation of Heavenly
blessing.

Hashem—*lit.* 'the Name;' Hebrew
colloquialism for G-d, to avoid
expressing Divine Names out of
reverence for their sanctity.

Hashgachah— lit. Supervision. In
our context term generally referring to Divine Providence. See
below, *Hashgachah Peratit.*

Hashgachah Peratit—lit. Individual Supervision. Term referring to
the Divine Providence governing every particular entity in the
universe.

Havayah—Colloquial epithet for
the *Tetragrammaton,* the ineffable
Name of G-d consisting of the
four letters Yud, Hei, Vav, Hei,
and generally signifying the
transcendence of G-d. (See *L.S.*,
vol. II: p. 10; III: p. 3*ff.*, notes 13,
15, 17.)

Helem Vehester—Concealment
and Obstruction. Generally
referring to the obstructions and
interferences encountered in the
course of man's *Avodah* and the
realization of the aims and purposes of spirituality.

Hey—Fifth letter of the Hebrew
alphabet.

Hidur [Mitzvah]—Glorification,
Beautification [of a Mitzvah], by
going beyond the minimum
standards for legal fulfillment.

Hilulah—Wedding; feast. In the literal sense it means a wedding-
feast, in an extended sense it is
used also to designate a spiritual

celebration as the reunification of the soul and its source, or its progressive ascent in the after-life (as on a *Yahrtzeit*—s.v.), or other festive occasions.

Hishtalshelut—Development; Evolution. In Kabbalistic-Chassidic terminology generally referring to its teaching of cosmogony—in terms of the progressively downward gradation of the Worlds, degree by degree, from the spiritual to the material.

His'talkut—lit. Removal; Departure. Term designating the departure of the soul from the body, used as a euphemism for the death of saints.

Isserles, R. Moses—*(Rema);* one of the principal codifiers (app. 1525-1572) whose additions to R. Joseph Karo's *Shulchan Aruch* are the standard authority for Ashkenazi halachic practise.

It'aruta dile'eyla—Arousal from Above. A stimulus or *Hamshachah* initiated by G-d, or elicited as a Divine response to human initiative.

It'aruta diletatah—Arousal from below. An initiative taken by man by performing *Mitzvot* and good deeds, which elicits a reciprocal response from G-d.

It-hapcha—Principle of converting or transforming (sublimating) the profane to holiness (see *Tanya*, ch. 27). See *L.S.*, vol. II, p. 17*f*.

Itkafya—Principle of controlling and subduing the forces of, or the urges to, the unholy (see *Tanya*, ch. 27).

Iyar—Second month in the Jewish

calendar, following after Nissan (*s.v.*).

Joseph Isaac of Lubavitch, R.—See *Rebbe.*

Kabalat haTorah—Receiving of the Torah; specifically designating the revelation at Mount Sinai when the Torah was given to Israel.

Kabalat Ol—Acceptance of the Yoke [of the Kingdom of Heaven]; concept of total submission and subordination to the Will of G-d.

Kabbalah—Tradition. In a wide sense relating to the totality of Jewish tradition transmitted from generation to generation. In the narrow, most widely used sense, referring specifically to the Jewish mystical tradition or esoteric dimension of the Torah.

Kal Vachomer—An argument *de minore ad majus*, a form of syllogistic reasoning in which the severity of the major or complex premise is derived from the minor or simple premise; one of the thirteen exegetical rules for expounding the Torah.

Kametz—Vowel in the Hebrew alphabet. In Sefardic pronunciation (generally adopted throughout the translation) an a, or in the case of a *kametz chatuf* an o; in Ashkenazy pronunciation, always an o.

Kavanah; *pl.* **Kavanot**—Intent; Devotion. (a) Concentrated devotion—'directing the heart and the mind'—in prayer, or conscious purpose in the performance of a religious precept, 'for the sake of Heaven, in accordance with the Will of G-d.'

(b) Concentration on the mystical devotions and meditations signifying the spiritual meanings and purposes of religious precepts.

Kelipah; *pl.* **Kelipot**—Shell(s). Term signifying evil and impurity. See *Mystical Concepts in Chassidism*, ch. X.

Kelipat Nogah—Irradiated or Translucent Shell; the intermediary level between holiness and impurity *(kelipah, s.v.)*, itself not-quite-impure and not-yet-holy. The mundane aspects and entities that are permitted but not enjoined fall into this category and must be elevated (by proper usage) to the level of holiness. See *Mystical Concepts in Chassidism*, ch. X.

Kelot Hanefesh—Expiration or Flight of the soul, in the context of a consuming yearning to become absorbed in Divinity. "His heart will glow with an intense love, like burning coals, with a passion, desire and longing, and a yearning soul, towards the greatness of the blessed *En Sof.*' This constitutes the culminating passion of the soul, of which Scripture speaks, as 'My soul longs, even faints... (Psalms 84:3), 'My soul thirsts for G-d... (Psalms 42:3), and 'My soul thirsts for You...' (Psalms 63:2). (Tanya, ch. 3)

Keri'at Yam Suf—Splitting of the Sea for the Jewish people at the time of the Exodus.

Keter—Crown. Highest of the ten *Sefirot*, generally signifying the Divine attribute of transcendence. See *Mystical Concepts in*

Chassidism, ch. III, section 3.

Kislev—Ninth month in the Jewish calendar.

Kohen Gadol—High Priest

Korban; pl. Korbanot—Sacrifice(s).

Lag Ba'Omer—'Thirty-third day of the Omer' (see below, *s.v. Omer*). Term for the 18th of Iyar (s.v.), which is a joyous day commemorating the cessation of a fatal plague among the many disciples of R. Akiva *(Tanna of the second century)*. This day is also the *yahrtzeit (s.v.)* and *hilula (s.v.)* of R. Shimon bar Yochai *(see below, s.v. Rashby)*.

Lishmah—An action done for its own sake, not for the promise of reward; often in reference to the study of Torah.

Luchot—Tablets, referring to the two Tablets of the Covenant on which G-d engraved the Ten Commandments.

Luria, R. Isaac—see Ari.

Lurianic—Relating to the teachings of R. Isaac *Luria*.

Ma'amar, *pl.* **Ma'amarim**—In *Chabad-Chassidism* formal discourses delivered by *Rebbe* to expound Chassidic doctrines.

Ma'aseh Merkavah—Work of the Chariot; term designating the principal subject-matter of *nistar*, Jewish mysticism. Specifically it refers to the Theophany described in the first chapter of Ezekiel (though generally also including the sixth chapter of Isaiah), describing the prophetic vision of the Divine Throne-chariot.

Mah—(a) 'What?'; a concept signifying the essential spirituality of man which manifests itself in

total self-negation and complete submission to the Divine.
(b) The number 45, a short form signifying one form of the Ineffable Name *Havayah*, when each of its letters is spelled phonetically like this: יו"ד ה"א וא"ו ה"א —as the numerical equivalent of all these letters is 45. This Name relates to the pristine transcendence of G-d. (See *L.S.*, vol. II: p. 53, note 34.)

Maharash—Acronym for Moreinu Harav Shmu'el (Our Master R. Shmu'el): R. Shmu'el Schneersohn of Lubavitch (1834-1882), son and successor of *Tzemach Tzedek*, thus fourth leader of Chabad-Chassidism.

Maggid—Preacher. In Chassidic history and thought, 'the *Maggid*,' unqualified, always refers to R. Dov Ber, the Maggid of Mezhirech (?-1772), disciple and successor of the *Baal Shem Tov*, thus second leader of the Chassidic movement. The *Maggid* was the principal master of *R. Shneur Zalman of Liadi*.

Makif—Encompassing. An aspect or effluence which encompasses its subject in a pervasive and transcending form. See *Orot Makifin*.

Malchut—Sovereignty. One of the Sefirot, designating the Divine attribute of sovereignty or kingship.

Marcheshvan—Eighth month in the Jewish calendar.

Mashiach—The anointed redeemer of Israel.

Mashpi'a—One who exerts influence. In Chassidic terminology a spiritual guide and counsellor.

Matan Torah—Giving of the Torah; the Revelation at Mount Sinai when the Torah was given to Israel.

Matzah—Unleavened bread (as opposed to *chametz*—s.v.), prescribed for *Pessach*.

Mechilta—Tannaitic Midrash on the Book of Exodus.

Mechitzah—Partition. Generally referring to the physical partition required by Jewish law to separate the sexes in places of worship.

Mehadrin—Term signifying an especially meticulous observance of Torah and *mitzvot* with *hidur* (s.v.).

Mekabel—lit. Recipient. In Chassidic terminology the recipient of spiritual guidance from *Mashpi'a* (s.v.).

Menachem Av—see above s.v. Av.

Menachem Mendel of Lubavitch, R.—See *Tzemach Tzedek*.

Menorah—Candlestick. Generally referring to the seven-branched candelabrum in the Sanctuary, though also to the eight-branched candlestick used for the lighting of the candles on *Chanukah*.

Mesirat Nefesh—Self-sacrifice. Concept signifying total submission to the point of a willingness to lay down one's life if *necessary*, for the realization of G-d's purposes .

Midot—Attributes. (a) The seven 'lower' *Sefirot* or 'emotive' attributes of G-d (Mercy, Justice, Compassion etc.). (b) The emotive soul powers (dispositions; affections or character-traits) in man, analogous to those *Sefirot*, in contradistinction to the *Mochin.* See *Mystical Concepts in Chassidism,* ch. III, sections 2 and 4-7.

Midrash, pl. Midrashim—Exegetical works of Scriptural interpretations set forth by the *Tannaim* and *Amoraim,* embodying various traditions of Biblical times; systematically arranged in the order of the Scriptures.

Mikdash—Sanctuary; generally synonymous with *mishkan (s.v.),* though also with *Bet Hamikdash (s.v.).* See *L.S.,* vol. II, p. 133, note *b.*

Mikveh—Pool for ritual immersion.

Minchah—Daily prayer to be recited after noon, before sunset.

Minyan—Quorum of at least ten male adults, required for certain religious observances.

Mishkan—Dwelling-place; Tabernacle. The sanctuary built by the Jewish people in the desert manifesting the 'indwelling' of the *Shechinah* (Divine Presence).

Mishnah—Basic collection of the legal pronouncements, discussions and interpretations of the *Tannaim,* edited by R. Judah Hanassi (the Patriarch) early in the third century.

Mitteler Rebbe—Intermediate *Rebbe;* R. Dov Ber Schneuri of Lubavitch (1773-1827), son and successor of *R. Shneur Zalman of Liadi,* thus second leader of *Chabad*-Chassidism. The term *Mitteler Rebbe* signifies the 'middle one' of the first three generations.

Mitzvah, pl. Mitzvot—Commandment(s); Precept(s). Religious obligations of the Jew, and in colloquial use referring to good deeds in general.

Mitzrayim—Egypt. As an idiom of *meytzarim* (boundaries; limitations), this term also signifies the concept of confining restraints and restrictions of spiritual aspirations and goals, thus a state of mental and spiritual exile.

Mochin—Brains. The collective term for *Chochmah, Binah* and *Da'at (Chabad)*—the three 'intellectual' *Sefirot,* and correspondingly the three soul-powers related to man's intellect, in contradistinction to the *Midot.* See *Mystical Concepts in Chassidism,* ch. III, sections 2 and 4.

Modeh Ani Lefanecha — 'I give thanks unto You... ' First prayer recited upon awakening, expressing gratitude for the restoration of the soul.

Nassi, pl. Nessi'im — Leader(s); Patriarch(s). In Chassidic terminology referring to the Chassidic leaders *(Rebbes).*

Nefesh—Soul. In the wider sense referring to the soul in general. In the narrow sense referring specifically to the lowest of the five grades in man's soul. See *Nefesh-Ruach-Neshamah.*

Nefesh Habahamit—Animal Soul. The basic life-force in the body, responsible for the physical nature and desires in man, in contradistinction to *Nefesh Ha'elokit (s.v.).* Discussed at length in *Tanya,* see there especially ch. 1, and 6-9.

Nefesh Ha'elokit—Divine Soul. The Divine component with which every Jew is endowed, and responsible for his purely spiritual aspirations (in contradistinction to *Nefesh Habahamit (s.v.)*). Discussed at length in *Tanya*, see there especially ch. 2-4, and 9.

Nefesh-Ruach-Neshamah-Chayah-Yechidah— These are the five terms Scripture uses to refer to man's soul. They are not, however, synonyms; each term denotes a different gradation of the soul—in ascending order from *Nefesh* to *Yechidah: Nefesh* is the basic life-force or natural soul in general, and specifically relates to the soul's basic or external manifestations in terms of the faculties of thought, speech and action. *Ruach* (Spirit) and *Neshamah* (Soul; Breath) are the spiritual life-force in man, relating to the *Midot* and *Mochim* respectively. *Chayah* (Living), often also referred to as *Neshamah leNeshamah* (Soul of the Soul), is the sublime root for the lower three grades. *Yechidah* (Only One; Unique) is the quintessence, the Divine spark as it were, the ultimate source of the soul—compounding yet transcending the lower grades. The higher grades of the soul are latently present in the *Nefesh*, in proportionally increasing concealment, but will become ever more manifest to the point of conscious awareness by man's continuous self-improvement and spiritual ascent. (For a fuller discussion of these terms and relevant references see *Kuntres Inyanah shel Torat Hachassidut (On the Essence of Chassidus)*, ch.

5 and 11, *et passim;* and note 53 in the English translation of *Igeret Hakodesh*, section V.)

Ne'ilah—Closing-prayer on *Yom Kippur*, recited with the conclusion of the day.

Neshamah—Soul. In the wider sense referring to the soul in general. In the narrow sense referring specifically to the Divine soul (as opposed to the basic life-force or natural soul), or the third of the five soul-grades. See *Nefesh-Ruach-Neshamah*.

Nigleh, Nigleh deTorah—The revealed or exoteric part of the *Torah* or Jewish tradition, touching specifically upon *Halachah*, in contradistinction to *Nistar*—the concealed or esoteric part of Torah.

Nissan—First month in the Jewish calendar (see Exodus 12:2), the spring-month during which the exodus from Egypt took place and is celebrated *(Pesach)*.

Nistar—The concealed or esoteric part of the Torah or Jewish tradition, in contradistinction to *Nigleh*. See *Sod*.

Nitzotz, *pl.*, **Nitzotzot (*or* Nitzotin)**—Spark(s): in Kabbalistic-Chassidic terminology the sparks of holiness or G-dliness inherent in everything, constituting everything's origin and sustaining quality, thus its true reality as created things. When something is used in its Divinely intended context, its sparks are said to be 'liberated' and re-absorbed in their Source, thus contributing to establishing the Divine unity which is the ulti-

GLOSSARY

mate purpose of creation. See *Birur;* and cf. *Mystical Concepts in Chassidism,* ch VII and XI.

Ohel Mo'ed—Tent of Meeting; one of the terms designating the *mishkan (s.v.).*

Olam Habah—The World To Come. Generally refers to after-life, in contradistinction to the here-and-now of *Olam Hazeh (s.v.).*

Olam Hazeh—This World. The here-and-now of the physical world, in contradistinction to *Olam Habah (s.v.).*

Omer—'Sheaf.' (a) Name of a measure. (b) Colloquial term for the period between Pesach and Shavu'ot (see below, *s.v. Sefirah; Sefirat Ha'Omer).*

Or, *pl.* **Orot**—Light(s). The mystics' favorite term for Divine emanations and effluences. See *Mystical Concepts in Chassidism,* ch. I, section 3.

Or Chozer—See *Or Yashar.*

Or Yashar—Direct Light. In Kabbalistic-Chassidic terminology a Divine Emanation or effluence extended from 'above downwards' in a 'direct' way, that is, manifesting the Divine Benevolence to His creations who are worthy to receive it; thus the *Or Yashar* is also called *Or shel Rachamim*—Light manifesting Compassion; *Or Hapanim*—Light from the (Divine) Countenance; and *Or shel Pnimiyut*—Light from the Innermost Point (thus denoting its sublime source and absolute benevolence). In contradistinction to *Or Yashar is Or Chozer*—the Returning or Reflecting Light: it 'radiates' *indirectly.* When the creatures are not worthy to receive the *Or Yashar,* the emanations of the *Or Yashar* 'return,' re-ascend 'from below upward,' and it is only the reflection shining from them in their withdrawal that extends to the worlds. That is, as G-d does not want to destroy the world, He will emanate to the world notwithstanding its unworthiness, albeit only as much as is needed for the world's continuing existence. In this context the *Or Chozer* is also called *Or Chitzoniyut* and *Or HaAchor*—the Light from the external or outermost aspect (as opposed to *Pnimiyut),* and *Or Hadin*—the Light of Judgment.

Orot Makifin—Encompassing Lights. The Divine emanations or effluences of an infinite order. They cannot be confined within limited creatures, thus are said to encompass them, albeit in a pervasive and transcending form. *See Mystical Concepts in Chassidism,* ch. V, section 2.

Orot Pnimiyim—'Inner lights,' Divine emanations or effluences immanent in creation and creatures relative to their limited capacities to absorb these. See *Mystical Concepts in Chassidism,* ch. V, section 2.

Pardes—Orchard; acronym for *Pshat, Remez, Derush, Sod*—the four levels or dimensions of meaning in the Torah. See those entries in the glossary.

Parshah, *pl.* **Parshiyot**—The weekly portion(s) of the *Chumash* (Pentateuch).

Pesach—Festival of Passover commemorating the Jewish people's liberation (Exodus) from Egyptian bondage, celebrated from the 15th of *Nissan* on.

Pesukei dezimrah—Verses of Praise; Biblical verses and psalms recited daily at the beginning of the morning-prayers following the principle that man should first praise G-d and then present his own petitions *(Berachot* 32a).

Piku'ach Nefesh—Saving endangered life

Pirkei Avot—'Chapters Of The Fathers.' Title of a tractate in the *Mishnah,* essentially dealing with moral teachings and instructions. This tractate is traditionally learned every Shabbat between Pesach and Shavu'ot, and in many communities also between Shavu'ot and Rosh Hashanah.

Pnimiyut—Inwardness; the inner core or essence.

Pnimiyut Hatorah—The inner dimension or soul of the Torah; the esoteric tradition in general, and *Chassidut* in particular.

Pshat—Plain, straightforward meaning of the Torah; one of the four levels known as *Pardes.*

Purim—Festival commemorating the deliverance of the Jewish people of the Persian Empire from the plot of Haman, as described in the Scroll of Esther; celebrated on the fourteenth of *Adar.* See also *s.v. Shushan Purim.*

Purim Katan—Minor Purim. In a leap-year the festival of *Purim is* celebrated in *Adar Sheni* (see *s.v. Adar).* The corresponding day in *Adar Rishon* is called *Purim Katan* and noted with minor celebration (see *L.S.,* vol. II: p. 145 *f.).*

Rambam—R. Mosheh ben Maimon (Maimonides; 1135-1204); principal Talmudic commentator, codifier, and philosopher.

Ramban—R. Mosheh ben Nachman (Nachmanides; 1194-1270); one of the principal commentators of the Bible and Talmud, and Kabbalist.

Rashby—R. Shimon bar Yochai; second century *Tanna,* disciple of R. Akiva. Author of *Zohar (s.v.).*

Rashi—R. Shelomo Yitzchaki (Solomon ben Isaac; 1040-1105); principal commentator of the Bible and the Talmud.

Ratzo Veshov—'Running and Retreating' (Ezekiel 1:14). *Ratzo* signifies the passionate advance (lit. running) to become attached to Divinity; *shov* signifies a retreat back into physical existence there to apply and realize the Divine intent for physical reality. (L.S., vol. II: p. 154*ff*).

Razin—Secrets. One of the terms for the mystical part of Torah— *(razin de'orayta,* the secrets or mysteries of the Torah).

Rebbe—Rabbi; Teacher. (a) Leader of a Chassidic group. (b) Unqualified references to 'the *Rebbe'* (or 'the *Rebbe,* my father-in-law') throughout *Likkutei Sichot* are to R. *Yoseph Yitzchak* (in translation also rendered Joseph Isaac) Schneersohn of Lubavitch (1880-1950), son and successor of *Reshab,* and father-in-law of the present Lubavitcher Rebbe שליט"א; sixth leader of *Chabad*-Chassidism .

Remez—Allusion; intimated meaning of the Torah; one of the four levels known as *Pardes.*

Reshab—Acronym for Rabenu Shalom Ber: R. Sholom Dov Ber Schneersohn of Lubavitch (1860-1920); son and *successor* of *Maharash,* thus fifth leader of *Chabad*-Chassidism.

Re'uta Deliba—Desire of the Heart, in the sense of the deep-seated devotion and desire from the innermost point of the heart to submit to the Divine Will.

Rishon, *pl.* **Rishonim**—The Ancient Teachers, specifically referring to the early Rabbinic authorities in the post-Geonic period— from the 11th century to approximately the composition of the *Shulchan Aruch* in the 16th century. The subsequent authorities are called *Acharonim*—the Later (or Recent) Teachers.

Rosen, R. Joseph—the Rogachover Gaon (1858-1936), rabbi in Dvinsk (Latvia); foremost Talmudist and author of commentaries and responsa noted for their ingenious subtlety and originality.

Rosh Chodesh—Beginning of the month .

Rosh Hashanah—Beginning of the Year. Generally referring to the Jewish New Year observed on the first of *Tishrei.*

Ruach—Spirit; one of the five grades in the soul. See *Nefesh-Ruach-Neshamah.*

Sages—Generally referring to the great body of teachers who taught and expounded the traditional laws and traditions of Israel from the time of Ezra to the completion of the Talmudic midrashic literature (app. 450 BCE—500 CE).

Seder—Order. In a specific sense referring to the traditional 'order' of procedures and celebration of the exodus on the first night [in the Diaspora: the first two nights] of Pesach.

Sefirah, *pl.* **Sefirot**—Term denoting the ten attributes or emanations through which G-d manifests Himself in both the creation and sustenance of the universe. See *Mystical Concepts in Chassidism,* ch. III.

Sefirah; Sefirat Ha'Omer—Counting; Counting of the *Omer.* The counting of the days beginning the second day of Pesach when an offering of an *omer* (sheaf) of the first-fruits of the harvest of barley is to be brought (Leviticus 23:9-14). 49 days are to be counted individually, to be followed, on the fiftieth day, with the celebration of *Shavu'ot* (Leviticus 23:15-21). The term *Sefirat Ha'Omer,* in short *Sefirah,* thus refers to this *mitzvah* of counting these days, or to this whole period of 49 days or Seven Weeks.

Shabbat Bereishit—The first Sabbath after *the* Festival of *Simchat Torah,* on which the *parshah* Bereishit (Genesis I-IV:8) is read—thus restarting the annual cycle of the weekly readings of the Torah.

Shabbat Mevarchim—'Sabbath of blessing'; last Sabbath of every month in the Jewish calendar, on which special prayers are recited to invoke the Divine blessings for the coming month. See vol I, p. 6, note *f*.

Shavu'ot—Festival commemorating the Giving of the Torah on Mount Sinai on the sixth of Sivan.

Shechinah—Divine Presence or Indwelling (Immanence) in creation.

Shechitah—Slaughtering. Term referring to the ritual slaughtering of animals as prescribed by Torah-law.

Shema—Term for the first verse or whole passage of Deuteronomy 6:4-9—or for the compound of that passage along with Deuteronomy 11:13-21 and Numbers 15:37-41—to be recited daily every morning and night.

Shemitah—Release, Remitting. Term for the Sabbatical Year (every seventh year in a specific counting of seven-year-cycles), subject to special laws and observances (Exodus 23:10*f.*; Leviticus 25: 1*ff.*; and Deuteronomy 15:1*ff.*).

Shemoneh Esrei—*lit.* 'Eighteen [Blessings].' Major-prayer (also called *Amidah*) recited daily.

Shevat—tenth month in the Jewish calendar .

Shevi'i shel Pesach—Seventh day of *Pesach*, celebrated as a *Yom Tov*, and commemorating *keri'at yam suf (s.v.)*.

Shevirat Hakeilim—'Breaking of the Vessels,' a central concept in Kabbalistic cosmogony which accounts for the multiplicity and the presence of evil in the universe. See *Mystical Concepb in Chassidism*, ch. VII.

Shmu'el of Lubavitch, R.—See *Maharash*.

Shneur Zalman of Liadi, R.—See *Alter Rebbe*.

Sholom Dov Ber of Lubavitch, R.—See *Reshab*.

Shov—see *Ratzo Veshov*.

Shulchan Aruch—Title of the standard code of Jewish law, compiled by R. Joseph Karo (1488-1575). An updated edition of a major part of *Shulchan Aruch* was compiled by R. *Shneur Zalman of Liadi* and is referred to by the same title joined with his name.

Shushan Purim—Purim of Shushan (Susa), celebrated on the fifteenth of *Adar* in all cities that were walled in the days of Joshua. It marks the original festival of *Purim* in Shushan, then the capital of the Persian Empire, which was not celebrated until the fifteenth of *Adar*, as distinguished from the 'regular' Purim on the fourteenth of *Adar* (see Esther 9:15-18).

Sichah, *pl.* **Sichot**—Talk(s). In *Chabad*-Chassidism generally denoting the 'informal' (in contradistinction to the formal *Ma'amar*) talks delivered by a *Rebbe* on a variety of subjects ranging from expositions of the Torah to pronouncements on topical themes.

Sidrah, *pl.* **Sidrot**—'Arrangement': the weekly portion(s) of the *Chumash* (Pentateuch); synonymous with *parshah*.

Sidur—*lit.* 'Order.' Term for prayerbook.

Simchat Torah—Rejoicing with the Torah; Festival celebrated in conjunction with *Shemini Atzeret* (in the Land of Israel on the same day, and in the Diaspora on the Second Day of *Shemini Atzeret)*, and marked by the completion of the annual cycle of reading the Torah and the immediate recommencing of the next cycle.

Siphre—*Tannaitic Midrash* on the Books of Numbers and Deuteronomy.

Sivan—Third month in the Jewish calendar.

Sod—Secret; the mystical or esoteric meaning of the Torah; one of the four levels of *Pardes.*

Sukot—Festival of Tabernacles, celebrated from *Tishrei* 15-22, commemorating G-d's care for the children of Israel in the desert after the Exodus, when they dwelled in *sukot* (booths). It is a festival noted for its special joy (*zeman simchatenu*—time of our rejoicing), and in Biblical times also the harvest-festival.

Talmid Chacham—Scholar; person learned in Torah and Jewish tradition.

Talmud—Comprehensive term for the *Mishnah*, and *Gemara* as joined in the two compilations known as the Babylonian Talmud (Talmud Bavli; completed in Babylon in 6th century) and the Jerusalem Talmud (Talmud Yerushalmi; completed in the Holy Land, beginning of the 5th century).

Tamuz—Fifth month in the Jewish calendar. The summer-solstice begins in *Tamuz.*

Tanna, *pl.* **Tanna'im**—Talmudic Teachers of the *Mishnah*-period, in contradistinction to the *Amora'im (s.v.)* who followed after them.

Tanya—Title of primary work of *Chabad*-Chassidut, composed by R. *Shneur Zalman of Liadi.*

Taryag—'613'—the number of Biblical *precepts,* consisting of 248 positive commandments and 365 negative commandments.

Tefilah —Prayer

Tefillin—Phylacteries; two leather cases containing Scriptural passages and strapped on the arm and head especially during the weekday morning-prayers.

Tehilim—Book of Psalms

Terumah—Heave-offering. Generally referring to the first levy on the annual produce, given to *kohanim* (Numbers 18:8*ff.*).

Teshuvah—Return. In the narrow sense, the act of repentance from sins of omission or commission. In the wider sense, it is taken literally as 'returning to G-d,' signifying a continuously progressive advance toward G-dliness, and thus applying to the non-sinner (or *Tzadik*) no less than to the sinner.

Tetragrammaton—Name of the Four Letters, the Ineffable Name—*Havayah.*

Tikunei Zohar—One of the volumes of the *Zohar*-literature.

Tikunim—another term for *Tikunei Zohar (s.v.)*

Tisha beAv—Ninth of *Av;* presently a day of fasting and mourning in commemoration of the destruction of the First and Second Sanctuaries, as well as other calamities .

Tishrei—Seventh month in the Jewish calendar, marking the beginning of the Jewish civil year *(Rosh Hashanah)*.

Tochachah—Chastisement; Rebuke. Common term for sections in the Torah (Leviticus 26:14-46; and Deuteronomy 28:15-69) describing the dire consequences that follow in retribution for disobeying and scorning the Torah.

Torah—Teaching. In the narrow sense the *Chumash* (Five Books of Moses; Pentateuch); in the general, comprehensive sense, the entire body of Jewish law and teachings. Often qualified in terms of: *Torah Shebiktav*—the Written Torah (Bible; Scriptures); *Torah Shebe'al Peh*—the Oral Torah (the exposition of the *Torah Shebiktav* and the traditions transmitted by word of mouth from the time of Moses until it was committed to writing in the *Talmudic-Midrashic* literature); *Pniymiyut Hatorah*—(see that entry, bove); *Nigleh deTorah*—(see that entry, above).

Torah Shebe'al Peh—Oral Torah; see *Torah.*

Torah Shebiktav—Written Torah; see *Torah.*

Tossafot—Title of a compilation of novellae on the *Talmud*, constituting a major commentary composed by leading rabbinic authorities in France and Germany—mainly during the 12th and 13th centuries.

Tzadik, *pl.* **Tzadikim**—Righteous person)s). In the wider sense a person whose good deeds outweigh the bad. In the narrow sense, as analyzed and explained in *Tanya* (esp. ch. 1, 10,

14-15), a saint devoid of any improper actions or who has altogether sublimated any innate evil.

Tzedakah—Righteousness. In colloquial use referring to charity.

Tzemach Tzedek—Title of voluminous collection of responsa composed by *R. Menachem Mendel of Lubavitch* (1789-1866), grandson and disciple of *R. Shneur Zalman of Liadi*, and son-in-law and successor of the *Mitteler Rebbe;* third leader of *Chabad*-Chassidism, and usually referred to by the title of his responsa as the *Tzemach Tzedek.*

Tzeniyut—Chastity; chaste or modest way of life.

Tzeyre—Vowel in the Hebrew alphabet, pronounced ey, ei or e.

Tzitzit—Fringes attached to four-cornered garments (Numbers 15: 37-41), like on *talit* (special garment donned for morning-prayers) or *talit katan* ("small *talit"* worn all day long).

Ufaratzta—"And you shall spread abroad [to the west and to the east, and to the north and to the south].' (Genesis 28;14); this term has become the slogan for the constant outreach activities of Chabad-Chassidim. The significance of this term as a slogan is explained in *L.S.*, vol. II: p. 125*ff.*

Worlds, the Four—In Kabbalistic cosmogony there are four principal stages or levels in the creation, one evolving from the other in descending order from a purely spiritual world to one which harbors the lowest level of the material world. These

Four Worlds are called *Atzilut, Beriah, Yetzirah* and *Asiyah,* denoting an ever-increasing occulation of Divinity. See *Mystical Concepts in Chassidism,* ch. IV.

Yahrtzeit—Ylddish term designating the anniversary of someone's passing.

Yechidah—The Unique One; highest of the five grades of the soul. See *Nefesh-Ruach-Neshamah.*

Yehei Shemey Rabba—'May the Great Name be blessed...'; principal response in the doxology of the Kadish-prayer.

Yerushalmi—Jerusalem (or Palestinian) Talmud, as distinguished from the more common *Bavli* (Babylonian Talmud).

Yetza Hara—Evil Impulse; the human inclination or impulse to do evil, rooted in the physical nature of man.

Yetzer Tov—Good Impulse; the human inclination or impulse to do good, rooted in the spiritual nature of man.

Yetzi'at Mitzrayim—Departure From Egypt. Term denoting the exodus.

Yetzirah—'[World of] Formation'; third in the hierarchy of the Four Worlds. See *Worlds.*

Yiddishkeit—Jewishness. Yiddish term denoting the traditional culture and way of life of Judaism.

Yom Kippur—Day of Atonement.

The Day of Judgment on the tenth of *Tishrei* which is set aside for repentance and atonement.

Yom Tov—Festival.

Yosef Yitzchak of Lubavitch, R.—See *Rebbe.*

Yud Shvat—Tenth of *Shvat, Yahrtzeit* of R. Joseph Isaac of Lubavitch, sixth Lubavitcher Rebbe.

Yud-Bet Yud-Gimel Tamuz—12th and 13th of Tamuz, days on which occurred the liberation of the *Rebbe* R. Yosef Yitzchak of Lubavitch (*s.v.*) in 5687 (1927) from his life-threatening imprisonment in Soviet Russia because of his self-sacrificing efforts to safeguard Torah-life; since then celebrated as a festival.

Yud-Tet Kislev—l9th day of Kislev; Chassidic festival known as the *Rosh Hashanah* (New Year) of Chassidut, marking the release from prison of the *Alter Rebbe* in 5559 (1798) when he had been incarcerated for disseminating the teachings of Chassidism. (See vol. I, p. 130, note *.)

Ze'eyr Anpin—'Small Image.' Kabbalistic concept denoting the compound of the first six *Midot,* and central to Kabbalistic cosmogony. See *Mystical Concepts in Chassidism,* ch. Vlll.

Zohar—Title of basic work of the *Kabbalah,* essentially composed by the second century *Tanna* R. Shimon bar Yochai.

APPENDIX

APPENDIX

Sources (dates of delivery) of the *sichot* in this volume

Bamidbar	A	I-X	Shabbat parshat Bamidbar 5714
	B	XI-XII	Excerpt from Letter to Neshei Chabad, Iyar 25, 5717
	C	XIII	Shabbat parshat Behar-Bechukotay 5713
	D	XIV-XIX	Shavu'ot 5713
	E*	XX-XXIII	26th Iyar 5720
	F*	XXIV-XXV	Shabbat parshat Behar-Bechukotay 5721
Shavu'ot	A	I-IV	Shabbat parshat Behar-Bechukotay 5718
	B-C	V-XVII	Shavu'ot 5718
	D	XVIII-XX	Shavu'ot 5711
	E	XXI-XXVII	Shavu'ot 5718
	F*-K*	XXVI-XXXV	Shavu'ot 5715
	L*-M*	XXXVI-XLI	Shavu'ot 5716
	N*	XLII-XLV	Shavu'ot 5712
	O*	XLVII-XLVIII	Shavu'ot 5714
	P*	XLIX-L	Shavu'ot 5715
	Q*	LI-LV	19th of Sivan 5722, to Graduates of Bet Rivkah School
	R*	LVI-LIX	Motza'ei Shabbat Bereishit 5714
	S*	LX	Shabbat Bereishit 5717
Nasso	A	I-IV	Yud Shvat 5713
Beha'alotecha	A	I	Yud Shvat 5716
	B	II-VII	Shavu'ot 5717
Shlach	A	I-V	Shabbat parshat Shlach 5715
	B	VI-VII	Shabbat parshat Shlach 5713

---

* *Sichot* marked with an asterisk are from the supplements in the original (Hebrew-Yiddish) text of *Likkutei Sichot*, vol. II.

	C*	VIII-XII	Shabbat parshat Shlach 5721
	D*	XIII-XXI	Shabbat parshat Shlach 5716
Korach	A	I-V	Shabbat parshat Korach 5714
Chukat	A	I-VIII	Yud-Bet Tamuz 5713
Balak	A-B	I-III	Yud-Bet Tamuz 5716
	C	IV-VI	Shabbat parshat Balak 5716
	D*	VII-VIII	Shabbat parshat Balak 5716

Yud-Bet Yud-Gimel Tamuz

	A*	I-III	Yud-Gimel Tamuz 5715
	B*	IV-VIII	Shabbat parshat Korach 5717
	C*	IX-XVIII	15th Tamuz 5717, to children of Camp "Gan Yisrael"
	D*	XIX-XXI	21st Tamuz 5721
	E*	XXII-XXVIII	Shabbat parshat Chukat-Balak 5722
Pinchas	A	I-III	Yud-Bet Tamuz 5714
	B	IV-V	Yud-Bet Tamuz 5713
	C	VI-X	16th Tamuz 5712
	D*	XI-XII	Shabbat parshat Balak 5716
	E*	XIII	Shabbat parshat Chukat-Balak 5722
	F*	XIV-XVI	Yud-Gimel Tamuz 5715
Matot	A*	I-IV	Shabbat parshat Matot-Massey 5716
Massey	A	I-VII	Shabbat parshat Matot-Massey 5717
	B*	VIII	Shabbat parshat Matot-Massey 5716

לעילוי נשמות

אביו ר' **מישאל**

ב"ר זאב יהודה הלוי ע"ה

נפטר ט"ז אלול, תשכ"א

ואמו מרת **שרה דבורה**

בת ר' שמואל ע"ה

נפטרה ביום וערש"ק פ' ויקהל

כ"ח אדר ראשון, ה'תשנ"ז

הורוביץ

ת.נ.צ.ב.ה.

◆

נדפס ע"י בן מכבד הוריו

הנדיב ר' **זאב שלום** הלוי

ה ו ר ו ב י ץ

ומשפחתו שיחיו

(פאלו, בראזיל)